The Savage Border

THE SAVAGE BORDER

THE HISTORY OF THE NORTH-WEST FRONTIER

JULES STEWART

SUTTON PUBLISHING

First published in the United Kingdom in 2007 by
Sutton Publishing Limited · Phoenix Mill
Thrupp · Stroud · Gloucestershire · GL5 2BU

British Library Cataloguing in Publication Data
A catalogue record for this book is available from the British Library.

Hardback ISBN 978-0-7509-4452-6
Paperback ISBN 978-0-7509-4489-2

Typeset in Goudy.
Typesetting and origination by
Sutton Publishing Limited.
Printed and bound in England by
J.H. Haynes & Co. Ltd, Sparkford.

To Helen

Contents

List of Illustrations

Acknowledgements

I would like to thank the following people for their advice and assistance with this book: Helen Crisp, Mark Baillie, Graham Wontner-Smith, Major John Girling, Rodney Bennett, Duncan McAra, Jonathan Falconer, Julia Fenn, Hilary Walford, Dr Humayun Khan, Douglas Learmond, the Field family and the staff at the Royal Geographical Society archives.

Many of the photographs reproduced in the plate section come from the personal albums of British servicemen who served on the North-West Frontier in the 1930s and 1940s.

Colonel Arthur Field OBE, MC, was a Royal Engineers subaltern officer attached to 12 Field Company, Queen Victoria's Madras Sappers and Miners, Indian Army. Like many of his contemporaries far from home and in a strange land, he was an avid photographer of life and events on the Frontier. He took his photographs using a Leica camera given to him as an engagement present by his future wife.

Major John Girling OBE joined the South Waziristan Scouts in 1945 at the age of 20. The Frontier was in his blood, his father having served in the 12th Pioneers during the Third Afghan War, while his grandfather soldiered in Afghanistan in the 1880s. After Partition, Girling stayed on as adjutant to the first Commandant. He served the newly created government of Pakistan until 1951.

A Scottish banker by training, Lieutenant Colonel Alexander William Swanson Learmond sailed to India in 1914. He was commissioned in the 51st Sikhs and served in Mesopotamia. The prospect of active service after the Amritsar riots made him reject a return to banking. He transferred to the 37th Dogras, serving in Afghanistan and Waziristan. He joined the Burma Military Police in 1937 and was Commandant in Mandalay, later leading part of the 'walk out' of Burma in 1942. He returned to Burma after the War, in the Military and Civil administration of Burma, and retired from the Indian Army in 1946.

Wing Commander William 'Lofty' Owen MBE, RAF, was a ground crew sergeant with 28 (AC) Squadron on the airfields and advanced landing grounds at Ambala, Manzai, Miranshah and Tank. Lofty recorded his duty overseas in Iraq and India (1934–9) with a camera he bought as a young aircraft apprentice at RAF Halton in 1923.

Through the lenses of these British servicemen, turned amateur photographers, we are given a unique insight into their lives on the savage border of the Empire at a crucial time in its history.

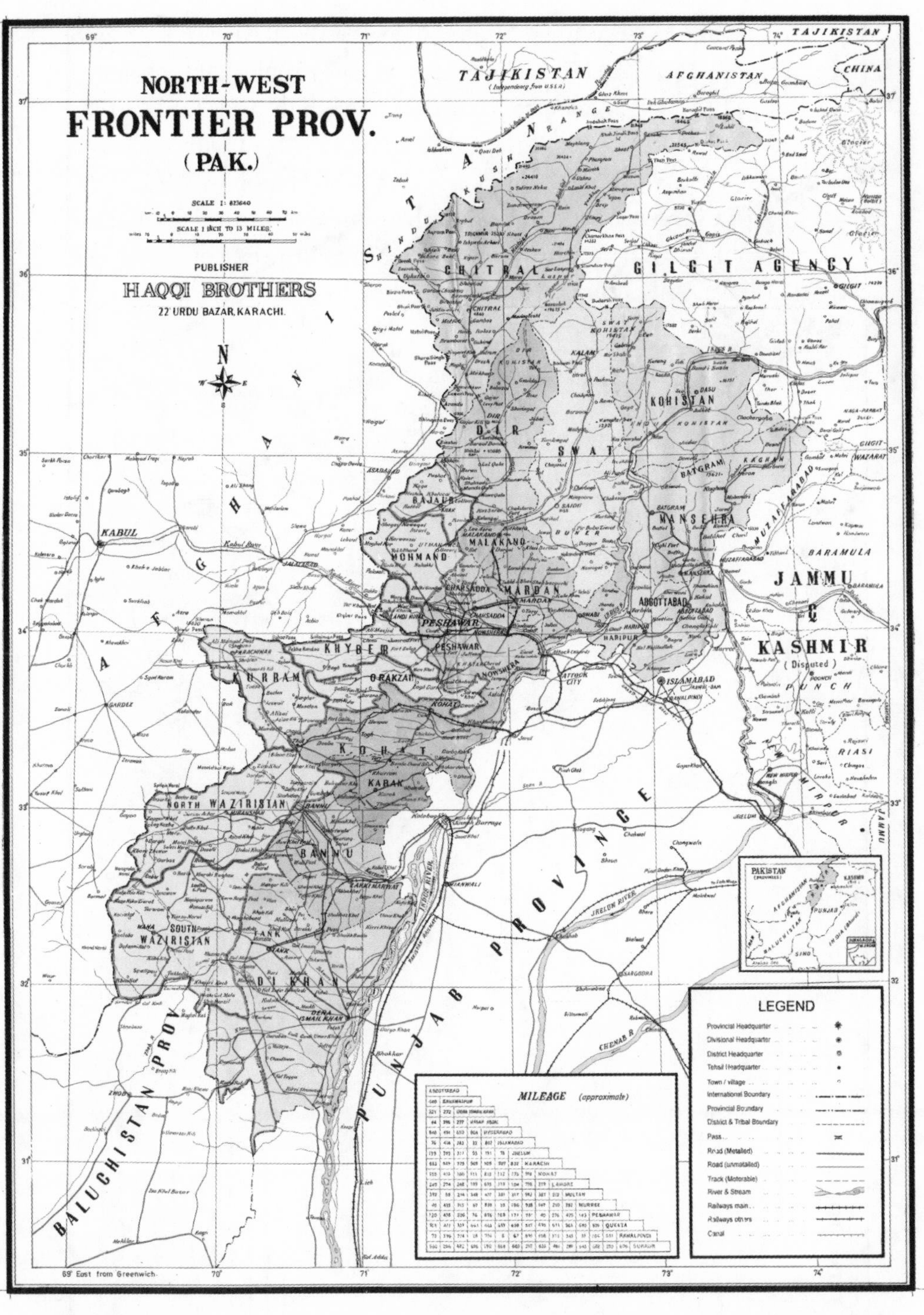
NORTH-WEST
FRONTIER PROV.
(PAK.)
SCALE 1: 823640
SCALE 1 INCH TO 13 MILES.
PUBLISHER
HAQQI BROTHERS
22 URDU BAZAR, KARACHI.
TAJIKISTAN
AFGHANISTAN
CHINA
AFGHANISTAN
HINDU KUSH RANGE
CHITRAL
GILGIT AGENCY
GILGIT
KOHISTAN
DIR
SWAT
BATGRAM
MANSEHRA
BAJAUR
MOHMAND
MALAKAND
CHARSADDA
MARDAN
PESHAWAR
NOWSHERA
ABBOTTABAD
HARIPUR
SWABI
ISLAMABAD
RAWALPINDI
ATTOCK CITY
KHYBER
KURRAM
ORAKZAI
KOHAT
KARAK
NORTH WAZIRISTAN
BANNU
LAKKI MARWAT
SOUTH WAZIRISTAN
TANK
D.I. KHAN
DERA ISMAIL KHAN
KABUL
JALALABAD
Kabul River
INDUS RIVER
JHELUM RIVER
CHENAB R.
JHELUM
SARGODHA
PUNJAB PROVINCE
BALUCHISTAN PROV.
ZHOB
JAMMU & KASHMIR (Disputed)
BARAMULA
MUZAFFARABAD
POONCH
RIASI
MIRPUR
NANGA PARBAT
PAKISTAN (PROVINCES)
MILEAGE (approximate)
ABBOTTABAD
BAHAWALPUR
DERA ISMAIL KHAN
HYDERABAD
ISLAMABAD
JHELUM
KARACHI
KOHAT
LAHORE
MULTAN
MURREE
PESHAWAR
QUETTA
RAWALPINDI
SUKKUR
LEGEND
Provincial Headquarter
Divisional Headquarter
District Headquarter
Tehsil Headquarter
Town / village
International Boundary
Provincial Boundary
District & Tribal Boundary
Pass
Road (Metalled)
Road (unmetalled)
Track (Motorable)
River & Stream
Railways main
Railways others
Canal
69° East from Greenwich

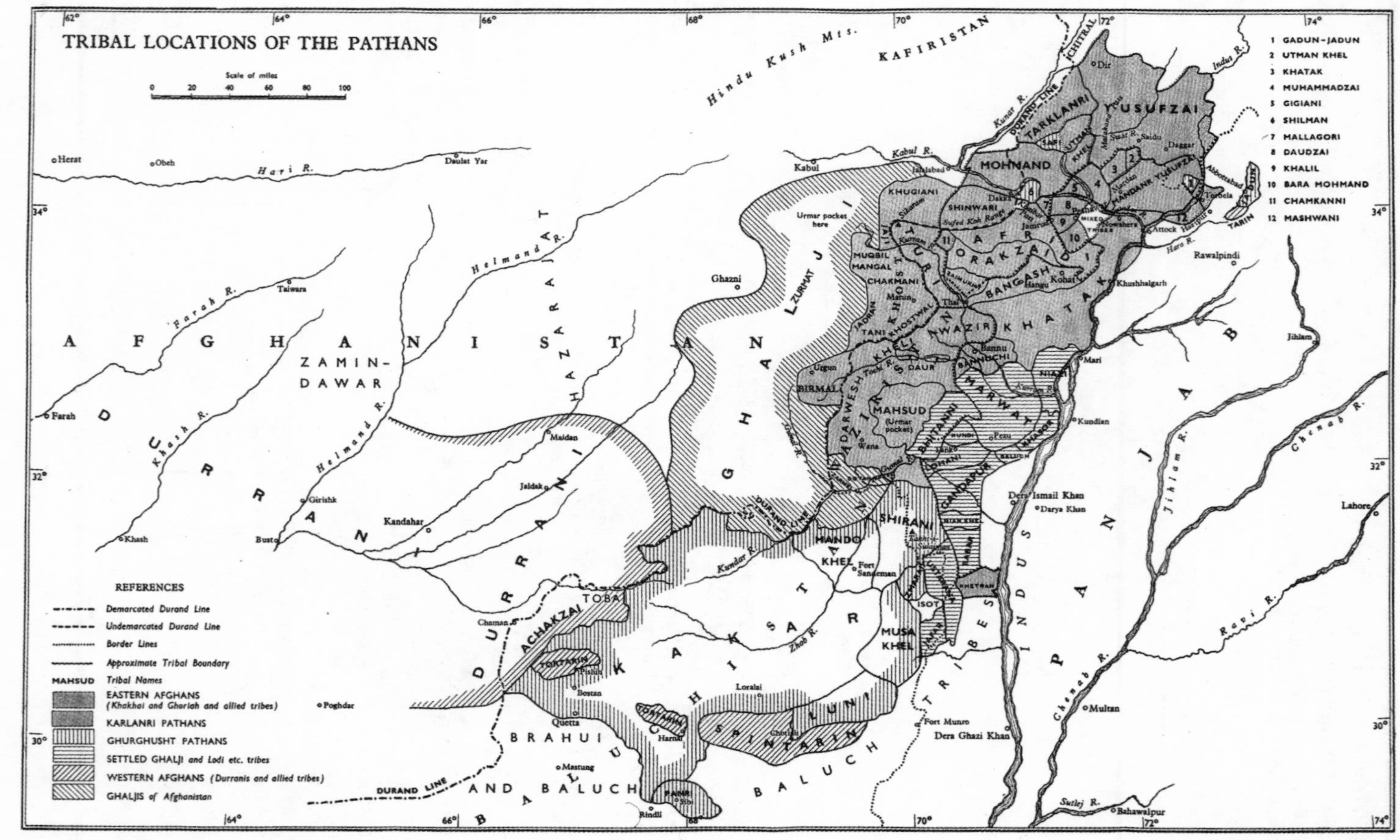

TRIBAL LOCATIONS OF THE PATHANS
Scale of miles
0 20 40 60 80 100
1 GADUN-JADUN
2 UTMAN KHEL
3 KHATAK
4 MUHAMMADZAI
5 GIGIANI
6 SHILMAN
7 MALLAGORI
8 DAUDZAI
9 KHALIL
10 BARA MOHMAND
11 CHAMKANNI
12 MASHWANI
REFERENCES
Demarcated Durand Line
Undemarcated Durand Line
Border Lines
Approximate Tribal Boundary
MAHSUD Tribal Names
EASTERN AFGHANS (Khakhai and Ghoriah and allied tribes)
KARLANRI PATHANS
GHURGHUSHT PATHANS
SETTLED GHALJI and Lodi etc. tribes
WESTERN AFGHANS (Durranis and allied tribes)
GHALJIS of Afghanistan
AFGHANISTAN
DURRANI
ZAMIN-DAWAR
HAZARA
GHALJI
ZURMAT
KAKAR
PANJAB
INDUS
BRAHUI AND BALUCH
BALUCH
TRIBES
KAFIRISTAN
Hindu Kush Mts.
CHITRAL
DURAND LINE
YUSUFZAI
TARKLANRI
MOHMAND
KHUGIANI
SHINWARI
AFRIDI
ORAKZAI
BANGASH
KHATAK
TURI
MUQBIL
MANGAL
CHAKMANI
KHOST
TANI
KHOSTWAL
WAZIR
DAUR
BANNUCHI
BIRMAL
MAHSUD
(Urmar pocket)
Urmar pocket here
DARWESH KHEL
MARWAT
NIAZI
BHITANNI
GANDAPUR
SHIRANI
MANDO KHEL
MUSA KHEL
ISOT
ACHAKZAI
TOBA
TORTARIN
SPINTARIN
LUNI
PANRI
Herat
Obeh
Daulat Yar
Taiwara
Farah
Khash
Girishk
Bust
Kandahar
Maidan
Jaldak
Ghazni
Kabul
Jalalabad
Dir
Saidu
Daggar
Abbottabad
Torbela
Attock
Nowshera
Jamrud
Dakka
Kohat
Hangu
Thal
Matun
Urgun
Bannu
Wana
Pezu
Khushhalgarh
Rawalpindi
Jihlam
Mari
Kundian
Dera Ismail Khan
Darya Khan
Fort Sandeman
Chaman
Pishin
Bostan
Quetta
Mastung
Harnai
Loralai
Sibi
Rindli
Poghdar
Fort Munro
Dera Ghazi Khan
Multan
Bahawalpur
Lahore
Hari R.
Farah R.
Khash R.
Helmand R.
Kabul R.
Kunar R.
Swat R.
Indus R.
Haro R.
Kurram R.
Tochi R.
Gumal R.
Kundar R.
Zhob R.
Jihlam R.
Chenab R.
Ravi R.
Sutlej R.
62°
64°
66°
68°
70°
72°
74°
34°
32°
30°

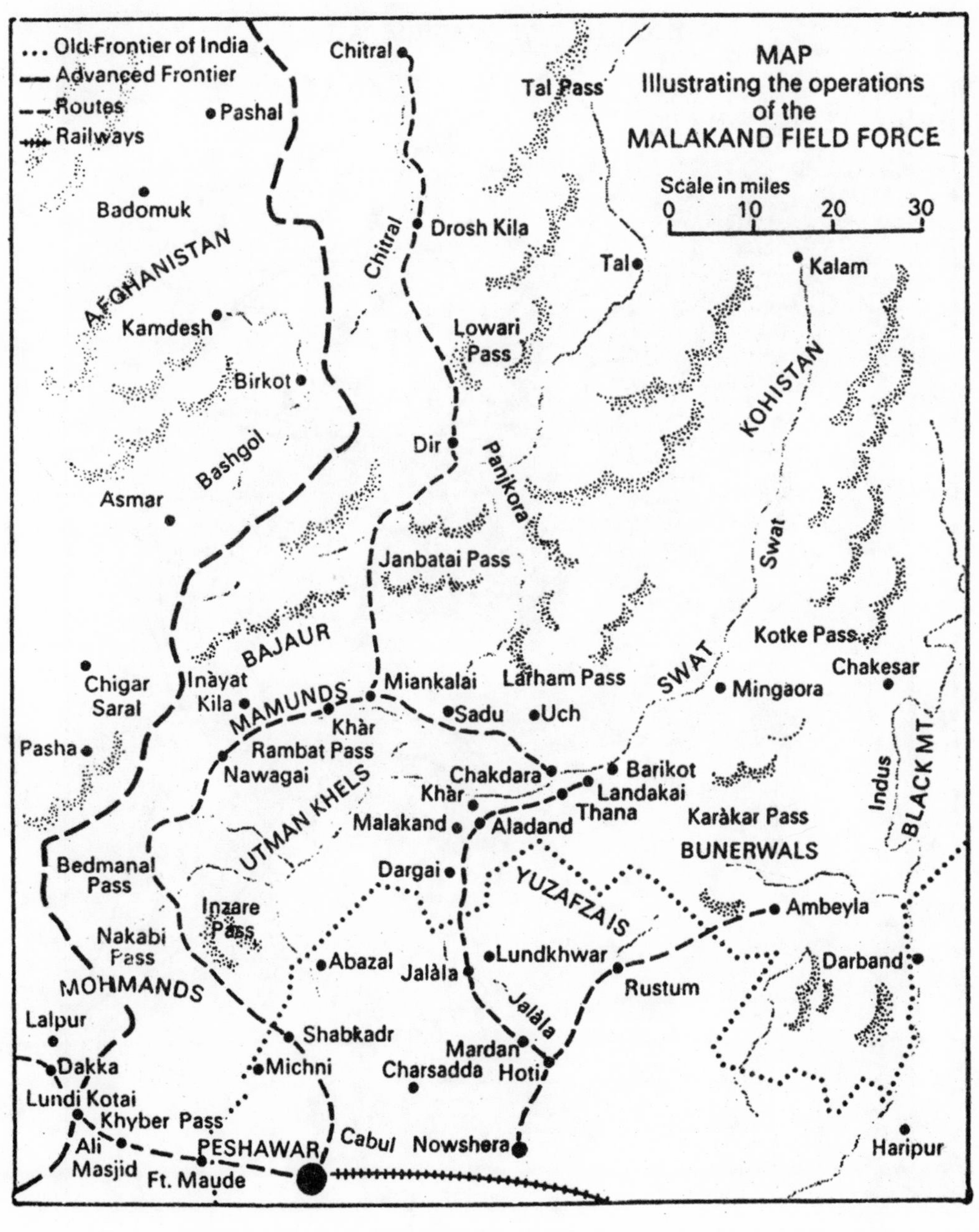

MAP
Illustrating the operations of the MALAKAND FIELD FORCE
... Old Frontier of India
Advanced Frontier
Routes
Railways
Scale in miles
0 10 20 30
Chitral
Tal Pass
Pashal
Badomuk
Drosh Kila
Chitral
AFGHANISTAN
Tal
Kalam
Kamdesh
Lowari Pass
Birkot
KOHISTAN
Dir
Panjkora
Bashgol
Asmar
Swat
Janbatai Pass
Kotke Pass
BAJAUR
Chakesar
Chigar Saral
Inayat Kila
Miankalai
Larham Pass
SWAT
Mingaora
MAMUNDS
Sadu
Uch
Khar
Rambat Pass
Pasha
Nawagai
Chakdara
Barikot
Khar
Landakai
UTMAN KHELS
Thana
Karakar Pass
Indus
BLACK MT
Malakand
Aladand
BUNERWALS
Bedmanai Pass
Dargai
YUZAFZAIS
Inzare Pass
Ambeyla
Nakabi Pass
Abazai
Lundkhwar
Darband
Jalala
Rustum
MOHMANDS
Jalala
Lalpur
Shabkadr
Mardan
Dakka
Michni
Charsadda
Hoti
Lundi Kotai
Khyber Pass
Ali Masjid
PESHAWAR
Cabul
Nowshera
Haripur
Ft. Maude

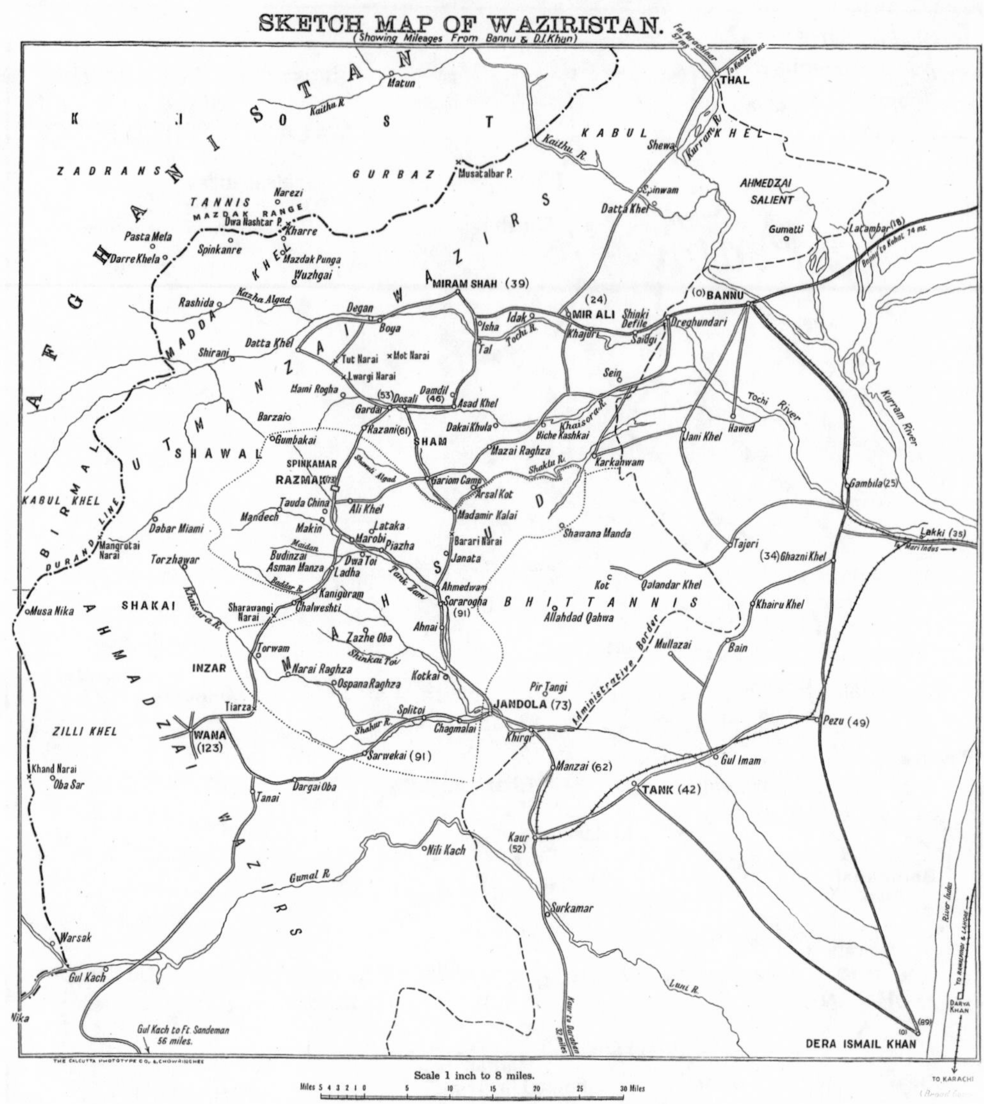

SKETCH MAP OF WAZIRISTAN.

Scale 1 inch to 8 miles.

Miles 5 4 3 2 1 0 5 10 15 20 25 30 Miles

1st. Class Metalled M. T. Roads

Other M. T. Roads

Limits of Mahsud Territory

ONE

People of a Lost Origin

The great phalanx tramped south towards the mountain barrier, churning a sea of dust in its wake as the multitude advanced across the Afghan plain. The grey, barren earth shuddered under the weight of five thousand mounted horse, led by the Faithful Companions, followed by many thousands more of infantrymen shouldering their twenty-foot pikes, wave upon wave of creaking chariots, great siege machines and countless camp followers and pack animals. For miles around, the land resounded with a cacophony of oaths, the braying of mutinous bullocks and the battle songs of the archers and javelineers. The buglers signalled up and down the columns for the foot soldiers to close ranks, quicken the pace, draw the cavalry into line away from the hillsides, where the Pathan tribesmen crouched behind their stone breastworks, poised to loose a deadly fusillade of stones and arrows at the approaching invaders.

In the fourth century BC Alexander of Macedon, the young conqueror of Asia, rode at the head of his host, an army of 120,000 men deployed in two divisions, one under Alexander's own command, consisting of 30,000 hand-picked, light-armed troops led by the general Craterus, and the other, the main force, some 90,000 foot soldiers and cavalry led by Hephaestin and Perdiceas. The army had spent many months marching across the vast wilderness of Afghanistan, and then over the foothills of the mighty Sofed Koh range, whence the men's gaze fell rapaciously on the mist rising from the lush Indus valleys beyond the hilltops.

As the columns drew near to the dark mountains, the 25-year-old scholar-warrior reflected on his nightly readings of Herodotus, the

Greek 'Father of History' who had chronicled these lands a century before Alexander was to set off on his mission of conquest. Herodotus spoke in his *Histories* of a tribe called the Apey Reti (today known as the Afridis), which dwelt in the Gandhara region west of the Indus, the modern vale of Peshawar. Herodotus warned travellers to this region of the tribesmen's savagery and hatred of outsiders, and of their fanaticism in battle. Discretion being the better part of valour, Alexander summoned up his genius of tactical instinct and divided his army into two bodies. His trusted generals Hephaestin and Perdiceas would lead the bulk of the force, ninety thousand foot soldiers and cavalry through the Khyber Pass, the homeland of the Afridis, while Alexander took a smaller élite force across the more northerly Kunnar Valley through Swat. Once this territory had been pacified, he would swing his column southward to link up with the main body of the army to begin the crossing of the Indus and the invasion of India proper.

The tribesmen who lay in wait for Alexander and his soldiers were no strangers to invasion. The Pathans, crouched on top of narrow defiles that gave passage into the Indus Valley, or behind stone breastworks with their daggers at the ready, had learnt to defend their homeland over centuries of warfare and internecine strife.

Sometime around 1500 BC the first stirrings were heard from the tribes that dwelt in the pastureland, by then exhausted, along the Caspian Sea. In time, these sedentary agriculturists became restless nomads, gathering force as they swept southward across the lands we now call Iran and Afghanistan.

The Aryans were on the march and there was no resisting this human horde driven by desperation, trampling underfoot all that stood in their path. At last, about a thousand years before the Macedonian king launched his expedition to the Indus, these early settlers began to establish themselves in the land of Gandhara, where they became known as the Men of Roh, the tribal name for the hill dwellers on the Suleiman range of the North-West Frontier.

The Aryans' martial culture was enshrined in their worship of warring storm-gods, beliefs that were later preserved in the Vedic religion, in which the god Indra was portrayed as a conquering deity, the scourge of the Aryans' enemies who smashed cities and slaughtered foes. Everything about these colonisers reflected their harsh environment. The fortunate ones made it across the ranges to the rich farmland of the Indus Valley. The lives of those who stayed behind in the parched hills became a daily struggle for survival, and over the years they were forged into one of the world's most feared warrior castes. This was to stand them in good stead against later waves of invaders, from Alexander to Genghis Khan, Tamerlane, the Mughal emperor Babur and eventually the British.

Then in the seventh century BC came another migratory wave of marauders from Central Asia to occupy a vast tract of land, stretching from the Helmand River that rises in central Afghanistan in the mountains west of Kabul, hundreds of miles east, to the plains of the Punjab in what is today northern Pakistan.

The tribesmen who settled in this inhospitable land built no cities or monuments, and they left no written records of their presence until well into the seventeenth century. Slowly they organised themselves into tribes, which today number about sixty, and numerous clans within each tribe, to defend themselves as much against incursions by rival tribesmen as against the common enemies who descended with regularity from the Asian steppes to plunder the rich lands of the Indus Valley.

Among these wild tribes, according to Herodotus, there was one that bore the name Pactyes, giving rise to speculation among ethnologists that these people were the forebears of the Pathans. 'Is the name that has come down to us in this ancient Greek version identical with the present-day Pathans?' asks one scholar. 'If it is, we have here a clue to the date at which the ancestors of the Pathans first established themselves in the Helmand basin.'[1]

Throughout the nineteenth and twentieth centuries, and indeed even to our own day, the ethnic origin of the Pathans has been a subject of much heated debate. Our knowledge of the tribes comes largely from relatively modern research, given the lack of written historical records and, above all, the hostile reception that awaits the interloper who dares venture into tribal territory along the North-

West Frontier. Even the Afridi tribe, the first to be identified in historical records among the Pathans, whose homeland is the relatively accessible Khyber and Tirah region of Pakistan's North-West Frontier Province, is still an enigma to scholars in search of their ethnic roots. The Afridis, like their brother Pathan tribes, are a Pashtu (or Pakhtu in this case, the harder northern variant) speaking people. But no one can say with any certainty if this was always so.

> Observations . . . support the belief that the Afridi tribes, though at present speaking Pashtu, contain a large, if not predominant racial element, which was established in Tirah long before the advent of those Afghan invaders who during Mohammedan times gradually pushed their way into the belt of hills and alluvial plains west of the Indus, and who have spread their Pashtu speech in places even across the great river.[2]

Sir Aurel Stein, the author of these comments and one of the most eminent archaeologists and orientalists of the early twentieth century, maintains that the Afridi tribesmen probably migrated from the Afghan highlands to the hill country along the North-West Frontier. Stein suggests that, with their often fair hair and frequently blue or light grey eyes, the Afridis bear a closer resemblance to the Dardic-speaking hill dwellers found south of the Hindu Kush mountains of Afghanistan than to the much darker and 'curiously Semitic-looking' type prevalent among Afghans proper living west and south-west of the Afridis' tribal homeland around the Khyber Pass. The Dardic speakers were those tribes that had fled the onslaught of the Aryans and established their fastness in Afghanistan's great range, where until relatively recent days they kept their ancient pagan faith and evaded conversion to Islam. Stein concludes that the Afridis were one of the Pathan tribes described by Herodotus, which inhabited the easternmost Persian satrapy, or province, of the Archaemenidian Empire that flourished between the sixth and fifth centuries BC. Stein's thesis is supported by the discovery of Archaemenid inscriptions mentioning Gandhara as one of the provinces of this early Persian Empire. We are therefore on relatively safe ground in assuming that the Afridis were in possession of their native land from very remote times, certainly before the sword-wielding Afghan horsemen of the seventh century AD galloped in to convert the tribes to Islam.

At some point, the Pathans began to weave a nexus of tales to explain their genealogy. About four hundred years ago we find the first references that planted the seeds of the Pathan genesis, not in the migrations of the pagan warriors who emerged from Central Asia, but in the venerable Hebrew patriarchs of the bible. The Pathans offer an elaborate biblical folklore linking their origins to the Ten Lost Tribes of Israel, from which they claim direct descent. The version that is told around the hearth, from mud dwellings of the barren hills of South Waziristan to the story-tellers' bazaar of Peshawar, goes like this: Saul, the first king of the Israelites, had a son named Irmia (Jeremiah), and he in turn had a son who was called Afghana. Saul was killed in battle with the Philistines and Jeremiah died at roughly the same time as his father. Afghana was brought up by King David and eventually rose to take command of the armies of Israel. Somewhere between the seventh and sixth centuries BC, about four hundred years after Afghana's death, which would be at the time of the captivity of the tribes of Israel, ten of the twelve tribes (the sons of Afghana) escaped, and several of them found refuge in the mountains of Ghor, in what is now Hazarat in central Afghanistan. These people, the tribesmen will tell you, were the progenitors of what was to become the Pathan nation. Moreover, the Pathans up and down the Frontier, who are overwhelmingly Sunni Muslims, refer to themselves in the most matter-of-fact way as *Ben-i-Israel*, or 'sons of Israel'. They acknowledge the founder of their race to be Qais, allegedly the thirty-seventh lineal descendant of Saul, who lived in Ghor at the time of the rise of Islam. Saul himself, according to Pathan lore, was the forty-fifth in descent from Abraham, a claim that is at total variance with biblical genealogy, while the former allows only thirty-seven generations for a period of 1,600 years. Nevertheless, the Pathans ignore this inconsistency, and according to their tradition, Qais himself was converted to Islam by Muhammad's emissary Khaled Ibn Waleed, whose daughter he married, and subsequently visited Mecca to receive a blessing from the Prophet. In the tenth century, the last of the Pathan tribes had embraced Islam. By tradition, Qais had four sons, Sarbanr, Bitan, Ghurghusht and Karlanri, and all the Pathan tribes trace their line of descent from one of these offspring. Thus the Sarbanri, or western Afghans, engendered the Saddozai and Muhammadzai families that ruled Afghanistan in the eighteenth and nineteenth centuries respectively. Another section of the Sarbanr dynasty, the eastern Afghans, gave rise to important tribes such as the Shinwaris and Mohmands, as well as the Yusufzais of Dir, Swat and Buner, and the Mandanr Yusufzais of the plains of Swabi and Mardan, the town that was to acquire fame in the days of the Raj as the spiritual home of the Corps of Guides, raised to keep the peace on the Frontier. The family tree of Bitan, Qais's second son, produced the Bhittanni tribe of Waziristan, and later the powerful Lodhi dynasty that ruled in Delhi in the fourteenth and fifteenth centuries. Ghurghusht was the patriarch of several tribes that migrated to the southernmost reaches of the Frontier, and also to the Peshawar district. Karlanri, the last of Qais's children, who was reputedly discovered in the forest as a newborn babe, was the forefather of the greatest hill tribes of the Frontier. The Afridis, Utman Khel, Orakzais, Daurs, Mahsuds, Utmanzais and Wazirs, and others, all look to Karlanri as their founding father.

What evidence do we have to substantiate this seductive theory of Jewish origin, which, it should be remembered, came to the attention of the western world at a time when the legend of the Lost Tribes and the biblical prophecies was very much in British minds? And, if archaeological shreds and fragments are to be found to support the claim to Israelite origin, is this a sufficiently sound foundation on which to construct a scientific thesis? The debate, which first came to the western public's notice in the early nineteenth century, split open a hornets' nest in the ethnologist community.

It was in 1808 that the intrepid traveller the Honourable Mountstuart Elphinstone assembled an embassy to Afghanistan, an entourage of great magnificence in the classic style of his day. Seated bolt upright on his mount, the gaunt, hawk-like Elphinstone rode out of the gates of Delhi at the head of what resembled a small army, made up of a secretary, two East India Company assistants, a surgeon and an infantry captain and seven officers commanding an escort of 450 mounted cavalry and infantrymen. The mission's objective was to gather intelligence about the unknown territories that lay beyond the borders of the Raj and to make such inquiries 'as were likely to be of use to the British Government'. This meant exploring the opening of trade routes with Central Asia as well as assessing the mood of the local potentates towards the Raj. On his journey, Elphinstone accumulated a vast store of knowledge on the Afghans and their cousins of the Frontier, which at that time lay hundreds of miles beyond British India's territorial limits. At the court of the Amir of Kabul, Elphinstone was regaled with stories of the Pathan bloodline, which he interpreted as plausible, but only up to a point, beyond which the tales became riddled with historical inconsistencies. He brought back accounts of warrior tribes whose version of Hebrew ancestry does not, according to the traveller, essentially differ from Scripture. 'It is known that ten of the twelve tribes remained in the east after the return of their brethren to Judea,' he writes.

> The supposition that the Afghans are their descendants explains easily and naturally both the disappearance of the one people, and the origin of the other. The rest of the story is confirmed by the fact that the Jews were very numerous in Arabia at the time of Mohammed, and that the principal division of them bore the appellation of Khyber, which is still the name of a district in Afghanistan, if not of an Afghan tribe.[3]

It is obvious from Elphinstone's description of the Khyber that the North-West Frontier, which four decades later was annexed to British India, was deemed in the early years of the nineteenth century to be part of the *terra incognita* that made up Afghanistan.

The debate between proponents of the Israelite origin theory and those who dismissed it as fanciful raged well into the twentieth century. As late as the 1950s, prominent individuals such as Itzhak Ben-Zvi, the second president of Israel, were outspoken in their acceptance of the Pathans' Jewish roots. Prior to that, the nineteenth-century explorer William Moorcroft mysteriously came across an ancient copy of the Old Testament in Hebrew on his travels in Afghanistan. Moorcroft's contemporary, the distinguished orientalist Sir William Jones, put forth his arguments in favour of the Pathan version of their descent on the basis of shared names with the ancient Hebrews, certain religious traditions and similarities between the Pashtu and Aramaic languages. The Central Asian explorer Joseph Wolff, a converted Jew and the son of a German rabbi, was, on the other hand, an emphatic disbeliever of the Ten Lost Tribes story. A hundred years after Elphinstone's expedition to Kabul, archaeological digs near Herat, in western Afghanistan, unearthed some remarkable gravestones bearing Hebrew as well as Persian names. Furthermore, the Kabul Museum, before it was savagely demolished by the Taliban, contained a black stone discovered in Kandahar with Hebrew inscriptions inexplicably carved on it. The Honourable Elphinstone himself must be cast alongside the sceptics. This is his word on the subject: 'I fear we must class the descent of the Afghans [Pathans] from the Jews with that of the Romans and the British from the Trojans, and that of the Irish from the Milesians or the Brahmins.'[4] It is perhaps a happy circumstance that the compelling mystery of the Pathans' ethnic origin is destined to be left unsolved for the foreseeable future. Given the tribesmen's historical hostility to outsiders, no comprehensive anthropological study of these people has ever been carried out.

Given the lack of unity among the Frontier tribes, it comes as no surprise that the theory of Israelite origin is only one of a pot-pourri of less widespread tales of Pathan origin. Several tribes adhere to the concept of Aryan genealogy, and still others are happy to consider themselves as descendants of the Arabs, Persians or Greeks. The Mohmands, for instance, firmly believe they can trace their ancestry directly back to followers of the Prophet Muhammad, while many of the tribes bear names with clear links to great Old Testament figures. Shinwari, for instance, comes from Simeon; Yusufzai translates as 'sons of Joseph', the suffix *zai* being a corruption of the Pathan word *zoe*, meaning 'son'; and *Afridi* is itself a derivative of 'Ephraim'. It is the Afridis, however, who stand out as the principal proponents of the Jewish origin theory. Their case has been taken up by genuine as well as amateur authorities from the early nineteenth century onward. Thomas Pennell was a physician and missionary who spent sixteen years in charge of a medical station at Bannu, in North Waziristan. Pennell had a fascination for what he perceived to be unmistakable ethnic links between his Pathan patients and the Jews. 'Often in looking round the visitors to our out-patient department one sees some old greybeard of pure Afghan descent, and involuntarily exclaims: "The man might for all the world be one of the old Jewish patriarchs returned to us from Bible history!"'[5] Pennell was struck by the many commonly shared customs and observances of the Pathans and Hebrews. In particular, he cites two that in the Islamic world are unique to the Pathans. The first is the sacrifice of an animal, usually a goat or a sheep, in case of illness, after which the blood of the animal is sprinkled over the door posts of the house of the sick person, to ward off the angel of death. The other is to take a heifer and ceremoniously place upon it the sins of the people, after which it is driven out into the wilderness.

Much later, in the 1950s, the American diplomat James W. Spain found himself seduced by the Pathans' exotic genealogical tree. After a posting with the US Embassy in Karachi, the original capital of Pakistan, Spain devoted nearly a decade of his life to researching the history and customs of the Frontier tribes. He never accepted the Pathans' literal version of their biblical lineage, but he was impressed by the remarkable consistency of their tales, which he surmised had been composed almost entirely from the same origin about four centuries previously. 'Every true Pathan can fit himself and his ancestors into this great family tree,' he says. 'Nonetheless, it is valuable since it provides a framework which reflects the real divisions of groups at that time and has preserved the actual lines of descent since.'[6]

The sceptic should be wary of rejecting out of hand this 'fable' of the Ten Lost Tribes. Attention must be drawn to the work of Sir Olaf Caroe, the doyen of Pathan historians, who served as the last British governor of the North-West Frontier Province before the transfer of sovereignty to Pakistan in 1947. As a native of the Scottish Highlands, albeit of Norwegian ancestry (his full Christian name was Olaf Kirkpatrick), Caroe found himself in familiar surroundings on the North-West Frontier. On his first journey to the Frontier, when he crossed the bridge at Attok, the gorge where the Kabul River meets the Indus at the site of the fort built in the sixteenth century under the reign of the emperor Babur, Caroe exclaimed that 'to cross the bridge at Attok is to come home'. Caroe was far more than a civil servant. His meticulous, scholarly research provides us with an authoritative point of reference to the Frontier tribes, embodied in *The Pathans*, a seminal work that traces this people's history from 550 BC to the second half of the twentieth century.

'Lest already the serious reader dismiss it as pure fable, I must here put some weight in the other scale,' writes Caroe about the Israelite origin theory.

> It is to be remembered, first, that with the exception of some modern Kabul writers, who at one time inclined to 'Nordic' theories under Hitlerian influence, the greater number of Afghan and Pathan commentators believe these traditions, the more so in relation to the tribal genealogies which grow out of the 'myth' when it reaches the Islamic era.[7]

The Pathans call their homeland *Yaghistan*, the 'Land of the Untamed'. The handful of surviving British soldiers who served on the North-West Frontier will tell you that the name is fully justified. No doubt the conquerors of past centuries whose armies clashed with these hill tribes would also endorse this view. The story goes in Pathan folklore that when God created the world there were many stones and rocks left over, and that these were all dumped down on the Frontier. The tribesmen's stoical acceptance of their existence in a largely desolate, hostile landscape belies a character as hard and enduring as the rocks that Allah caused to be scattered on their homeland.

This rugged landscape stretches from the mountains of Chitral in the north, where many of the inhabitants claim to be descendants of the remnants of Alexander's army that stayed behind and settled here. Indeed, one of the most common male names in this region is *Iskander*, the local translation of Alexander. What is today the North-West Frontier then descends some 400 miles south through a tangle of inhospitable hill and mountain country to untamed South Waziristan, the land of the much-feared Mahsud tribe. Here the hills are mostly devoid of cultivation, from the Kurram Valley to the north to the point at which the hills merge with the Suleiman Range near the towering landmark of Takht-i-Sulaiman, the 'Throne of Solomon'. At its widest point the Frontier runs from Kurram Agency on the Afghan border about 250 miles eastward to Abbottabad, so named for General Sir James Abbott, one of the great paladins of the Punjab.

The North-West Frontier lies in the epicentre of conflict zones. On its northern border, it touches the Wakhan Corridor, the elongated mountainous valley between the Hindu Kush and the Pamirs that was ceded to Afghanistan in 1893. This finger of land was demarcated to act as a buffer to prevent Britain and Russia's colonial empires meeting head on. Yet the two superpowers of their day were separated by less than half a dozen miles by the Corridor, which today serves as a wedge between Pakistan and Tajikistan, one of Central Asia's most politically unstable countries, and also as the gateway to China. To the south, the Frontier is bounded by the desolate tribal land of Baluchistan, where the Pakistani government is battling pockets of tribal revolt, and the Dera Ghazi Khan district of the Punjab. To the east lies Kashmir, one of the loveliest spots in South Asia, where the Pakistani and Indian armies confront one another on the world's highest battleground, the 20,700ft Siachen Glacier. The Frontier's western border straddles Afghanistan, a country that has not known peace for almost three decades.

Geographically, the Frontier is split into three regions. The Hazara district is the only portion of the Frontier found to the east of the Indus. Only about a quarter of the people in this district are Pashtu speakers, while the remainder speak Hindko, an ancient language of northern Pakistan. There is a narrow strip of land between the west bank of the Indus and the tribal hill country, whose main city is Peshawar, the administrative as well as the historic capital of the

Frontier. The tribal area itself, to the north and west, lies along the Durand Line, which for more than a century has stood as the official border between British India, now Pakistan, and Afghanistan.

Outside the cultivated farmland and bustling towns of the 'settled districts' – that is, the Frontier enclave in which the British colonialists established their presence – there is little of natural beauty in tribal territory proper. 'First, miles of cliff and stony slopes,' recalls one veteran Frontiersman in his memoirs of tribal warfare. 'Then open plains flanked by low, bare hills, and scored by deep ravines, after which you come to the great bare hills and cliffs of the Khyber . . .'[8] There are exceptions to this bleakness – for instance, the Tirah, the lush valleys and woodlands south of the Khyber Pass that are the jealously guarded preserve of the Afridi tribe. But for the most part, a visitor to the Frontier would be hard pressed to understand how anyone could survive, much less provide for a family, in this barren country that is home to several millions of Pathans. The answer is that the Pathans struggle desperately hard to eke out a living from traditional farming and trade and by long-standing tradition regularly engage in less savoury activities, such as smuggling, extortion and the drug trade, to make ends meet.

Yet the Frontier has always held a compelling allure for those who have given years of their lives to this harsh environment. Caroe, for one, found that the secret of the Frontier's fascination was in what he described as the tremendous scenic canvas brought into sharp relief by sharp, cruel changes of climate. 'Sometimes the assault on the spirit is that of stark ugliness and discomfort – appalling heat, a dust-storm across the Peshawar plain, the eroded foothills of Khyber or Waziristan,' he writes. 'More often it is an impression of beauty indescribable in its clarity and contrast with the barren emptiness that went before. The weft and warp of this tapestry is woven into the souls and bodies of the men who move before it. Much is harsh, but all is drawn in strong tones that catch the breath, and at times bring tears, almost of pain.'[9] There is no doubt that the Frontier, in the very bleakness that inspired Caroe's elegant tribute, possesses the power to rouse deeper emotions than might, for instance, a familiar and pleasant alpine meadow. 'The last free place on Earth' was how a

British journalist in the 1950s described his first exposure to the North-West Frontier.

Given the poverty of the land and the extremes of climate (temperatures can soar to more than 115°F in summer and plunge to well below freezing in the winter months), it is no wonder that the Pathans have been moulded into what more than one officer serving on the Frontier has acknowledged to be the world's toughest fighting men. Their ability to stalk an enemy with the stealth and cunning of a panther is legendary. 'Their power of moving concealed is astounding, not only in moving from cover to cover, but in slipping from light to shadow, and background to background,' recalls one British solider. 'It has to be seen to be believed. And their stillness in cover is equally striking.'[10] This predatory nature is graphically reflected in the Pathans' raiding tactics. Reliable British Army issue rifles, since the arrival of the Raj, have always been their most cherished booty, and camp sentries their chosen prey. When launching a raid on an arms depot under the cover of darkness, a party of Pathan warriors would often strip naked to avoid the tribesmen's baggy trousers rustling against the underbrush and thus giving away their presence. Apart from their daggers, they carried short twigs to use as a funnel should anyone have to relieve his bladder during the long waiting hours before the attack. The slightest noise that might cause a sentry to prick up his ears would send the raiders slithering silently back to their *nullahs*, the dry riverbeds that criss-cross the valleys and serve as escape routes. If the opportunity is missed on any given night, it is bound to come the next or the one after that, at any rate often enough to make it worth their while to watch for it. 'They have no work to do, no camp to get to, they have range upon range of hill to screen them for as long as they choose, and night has no terrors for them. They will return to the job day after day without anyone having an inkling of their presence, and when the real chance comes they seize it like lightning.'[11]

It should not be assumed that the Pathan tribes make up a homogenous race in respect of character and a belligerent nature. Historically, much depends on environment – that is, to what extreme a tribe is forced to prey on its neighbours to obtain its daily bread. As we have seen, not all the tribal land is made up of parched hills and barren scrub. There exist pockets of rich farmland, as well as grazing pasture up and down the Frontier, in Bajaur, the Khyber and elsewhere. The less warlike tribes tend to be found in these comparatively prosperous regions. In more recent times it became a matter of a tribe's proximity to the settled districts, in particular the major towns like Peshawar. Education and social services come into the picture as well. This author was told by a Mullagori tribesman, whose family hails from north of the Khyber Pass, that in his village in the past, any man who ventured out of his home without a firearm did so at the peril of his life. Over a period of a couple of decades, the village had been provided with schools, sanitation facilities and proper medical services. Today, he said, these who walked the streets with assault rifles slung over their shoulders would be laughed at.

Sir William Barton, who served as Commandant of the Khyber Rifles at the time of the Third Afghan War in 1919 and later held high rank in the North-West Frontier civil service, was one of the most experienced of British administrators in dealing with the mosaic of Pathan tribes. Barton held to the view that it would hardly be possible to produce a sketch of Pathan character to fit all the tribes, from the Indus to the Persian border and the Hindu Kush to Baluchistan. He explains:

> There is, for example, a vast difference between the mental and moral outlook of a rich young Khan from Peshawar, educated in England, who, on a visit to London, might give you an elaborate lunch at the Savoy, and an odoriferous Wazir lazily making his way from Birmal in the Amir's country [Afghanistan], to the Kurram valley with his sheep and camels.

Barton nurtures no romantic notions of these rough hill people, who in his view, and in that of the soldiers who crossed swords with the fierce Wazir tribesmen, would cut an infidel's throat with a blunt knife as soon as look at him. This mistrust and animosity towards outsiders are not confined to foreign intruders. As far as the tribesmen of the hills are concerned, any stranger is to be regarded as an adversary until the contrary is proven, a doctrine embodied in the Pathan language, whose word for 'cousin' (*tarbur*) is synonymous with 'enemy'. 'The Khan might not like his English guest politically,' says Barton, 'he might criticise the social exclusiveness of the Englishman, but the murderous instincts of his race have been atrophied by education and contact with civilised life.'[12]

This 'odoriferous Wazir', to which Barton referred, according to the earliest written records has for centuries past inhabited the wild tangle of hills of Waziristan that stretch for about 100 miles south of Kurram Agency, with Afghanistan as the western border and the tribal agencies of Bannu and Dera Ismail Khan to the east. The two agencies of South and North Waziristan, which together comprise the homeland of the Wazir tribe, cover an area of some 5,000 square miles, most of it wilderness, with the towns of Miranshah, Tank and Wana as the only outposts of civilisation in the entire territory. Given their remoteness and the fierce independent spirit of the inhabitants, North and South Waziristan have always been the most troublesome of the tribal territories, from a military and administrative perspective, starting in early British colonial days, right up to the present. Many mujahidin guerrillas who fought the Russian army during the Soviet invasion of Afghanistan in the 1980s, as well as Taliban remnants and Al Qaeda militants fleeing the US forces after the 11 September 2001 terrorist attacks, found a safe haven amongst the fanatical Wazirs. The Pakistani army has deployed a massive contingent of some eighty thousand troops in and around the borders of Waziristan, where they are battling to root out foreign terrorists and seal off the region to infiltrators from Afghanistan. Army operations in the territory have carried a high cost. Since 2004, hundreds of Pakistani troops have been killed in fierce engagements with the tribesmen. The Wazirs are not in the least intimidated by modern weaponry, which they can easily match with their own panoply of captured Soviet equipment and smuggled arms. The Pakistan Government is showing signs of impatience with their frustrated efforts to stem the influx of Al Qaeda terrorists across the Afghan border into Waziristan. Prime Minister Shaukat Aziz stated on a visit to Britain in 2006 that 'terrorists should not have to be intercepted in tribal territory' and that 'more action needed to be taken on the Afghan side'. For Kabul, turning a blind eye to guerrilla infiltration across the border from Afghanistan's radical heartland is a convenient way to keep up the pressure on Pakistan in the historical stand-off between the two nations.

The British always regarded the Frontier as a territory of maximum strategic significance for the defence of the Indian Empire. As late as 1927, a mere twenty years before Britain relinquished sovereignty of the subcontinent, the Simon Commission, which was set up to make recommendations on the future Indian Constitution, reinforced this concept. 'The North-West Frontier is not only the frontier of India,' the report stated. 'It is an international frontier of the first importance from the military point of view for the whole Empire.'[13] A prophetic statement in the light of how history has unfolded in the eighty years since the Commission submitted its report, and nowhere is this more pertinent than in the turbulent land of Waziristan. The region's strategic value also lies in its geographical location as a major crossroads between Afghanistan and Pakistan. The Tochi Pass connects Ghazni in Afghanistan with Bannu, while the Gomal Pass provides a trade route from Afghanistan to Dera Ismail Khan. Both these roads cut straight through the heart of Waziristan.

The historian Arnold J. Toynbee, who travelled extensively in this region in the early 1960s, attributes the fierceness of the Wazirs to a piece of historical bad luck, in his opinion a consequence of the tribe having stumbled on the badlands at the time of the migrations across the watershed of the hills dividing the parched Afghan flatlands from the fertile Indus Valley. Toynbee held that a tribe's character is a product of that tribe's lands. 'On these lands they [the Wazirs] have not been able to make a living by peaceful labour,' he writes. 'In order to live, they have had to rob either each other or, more profitably, their less indigent neighbours. There has been nothing but fighting to occupy their minds and employ their energies. So the nakedness of their land would explain the Ishmaelitish [desert Arab] way of life that they lead today.'[14]

On his journey to Kabul in 1808, Elphinstone came across these wild hill men and found them a peaceful and cordial lot. Four decades later, when the British Government came up against the Wazirs, the tribe swiftly gained a reputation for being one of the most singularly hostile on the North-West Frontier. Even in 1937, after many years of military campaigns against the Wazirs, several British Indian Army divisions found themselves involved in operations in Waziristan in what amounted to almost full-scale war. The most plausible explanation for this reversal of attitude is that Elphinstone would have been accepted as a transient visitor, an object of curiosity to a tribe that had never before come into contact with Europeans. Less than a generation after the Elphinstone expedition, the tribesmen got word of the annihilation of an entire British army on the retreat from Kabul, in the wake of the First Afghan War, at the hands of their kinsmen on the other side of the hills. From that moment the Pathans would have certainly looked upon the *feringhee* (European) as the enemy. From that episode came into common usage the Pathan proverb that was to serve as the tribesmen's watchword for the next hundred years of British presence on the Frontier: 'First comes one Englishman for *shikar* [hunting], then come two Englishman to draw a map, and then comes an army to take your land. So it is best to kill the first Englishman.'

The Wazirs are frequently referred to as the Darwesh Khel, *Khel* being the Pashtu word for clan. The tribe is divided into two great branches, the Utmanzai and Ahmadzai. Both branches take pains to distinguish themselves from their cousins, the Mahsuds of South Waziristan, who are regarded as the most extreme fanatics of all the Frontier tribes. The Mahsuds' cruelty, especially on the battlefield, became the stuff of barrack-room lore among the troops who crossed swords with this ferocious tribe. 'They are an extremely barbarous and warlike tribe, of the same origin as the Darwesh Khel Wazirs,' declares an official report issued in 1910.[15] This document is in itself an elaborate testimony to the Government's determination to catalogue every bit of data it had accumulated on the Pathan hill tribes. It contains almost five thousand entries classifying the Pathans first by tribe, then by clan of the tribe, division of the clan, sub-division of the division, section of the sub-division, down to other minor factions of the section, along with the number of fighting men of each faction, the locality of the tribe, the clan and so on.

The directory was compiled very much in the spirit of 'know thy enemy', for government records, particularly in the early days of British rule, showed nothing but a deep-rooted contempt for the Frontier tribes. Less than a decade after the Raj arrived on the scene in 1849, the official reports filed by government agents on the Frontier spoke with breathtaking arrogance of the Pathans as 'savages' and 'absolute barbarians'.

> They have nothing approaching Government or Civil Institutions. They have for the most part no education. They have nominally a religion, but Mahomedanism, as understood by them, is no better, or perhaps is actually worse, than the creeds of the wildest races on earth. In their eyes the one great commandment is blood for blood, and fire and sword for all infidels, that is, for all people not Mahomedans. They are superstitious and priest-ridden. But the priests [Mullahs] are as ignorant as they are bigoted, and use their influence simply for preaching crusades against unbelievers, and inculcate the doctrine of rapine and bloodshed against the defenceless people of the Plain. The hill men are sensitive in regard to their women, but their custom in regard to marriage and betrothal is very prejudicial to social advancement. At the same time they are a sensual race. They are avaricious. For gold they will do almost anything, except betray a guest. They are thievish and predatory to the last degree. The Pathan mother often prays that her son may be a successful robber.'[16]

The most significant aspect of this inflammatory diatribe is that it smacks quite distinctly of sour grapes. It was issued a century after Clive's victory at Plassey, the battle that launched Britain on its conquest of India. Suddenly, after a hundred years of seemingly unstoppable expansion, the Raj's self-confidence had been shattered by a tribe of 'savages' and 'barbarians', who refused to capitulate or let themselves be co-opted into collaboration with the British masters.

The tales of Mahsud atrocities committed against their own people as well as the British occupiers are legendary. Major Walter James Cummings, an Indian-born British officer who served in Waziristan after the First World War, tells the story of coming across the aftermath of a Mahsud raid on a local village.

> We arrived at the village shortly after dawn, the Mahsud raiders had made off a few hours before we arrived. The women of the village were still screaming from fear and pain at the ghastly handling they had all received at the hands of the gang. The Mahsuds had torn and ripped the gold ornaments out of the noses and ears of the owners and in one case a woman's finger had been cut off to get a gold ring. Some of the men folk who had shown resistance had been shot out of hand and their bodies flung out on to the roadway whilst their dwellings were pillaged.[17]

Traders and travellers passing though Mahsud country did so at great peril to their lives. Strength in numbers was no deterrent to the marauding tribesmen, as was verified each year when the great caravans of Powindah traders crossed the Zhob and Gomal passes through the Suleiman hills into Waziristan. Every autumn, these tribes of warrior traders came leading many thousands of camels laden with merchandise from Bokhara and Kandahar, to the Indian markets of Multan, Rajputana, Lahore, Amritsar, Delhi, Cawnpore, Benares and Patna. The Powindahs, whose name derives from the same root as the Pashtu word 'to graze', belong chiefly to the great tribe of Ghilzai Pathans of Afghanistan, the backbone of the Afghan nation, and they were well capable of defending themselves. But after days of harassment by Mahsud raiding parties, once encamped inside the supposed sanctity of British territory they would often let their guard down. That is when the tribesmen would strike, giving the British yet another headache by forcing them to chase the raiders back across the administrative border.

The Mahsuds' relentless pursuit of revenge and terrifying predilection for cruelty were two traits that stood out in the minds of British veterans of the Frontier. The novelist John Masters was posted to Waziristan with the 4th Gurkhas, during which time he took part in a number of Frontier skirmishes and set battles with these tribesmen. 'They never took prisoners but mutilated and beheaded any wounded or dead who fell into their hands,' he recalls. 'They took advantage of the rules to disguise themselves as peaceful passers-by, or as women. They simulated death and pounced on anyone foolish enough to relax his guard.' A British Army officer lay severely wounded after a sharp battle, and when he was found next day, 'he had been castrated and flayed, probably whilst alive, and his skin lay pegged out on the rocks not far from camp'. Masters writes that, if the tribesmen captured any soldiers other than Muslims, and especially if the prisoners were Sikhs or British, they would routinely castrate and behead them. 'Both these operations were frequently done by the women. Sometimes they would torture prisoners with the death of a thousand cuts, pushing grass and thorns into each wound as it was made.'[18]

The Mahsuds are sufficiently fanatical to put a halo round the heads of all those who have been prominent in opposition to the British. Similarly, there is little love lost between this tribe and its Pathan brethren. One explanation for their belligerence is the fact that the Mahsuds exist in complete isolation, more so than any of the other Pathan groupings on the Frontier. The Mahsud tribe dwells in what is now South Waziristan and finds itself encircled on the north, south and west by the Wazirs of North Waziristan. Closing the circle to the east are the Bhittannis, a small tribe who have traditionally allied themselves with their neighbours. Though lacking the martial spirit of the Wazirs and Mahsuds, the Bhittanis are referred to locally as 'the jackals of the Wazirs', a term in all likelihood conceived by the Mahsuds themselves.

Fear of encirclement by hostile neighbours is one important factor behind the Mahsuds' truculent character, but there are other reasons for this tribe having earned its reputation as the terror of the Frontier. From the day the British took possession of the North-West Frontier, successive rulers of Afghanistan became engaged in constant intrigue in Mahsud affairs. Their aim was to exploit the tribe's hostility towards outsiders in order to keep up the pressure on British India, which after all had fought three full-scale wars with Afghanistan during the Raj. A less apparent, but perhaps the most powerful, motive for the Mahsuds' aggressiveness is their relentless pursuit of the blood feud, a subject to be dealt with in another chapter. 'Indeed I believe this to be the root of the economic difficulty, which is the bane of the whole tribal belt,' wrote Sir Evelyn Howell, a former Political Officer on the Frontier.

> No man whose hold on life is as insecure as that of the average tribesman, whether Mahsud, Afridi or what you will, can readily command capital, nor if at any time a sum of money comes into his hand can he lay it out on such things as water-courses, orchards or improvements to the land of any kind. He is compelled to spend it on weapons, whether of defence, such as towers and *kots* [forts], or of offence, such as the latest pattern of military rifle. The retarding influence does not stop at that. It is also a powerful check not only on individual initiative but also on all forms of collective enterprise. Nothing is more remarkable throughout Waziristan – and I believe the same to be true of Tirah – than the traces of terraced fields which are a clear demonstration that once men grew corn where now there is no tillage. What is it if not the blood feud – and the temper from which the blood feud springs – which has kept the active, intelligent and – till we spoilt him – industrious Mahsud, whose coming is comparatively recent, from turning his land to as good an account as did its former occupants?[19]

The fourth tribe of Waziristan that is worthy of consideration is the Daurs. This relatively small band of tribesmen has the dubious distinction of being despised by all their neighbours, who even cast doubt on the Daurs' claim to a Pathan lineage. The other tribes believe that the Daurs are at best illegitimate or half-caste Pathans, their forebears having sprung from a concubine of one of the early tribal patriarchs. The fact that the Daurs committed a gross infamy by petitioning the British to take them under the protection of the Raj to a large extent accounts for this animosity. The Government saw fit to ignore this request, which would have involved stationing large contingents of troops in tribal territory. The reality is that the Daurs bear a much closer resemblance to tribesmen of the settled districts than to their untamed cousins of the hills. They cultivate one of the very few fertile areas in Waziristan, the Tochi Valley, while during and after British rule they engaged in normal channels of commerce, trading their footwear and leather goods in the bazaars. The Daurs gave the authorities little trouble, thus lending support to the theory advanced by Frontier veterans such as Howell and Caroe that economic progress is the indisputable civilising factor in the lives of the Pathan tribesmen.

Travelling north through the tribal belt from Waziristan, one crosses an imaginary linguistic line, running roughly east–west, where the Indus meets the Kurram River. This divide separates the softer Pashtu variant from the more guttural Pakhtu spoken by the tribes of the Khyber and adjacent areas. Despite the existence of the two distinct dialects, it is common practice to refer collectively to the Pathan language as Pashtu.

Second only to the Mahsuds in warlike spirit is the mighty Afridi nation of the Khyber. The Afridis put forth a case for being of the purest Pathan lineage, a claim that is disputed on linguistic grounds by noted ethnologists such as Sir George Grierson, Sir Aurel Stein and others. Some scholars argue that Tirahi was the original language of a large number of Afridis living in the hills of Tirah south of the Khyber Pass. It has been reasonably established that Tirahi was a Dardic tongue, suggesting that these people inhabited their present homeland well before the Afghan invaders pushed the Pashtu language across the hills west of the Indus in Muhammadan times. 'We know that, both on the upper Indus and in the valleys drained by the Swat river, tribes who now speak Pashtu and proudly claim to be Pathans were of Dard stock and Dardic speech until their comparatively recent conversion to Islam,' says Stein.[20]

The Afridis command the Khyber Pass, and this political reality in itself means that relations with the tribe take on a crucial strategic importance, for the successive governments of Pakistan as well as for the British during their years of Frontier rule. The Khyber Pass was always a strategically vulnerable spot for British India. Throughout history, it has accommodated almost every imaginable mode of road transport, from chariots to elephants, elaborately painted Pakistani lorries, the Rolls-Royce of a fleeing Afghan monarch, not to omit tanks. Apart from being the historic point of entry for invading armies, the pass has always served as the main trade route to the Indian subcontinent from Central Asia. The sea lanes of India were by the mid-nineteenth century well protected by the British navy, to the east lay hundreds of miles of dense Burmese jungle, and to complete this defensive ring the Himalaya range to the north stands as perhaps the world's most formidable barrier to land invasion. The North-West Frontier, on the other hand, and in particular the Khyber Pass, afforded comparatively easy access to India and was therefore considered paramount to the defence of the Raj. The Afridis control the pass and its surrounding territory; hence the need to maintain friendly relations with the tribe.

The British came into contact with the Afridis in 1839 at the time of the First Afghan War, ten years before the annexation of the Punjab and, with it, the North-West Frontier, which was loosely held under Sikh domination. As with all the Pathan tribes, it would be wrong to assume that every one is a homogenous unit with identical character traits. The Afridis are divided into six main clans and numerous sub-sections. They have been described as 'pleasant-looking men' with 'a Hebraic cast of features and a partiality for full beards', which, when added to the grace with which most of the older men wear their flowing garments, convey an impression of an assembly of Old Testament prophets.[21] Yet this uniformity runs skin-deep only. Each clan has its own habitat and, generally speaking, the closer its territory lay to the settled districts of British India – in this case the town of Peshawar – the more amenable the clan would be to dealing with the *feringhee* in a reasonably peaceful fashion, thanks in no small measure to the allowances (a euphemism for bribes) they were allotted by the Government in exchange for undertakings to keep on good behaviour.

It is not by chance that the Zakka Khel clan was regarded as the scourge of established law during the years of British rule. Its villages are the most remote of all the Afridi clans from the administrative border area. They are also a more self-sufficient people than their brethren; hence they had little need to establish trade channels with British-controlled territory.

Major-General Sir George Roos-Keppel, during his tenure as Political Agent of the Khyber in the early twentieth century, found this clan to be the most troublesome and difficult with which he had to deal during his long career on the Frontier. In his experience, any show of liberality and patience was taken as a sign of fear or weakness. Bitterly hostile as the Zakka Khel were to everything and every person connected with British rule, they would prefer to linger in isolation and to have no relations with Government.

The Zakka Khel territory, now as in the past, occupies part of the Khyber Pass road and is by far the most extensive and politically sensitive area of the Khyber, covering as it does the whole of the fertile Bazar Valley and a large part of Tirah, the region's prime poppy-growing area. The clan has effective control of the Khyber Pass and this allows the Zakka Khels to travel throughout the Khyber Agency without having to traverse land belonging to any other Afridi clan.

The British were obliged to keep the Zakka Khels sweet and therefore this clan received the lion's share of the tribal allowances. When, in 1880, the Government agreed to grant the Afridis a monthly stipend of 7,155 rupees in exchange for an undertaking to keep the Khyber Pass open to caravan traffic, it was thought wise to hand over 1,700 rupees, roughly a quarter of this allowance, to the Zakka Khels, one of eight Afridi clans. Even the Khyber Political Agent Colonel Sir Robert Warburton, who almost alone among Frontier officials of his day could muster words of praise for the Afridis, wrote of his contempt for this particular clan. He dismissed the Zakka Khels as 'the greatest thieves, housebreakers, robbers and raiders amongst all the Khyber clans, their word or promise never being believed or trusted by their Afridi brethren without a substantial security being taken for its fulfilment'.[22] It was, after all, the Zakka Khels who had rallied the Afridis to rise up against the British in 1897, and it was this same clan that never accepted the terms of submission laid down by Government, preferring to continue to stage raids and commit atrocities in the settled districts long after the formal end to hostilities.

The Orakzai tribe occupies an area of some 700 square miles adjacent to the Afridis, mostly south of the Khyber Pass, as far as the hills of the Kurram Valley. The main town of the Orakzai Agency is Darra Adam Khel, a popular destination with adventure travellers who delight in having their photo taken fondling one of the automatic weapons produced in the town's arms factories.

The Orakzais, who are divided into seven clans, were traditionally allied to the Afridis in their feuds with the British, but were deemed to be less warlike and therefore of inferior fighting quality. At one point, this tribe raised a peculiar problem for the British Government. This was related to the fact that a minority of the Orakzais, comprising about 10 per cent of the tribe, belong to the Shi'a sect of Islam, as opposed to the majority of Sunni Muslims who make up the Pathan nation. The tribe takes its name, which in Pashtu means the 'lost son' (*orak zoi*), from a legend of their ancestor, Sikandar Shah, a prince from Iran who was lost in the wilderness and after many adventures came to rule over Tirah. Some historians believe that the Shi'a Orakzais are remnants of the Roshaniyya movement (literally the 'Illuminated Ones'), a powerful sixteenth-century secret cult that arose in the mountains of Afghanistan under the leadership of one Bayezid Ansari, whose family claimed descent from the early Muslims who assisted the Prophet Muhammad after his flight from Mecca. The Roshaniyya heretics found a refuge in Tirah some five hundred years ago when they were driven out of their Afghan stronghold by more orthodox tribes. Caroe, for instance, who had much to do with the Orakzai Shi'as, is inclined to accept that this occult Afghan movement was a catalyst for the beginnings of Shi'a sectarianism on the borders of Tirah. Be that as it may, the conundrum posed by the Orakzai religious minority was one of how to deal with the extraordinary request, made in 1904, that the British Government take over their territory and thus protect them from the alleged persecution of the majority Sunni Orakzais. There was no doubt about the long-standing feud that existed between followers of both sects, and this factor meant the request merited serious consideration. Large-scale tribal conflict on the border of British India, with a hostile

Afghanistan waiting in the wings to reap the spoils of turmoil, was not a welcome proposition for the British authorities.

Sir Harold Deane, who served as the first Chief Commissioner of the North-West Frontier Province, was one Government administrator who favoured annexing Orakzai territory. His strategy was to secure a firmer political control over the adjacent Afridis, mainly the Zakka Khels and several other recalcitrant clans. The Commander-in-Chief Lord Kitchener received this proposal with enthusiasm, while the Viceroy Lord Curzon, who was at the time on home leave in England looking after his ailing wife, saw little merit in becoming embroiled in inter-tribal factionalism. In the end, as was the case with the Daurs of Waziristan, the request for Government protection was turned down. Lord Ampthill, the acting Viceroy, took the view that this would have involved a 'distinct departure from the existing Frontier policy . . . prohibiting the undertaking of any new responsibility unless absolutely required by actual strategic necessities, and forbidding any unnecessary interference with the tribes'.[23]

A Pathan named Lukman and his three brothers were out hunting one day when they spied four young, veiled women coming up a forest path towards them. The brothers decided they should draw lots for the girls and Lukman, being the eldest, demanded that he have first choice. When he lifted the veil of the one he thought would be the most beautiful, whose name was Sibuka, he was dismayed to find that she was the plainest of the four. At that point his brothers began to taunt him, chanting *Lukman pa khatte keh lar*, or 'Lukman has landed himself in the mud'. Two of the brothers, Usman and Utman, came to be the progenitors of the Afridi and Utman Khel tribes. Lukman, on the other hand, was the founding father of the Khattaks (from *khatte*, or 'mud'), the only major tribal grouping established within the borders of what was at that time the British administered area of the Frontier. The Khattaks' willingness to accept this less than flattering version of their genealogy indicates a spirit untroubled by the fanaticism of some of the other tribes. Unlike the hothead Mahsuds and some sections of the Afridis, the Khattaks, who inhabit the south-eastern portion of the Peshawar district and lands adjacent to Kohat, were known to be quiet and loyal subjects of the British Raj, furnishing many recruits to the Indian army. They are also the only Pathan tribe whose recorded history indicates that, as opposed to later migratory arrivals, they were present from earliest times in what makes up today's North-West Frontier Province.

The venerable scholar of Indian history C. Collin Davies held the Khattaks in the very highest regard as 'the most favourable specimens of Pathans on the whole Frontier'. They are, in his opinion, 'hard working and industrious . . . brave, active and trustworthy, and make good soldiers'. Writing in the late 1920s, Davies surmised that this benevolent character was the result of 'nearly eighty years' contact with the benefits of British administration in the settled districts'.[24] In this case, 'benefits' can be taken as a euphemism for goods and services. The Khattaks always enjoyed close trading ties with Peshawar and other British settlements. It was this commercial relationship, rather than any benevolence inherited from living in close proximity to the British, that kept the tribesmen on peaceful terms with Government.

The Khattaks comprise a unique community among the Pathans, for more than any of their kinsmen they organise themselves along hierarchical lines, owing allegiance to a recognised tribal leader. They are also the only Frontier tribe divided linguistically between the harder northern Pakhtu and softer Pashtu variety of the south. For more than eight centuries the tribe has followed the rule of a supreme chieftain, being less given than most Pathans to resolving their problems through collective decision-making, as laid down in the tribal council or *jirga* by village elders and maliks. 'The Khattaks attained a relatively high degree of social organisation and culture at an early date,' according to one writer, who describes them as a sturdy and light-skinned people, noted for their cleanliness. 'The sub-divisions of the tribe are more complex than those of the other Pathan groups, and a kind of aristocracy of blood exists.'[25]

This is not to infer any pacifist tendencies on the part of the Khattaks, who throughout history have been at daggers drawn with most of their neighbouring tribes. This is particularly true of the Afridis, with whom the Khattaks fought three major wars, while the

Yusufzais hardly knew peace for the better part of a century, thanks to constant attacks by Khattak warriors. This was the state of affairs in Khattak country until the arrival of the British in the mid-nineteenth century, when the tribe was persuaded to shift its energies to the salt trade, commerce and farming.

The Yusufzais are one of the proudest of the tribes, a blue-blooded Pathan aristocracy dwelling in the plains and hill country between the Kabul River and the northern extreme of the Frontier's tribal belt on the border with Chitral. They are said to have descended from the ancient Gandhara Greco-Buddhist civilisation that emerged and flourished in the Vale of Peshawar. Some 1,600 years ago, the Yusufzai set off on a westward migration to the Helmand Valley in southern Afghanistan, seeking new agricultural land, and there they mixed with the people of Hazara, who are mostly of Mongolian origin and can trace their ancestry to the great hordes of Genghis Khan. More than another thousand years were to pass before the Yusufzai began to return to their ancestral home, travelling via Kandahar and Kabul to the plains around Peshawar, where they made themselves masters of this region, having driven lesser tribes across the Indus. The Afghan sojourn persists in the Yusufzai mind and folklore even today: if asked who he is, the Yusufzai tribesman will proudly state that he is an Afghan, not a Pathan. The Yusufzai also rule over large tracts of mountainous country in Dir, Swat and the fertile valley of Mardan, and altogether number in the region of a million souls, the largest and certainly one of the oldest of the Frontier tribes. The hill people, often known as the Bunerwals, as distinguished from the Mardans of the plains, are regarded by many as the 'true Yusufzais'. They are to be found in the remote northern tribal reaches, in which the British did not set foot for fully half a century following the annexation of the Punjab. The general opinion at the time was that they were superior to their neighbouring Yusufzai cousins, who reside in the plains of Swat. Warburton, the Warden of the Khyber, considered them to be the finest race on the North-West Frontier. He wrote in an official briefing:

> Simple and austere in their habits, religious and truthful in their ways, hospitable to all who seek shelter amongst them, free from

> secret assassinations, they are a bright example of what good materials a Pathan tribe can be developed into, clinging with the fondest affection to their country and ancient customs handed down to them by their forefathers. . . . Their word once given through the general council of the tribe may be depended on with greater certainty than that of any other border race, even when unaccompanied with the usual security for the fulfilment of the contract. Though poor, they are utterly free from those thievish propensities which disgrace nearly every other tribe on the Peshawar border.[26]

The Yusufzai can be thought of as the landed gentry of the Frontier rather than a trading people. Many of the tribesmen still live under a system of individual land tenure, each man owning a share in the tribe's common land, although these small freeholds began to disappear in the nineteenth century when the British enacted a programme of land redistribution.

The Yusufzai have always defended their territory tooth and nail against all invaders, from the Moghul emperor Babur to the British. As warriors of great prowess and dignity, they have gained the respect of their foes, and they embody the love–hate relationship that characterised nearly a century of social and political intercourse with the Raj. Caroe eulogised this tribe with characteristic affection: 'To know and respect, and be known and be liked by the leaders of Yusufzai society means that a man has entered into a sort of Pathan freemasonry, and has reached a position in which the very quintessence of the Pathan spirit begins to be revealed to him.'[27]

The Mohmands are one of the most problematic tribes the British, and indeed the Pakistani authorities who inherited the Frontier in 1947, have had to confront. The problem is one of divided loyalties, since the Afghan boundary that was demarcated by the British in 1893 cuts straight through Mohmand territory, leaving part of the tribe in Afghan territory, another portion in North-West Frontier tribal lands and the rest in the settled districts north of the Khyber around Peshawar. The Afghans never accepted the partitioning of

Mohmand territory and therefore made repeated efforts to incite the tribesmen who were left cut off from their kinsmen to revolt against the British masters. For this reason the Mohmand tribesmen are reckoned even today to be untrustworthy. This is reflected in the fact that they are the only tribe whose young men are not accepted for service in the Khyber Rifles, the native levy that protects the sensitive border region with Afghanistan. The Mohmands' political links to Afghanistan are clear-cut: in the past, the tribe was ruled by hereditary chieftains appointed by the successive Amirs of Kabul, who doled out allowances to the tribal maliks. This cosy relationship with Afghanistan created deep tensions between the Mohmands and the British, who found it necessary to avenge successive tribal raids by mounting three punitive expeditions against these people in the first five years of British rule on the Frontier. Hostilities were triggered by Britain's expropriation of some areas of tribal territory. Some of this land was later returned to its owners, but this did little to quell the resentment that had been aroused mainly through Afghanistan, whose rulers can even now rely on the Mohmands to act as their most reliable agents provocateurs in Kabul's frequent squabbles with Pakistan. In times past, as well as today, the Mohmands have eagerly rallied round Afghan rabble-rousers agitating for an independent Pathan state.

South-west of Peshawar and the Khyber Valley lies the native land of the Turis, a Shi'a tribe, descendants of early Turkic conquerors who made their home in the Kurram Valley. The Turis believe themselves to be descendants of Toghani, a Turkic prince who settled the tribe in this rich valley before the Mughal emperor Babur marched from his stronghold at Kabul on his invasion of India, which would place the migration some time in the early sixteenth century. The Turis' tribal ways persisted untouched for three centuries, until surrounding tribes brought pressure to bear on their independent-minded neighbours to accept the general Pathan social, legal and religious code known as Pakhtunwali. Being Shi'as, the Turis suffered constant persecution at the hands of their Pathan Sunni neighbours, who also coveted their land, which is the most fertile of all the tribal territory. But prior to their voluntary 'domestication', in the late nineteenth century, the gentle Turis could give as good as they got.

They have been described as not very big or very good-looking specimens of Pathans, with 'somewhat of the look of the savage about them'. The Turi, writes one historian who was witness to the tribe's conversion to the British cause, went about profusely armed, 'with a couple of brass-bound carbines at his back, two or three pistols in front, knives of many sizes and sorts in his waist-belt, and a sword by his side. The newly-born Turi is introduced to ordinary life by a number of shots fired over his head, to accustom him to the sound, and prevent him shrinking when his turn comes to be shot at.' The Turi, who according to this contemporary observer was a breeder of excellent horses, had to carry his entire wardrobe packed under his saddle, along with food to sustain man and beast for several days, some spare shoes, nails and a hammer, an iron peg and a picket rope – in short, 'all the requisites to enable this distinguished highwayman to carry on distant and daring raids, which is the Turi road to distinction'.[28]

It is no bad thing that this once rapacious tribe chose to cast its lot with the Raj, and this came about in the following way. Shortly after the annexation of the Punjab in 1849, the Afghans announced their claim to the Kurram Valley and adjacent areas, and even went so far as to dispatch several columns of troops to back their demands. The prospect of being drawn into open warfare alarmed the Turis to such an extent that they offered to pay the Indian Government an annual tribute in return for inclusion of their country in British territory. As a consequence, the Turis welcomed the arrival of the British as liberators more than oppressors and they very quickly made common cause with the new rulers. Through close contact with the British-administered districts of Kohat and Bannu, the Turis gradually came to resemble one of the 'settled tribes'. In 1892, having by then lost many of their independent tribal customs, the Turis struck a formal agreement to bring their territory under British administration. A native levy, the Kurram Militia, was raised the following year to guard the newly acquired Kurram route, an important passage into Afghanistan that gave the Government access to the cities of Ghazni and Kabul through the Peiwar Kotal Pass.

A detailed analysis of the history, customs and traditions of the Pathans of the North-West Frontier would fall well outside the scope of this narrative. They are also far too many in number, with at least sixty distinct tribes, not to mention thousands of clans, sections and family groupings, making up the Pathan nation, which indeed spills over into parts of the neighbouring province of Baluchistan. It is useful to take a glance at the major tribes and the conditions, physical and social, that have over the centuries shaped their character. As the world's largest tribe, with some twenty million people claiming Pathan lineage on both sides of the Afghan–Pakistan border, one would expect to encounter a high degree of diversity, and this is indeed the case. On the surface of it, the rampaging Mahsud of South Waziristan would appear to have little in common with the law-abiding Daurs, who sought the protection of British India. Certainly there is precious little in the way of fraternal feeling between the majority Sunnis and the Orakzai or Turi Shi'as. Yet there exist a number of shared bonds among all the tribes. Caroe wrote of 'the force of Pathan character, the bravery of the Pathan soldier, and the shrewdness of Pathan assessments of political realism'.[29] The Pathans of whatever tribe are as one in their ability to unite in the face of a common enemy, in their adherence to a strict tribal code of conduct and in their highly developed sense of pride and courage in battle.

These are the people who inspired fear, respect and admiration in the hearts of trespassers who, throughout history, from Alexander to Tamerlane, from Imperial Britain to the Soviet Red Army, came into conflict with the Pathans. In spite of the hardships and dangers these invaders suffered, which could result in a wounded soldier left behind having to endure a painful and lingering death at the hands of Pathan torturers, there is no denying the Frontier's seductiveness. Men like Arthur Swinson, whose credentials as a sober historian are beyond reproach, could slip into raptures of hyperbole over the romance of the Frontier. In the late 1960s, Swinson produced a book to accompany the popular Thames Television programme *Frontier*, an action adventure series, according to its producers, 'set in the dangerous Khyber Pass area of Imperial India'. Forty years on, the book's promotional blurb must leave the reader red-faced with embarrassment:

> High in the dangerous, half-explored mountains of India's North-West Frontier was the decaying fortress of Saragoda – besieged by fifteen thousand bloodthirsty Yarkhuni tribesmen, whose leader had murdered his brother to seize command. Behind the fragile walls was a tiny garrison under the command of Colonel Whiteley. Among the officers, on his first service at the Frontier, was the daring young Lieutenant Clive Russell. The garrison was weakened by desertion and the sinister intrigues of the civilian Captain Horace Stoughton.[30]

To this stirring outpouring of *Boy's Own* rhetoric one can but add, 'Now read on'.

TWO

A Frontier is Born

Warfare is a time-honoured way of life for the Afghan. For centuries, amirs and warlords have clashed on the plains and highlands to assert their sovereignty over this or that fiefdom, citadel or mountain pass. Rival tribes and feudal chieftains held sway over this kingdom, which was nominally under the rule of the Amir of Kabul but in reality belonged to whoever could field the most powerful *lashkar*, or tribal fighting force. To the Afghan, the concept of nationhood was as alien as the column of 19,000 red-coated cavalry and foot soldiers of the Bengal and Bombay armies that, one fine spring morning in 1839, debouched from the Bolan Pass on the march to Quetta. The expeditionary force of the East India Company passed unopposed by the Baluch tribesmen, who, from their cliff-top eyries, contemplated with curious detachment the *feringhees* almost as if they knew that the British force was advancing to its annihilation. The column stretched to the horizon, for this was a military expedition in the grand style: the soldiers of the Raj were accompanied by no fewer than 38,000 camp-followers and 30,000 camels, not to overlook the 16th Lancers' pack of foxhounds. 'One brigadier required sixty camels to tote his personal belongings,' writes a chronicler of the ill-fated event. 'The staff of General Sir John Keane, commander of the invasion force, required 260 pack animals. Two camels were designated simply to carry a regiment's cigars. Each officer was allowed ten servants, but the rule was customarily broken and some young lieutenants brought as many as forty.'[1]

In that year the Governor General Lord Auckland, an intense and donnish bachelor, and Maharajah Ranjit Singh, the depraved, one-eyed ruler of the Sikhs, marched together as unlikely allies at the head of the Army of the Indus. Ten years later, the warrior caste Sikhs were to bow their knee in submission to the Raj after the loss of the Punjab, their homeland, to British India. A third dignitary rode with the entourage: a cunning Afghan prince named Shah Shuja, who with a hungry look in his eye impatiently spurred on his white charger, for he was returning to his native land at the invitation of the British, intent on seizing the throne of Kabul from his hated cousin the Amir Dost Mohammed.

As ruler of Afghanistan, Shah Shuja had not exactly endeared himself to his subjects. A tribal rebellion in 1812, mounted with the support of Mahmut, the Khan of Herat, forced Shah Shuja to seek refuge at the court of Ranjit Singh in Lahore. Following the defeat of Shah Shuja's forces, Afghanistan slipped into its customary state of anarchy. This state of affairs continued for almost a quarter of a century until, in 1826, the deposed Amir's older cousin Dost Mohammed took power. This was in essence a traditional battle between two rival dynasties: the Saddozai line embodied in the person of Shah Shuja, and Dost Mohammed as the head of the Durrani tribe. Shah Shuja spent his years in exile dreaming of restoring the Saddozai lineage, and in 1834 he launched an expedition on Kandahar supported by a Sikh army that had been provided for the occasion by Ranjit Singh, who had his own agenda for stirring up turmoil in Afghanistan. By this time the Sikhs had occupied Peshawar, a city that was always regarded as the jewel in the Afghan crown. The Court of Kabul was seething with animosity over this loss, therefore for the Sikhs it made perfect tactical sense to keep the Afghans tied down in conflict on their home territory. The mission ended in disaster, with the invaders routed by tribesmen loyal to Dost Mohammed, who over time proved himself to be one of Afghanistan's most enlightened monarchs.

The Amir flew into a fit of rage over the loss of Peshawar and declared a jihad, or holy war, to avenge his humiliation. He dispatched his favourite son, Akbar Khan, a slight, feline creature with a wispy moustache, almond eyes and a deep hatred of foreigners, to seek out and destroy the Sikh army. At first things went well for the Afghans, who inflicted a smart defeat on the enemy and killed the brilliant Sikh general Hari Singh. But the Sikhs rallied their forces and overwhelmed the invaders, with the result that Dost Mohammed lost most of his domains in the Punjab, Kashmir and Sind.

By now reports were trickling into the East India Company's offices in Calcutta concerning Russian machinations in Persia and Afghanistan, all of which brought Tsarist forces dangerously close to the borders of British India. The Great Game, that romantic nineteenth-century cold war of intrigue between the Russian and British empires in Asia, was under way. The Persians, supported by a regiment of Russian troops, had laid siege to Herat. A fascinating character in this particular drama was Eldred Pottinger, a 26-year-old British Army officer who, when on a spying mission in Persia, slipped into the besieged city in disguise and organised its successful defence.

Meanwhile in Kabul, the arrival of a Russian agent, Captain Ivan Vitkievitch, sounded the alarm bells at General Staff headquarters. This was the final straw, as well as the excuse Auckland was looking for to halt the Russians in their tracks. Never mind that the Persians and their Russian allies had lifted the siege of Herat, or that the Russian mission to Kabul had proven so outstandingly unsuccessful that, directly Vitkievitch returned home, he destroyed his papers and put a revolver to his head. The Governor General wanted war, and in the end he got more than he had bargained for.

By March of 1839 the Army of the Indus had begun to gather momentum: April saw the fall of Quetta; the assault on Ghazni, Afghanistan's second city, took place in July; and on 7 August the column of red coats was piped through the gates of Kabul. The British forces were under the command of Major-General William Elphinstone, an ageing soldier, crippled by gout, whose last battle experience had been at Waterloo. Dost Mohammed was exiled, Shah Shuja was installed on the throne, the Army built its cantonments with all the amenities required of an occupying force, and for a while it seemed that the British were in control of the situation. As the months rolled by, however, things turned sour, as the Afghans began to stage ever-bolder retaliatory raids and outrages against the invaders. At last, in the depths of winter in 1842, Elphinstone was forced to withdraw the Army of the Indus from Kabul, having obtained from the Amir's son Akbar Khan undertakings of safe passage back to India.

It was not to be. Barely had the first contingent ridden out of the city gates, which they had triumphantly entered three years earlier, than the Afghans started to rain down volleys of musket fire on the troops. The slaughter continued day after day, as the besieged British forces trudged through the snow in sub-freezing temperatures, marching east towards the land they were destined never to reach. By 13 January, less than a week into the retreat and only 29 miles from the safety of the British-held fort at Jalalabad, all that was left of sixteen thousand soldiers, their families and camp-followers, were twenty men still capable of bearing arms. They, too, succumbed to the dagger-wielding Afghans, and only one man, a 33-year-old Scottish surgeon named William Brydon, escaped to tell the horrific tale of the Army of the Indus's annihilation. The final blow to Auckland's policy was Shah Shuja's murder at the hands of an Afghan mob.

Auckland was beside himself with rage when he received the news of the disaster and, as might be expected, revenge was swift. Within three months, the Army of Retribution under the command of General George Pollock was fighting its way through the Khyber Pass to liberate the handful of British subjects who had given themselves up as hostages in Kabul, and to wreak vengeance on the Afghans. Contemporary reports speak of an orgy of destruction and pillage committed by British forces on a magnitude with the wildest Afghan excesses. It would seem that the only justification for this second invasion of Afghanistan was to prove that, in the end, the last battle always went to the British. For no sooner had Kabul been looted and the hostages freed than the Army of Retribution marched home and left the Afghans to their own devices. 'Afghanistan was abandoned, Dost Mohammed restored, and the utter futility of the whole episode revealed,' notes one historian.[2]

The British generals who led their troops into Afghanistan had little time to reflect on the consequences of their first encounter with a frontier that was to become the soft underbelly of British India and a festering sore for the Raj over the next century. 'It was during these operations that the British obtained their first close look at the Khyber and realised what a formidable obstacle it was,' writes Arthur Swinson. 'No one, not even a large force, could enter the Khyber without trepidation, and the Afridis and Shinwaris, perched high on the observation posts, made it quite clear that no intruders were welcome.'[3]

The North-West Frontier was not at that time anyone's political boundary, though, taking into account bonds of race and religion, the allegiances of the Pathan tribes would naturally lean towards Kabul. The Pathans prided themselves on being a superior breed, a true warrior caste, and they felt nothing but contempt for the effete Hindus of the plains. But these fanatical tribesmen were unaware of the Great Game politics gathering momentum in the far distant Punjab and elsewhere in India, and of the impact that these conflicts were to have on their way of life over the next hundred years.

The intoxication of having avenged the honour of British arms in Afghanistan drove Calcutta on to greater imperial expansion. General Sir Charles Napier was dispatched to Sind in 1843, where he vanquished a numerically superior foe and claimed the province for the East India Company. The recently launched satirical magazine *Punch* published a cartoon of Napier striding through the carnage of the battlefield with the Latin caption '*Peccavi*', 'I have sinned'.

Next it was the turn of Britain's former allies, the Sikhs. In 1845 sovereignty of the Punjab rested in Sikh hands but under a form of British guidance that fell short of direct occupation. In that year, a Sikh revolt touched off the first of two wars with the East India Company's sepoy army. The conflict ended in 1849 with the Sikhs suffering a crushing defeat and the formal annexation of the Punjab, thereby extending British India to its 'natural frontier', the Indus. Almost as if by default, the conquest of the Punjab, the Land of the Five Rivers, placed into British hands the remote and uncharted hill country to the north-west that gave access to Afghanistan. Little was known about this historic crossroads between India and Asia, and even less of the tribes that inhabited its hidden valleys and arid hills.

In that same year the British forces entered Peshawar, the city that had alternately been the prized possession of Sikhs and Afghans, and that was now to become the nerve centre of British India's outpost on the North-West Frontier. The first step was to build a cantonment, a peculiar British phenomenon in the Indian subcontinent. Wherever the Raj occupied new territory, it set up garrison towns on the edge of the old quarters of cities, special enclaves consisting of barracks, bungalows, churches, clubs and cemeteries. The Peshawar Club still stands in the cantonment, a sprawling red-brick complex of quiet, melancholy elegance surrounded by the scent of rare shrubs and flowers. The antlered skulls of hunting trophies hang rather sadly from the panelled walls, adorned with twenty or more prints of Masters of Hounds. Nearby is the old Mughal garden, with its ancient trees and many rose bushes. Victoria Memorial Hall, now the Peshawar Museum, is between the site where the old classic hotel of the Raj, Dean's, once stood, and the Old City and its teeming bazaars. To the west, along the Jamrud Road leading to the Khyber Pass some 30 miles away, can be found the old cemetery. Its near nine hundred inscriptions speak eloquently of the perils of Frontier life: 'concussion of brain at polo', 'delirium tremens assisted by an attempt at suicide', 'shock caused by a stab wound (not self-inflicted)', 'death from a wound inflicted by an assassin as he was returning from the city'.

The first British arrival in Peshawar had been Mountstuart Elphinstone, the envoy who in 1809 came to pay his respects at the court of the Amir Shah Shuja. At that time Peshawar served as the winter capital of Afghan royalty, and it was in the hilltop Bala Hissar fortress that dominates the western entrance to the city that Elphinstone presented his credentials to the ill-fated Afghan ruler.

Following the ouster of the Afghans, the city and the trans-Indus country up to the hills was held by the Sikhs under Ranjit Singh from 1818 until the triumphant entry of the British forces thirty-one years later under the command of General Sir Walter Gilbert. The five districts of Hazara, Peshawar, Kohat, Bannu and Dera Ismail Khan were created and administered on the same system of direct rule as the rest of the Punjab. But a tense question hung over the territory beyond the sanctuary of these settled districts. How would the Pathan tribes take to a European colonial power claiming sovereignty, albeit not outright seizure of their land?

The answer was not long in coming. The occupation of Peshawar was followed by a series of clashes with almost every tribe along the North-West Frontier, touching off what was to become a replay of the Hundred Years War, and with similar results to the one fought between England and France. For in the end – that is, with the withdrawal of Britain from Pakistan and the North-West Frontier – it marked the failure of another attempt by the English to control foreign territory.

Within six months of taking over the Punjab, the British ran up against the Baizais, a particularly refractory Yusufzai clan living in the Swat valley, the 'Switzerland of Pakistan' nestled in the foothills of the Hindu Kush, 100 miles to the north of Peshawar. The Baizais staged a rebellion over being forced to pay taxes to the Raj, an unacceptable demand from the tribesmen's point of view, as their land happened to lie outside British territory. A heated exchange took place between Government envoys sent to collect their tribute, and the tribal maliks who steadfastly refused to pay up. This resulted in a protracted stand-off, with which the Government eventually lost patience, sending in more than 2,300 native sepoys and British regulars under Lieutenant-Colonel J. Bradshaw, an experienced India hand who had commanded the 1st Battalion of the King's Royal Rifle Corps in the battle of Gujarat during the Second Sikh War. The battalion gained some notoriety in this campaign for its unremitting pursuit of the Sikhs' Afghan allies as far as the Khyber Pass, the troops having endured much suffering on a march of nearly 500 miles in six weeks.

In December of 1849 the first of many punitive expeditions, carried out by some two hundred riflemen of the 1st Battalion, was dispatched to the Baizai country. This incursion set the tone for a century of quick in-and-out campaigns adopted as standard retaliatory tactics for punishing outrages committed by the Pathan tribesmen. This policy went under the unsavoury name of 'butcher and bolt', an acknowledgement that from the very outset the Army realised there was little to be gained by attempting to control the tribes' seditious activities through permanent occupation. On this occasion the roar of the British lion quite literally shook the Baizai villages to their foundations. The tribesmen's homes were systematically blown up, their crops destroyed and their farm animals carried off by the troops. Bradshaw could look with satisfaction upon his handiwork. This is how one contemporary junior officer sums it up: 'No serious fighting took place before the tribesmen were reduced to submission and, although further troubles arose at intervals during the course of the next few years, no military expedition was necessary, the fine demanded for any act of misconduct that occurred being invariably paid without prevarication.'[4] The day was not without its touch of gallantry, when Rifleman Michael Burke captured the Baizai battle standard that is now displayed in the Regimental Museum in Winchester. The Museum's silver centrepiece, mounted on a mess elephant's tusk, was presented to the 1st Battalion in commemoration of Burke's exploit.

The first tribal rebellion the Raj had to deal with since taking possession of the North-West Frontier had been quelled with the loss of only eight sepoys. It could have been described as a 'minor skirmish' compared with what was in store for the Army in the coming months. The Government of India had by no means heard the last of the Yusufzai clans of Swat and certain shadowy forces lurking in the background that fanned the flames of revolt. These idyllic valleys were in fact to become the staging ground for the great Pathan uprising of 1897, an insurrection of the major tribes that pushed the Government to the brink, nearly precipitating the loss of Frontier authority for the British.

The Government of India's first New Year's Eve in Peshawar, in 1849, was celebrated in high spirits, with staff officers congratulating one another on their resounding success in putting down a handful of insubordinate tribesmen. But the festive mood did not last long. Less than two months after the dust had settled on the Swat expedition, the Peshawar garrison was alerted to a serious incident in the strategic Kohat Pass, the only direct road link connecting Peshawar to the southern district that does not require a crossing of the Indus.

One winter morning in 1850 an Afridi raiding party, whooping their war cries and waving long-barrelled matchlocks over their heads, descended on a party of Indian workers who were repairing the road near Kohat. The attack was a particularly audacious one because it had been perpetrated in British territory (Kohat being one of the original five administrative districts of the North-West Frontier) and the victims were British subjects. The Government was doubly outraged over the affair because this particular Afridi faction had been singled out, at the time of annexation of the Punjab, to safeguard the road through the pass, a duty for which they were rewarded with a handsome yearly allowance. The reason for the raid was a dispute over the payment, which the Afridis considered insufficient.

The Army's reaction was a piece of overkill on a truly monumental scale, involving two of the Empire's most distinguished soldiers. The Government was determined to teach the rebellious tribesmen a lesson they would not soon forget, an aspiration that of course proved itself no less quixotic than the outcome.

The expeditionary force that marched out of Peshawar's Bala Hissar gate on 9 February was under the command of the illustrious Brigadier-General Sir Colin Campbell, a veteran of the Sikh wars who seven years later was to lead the relief of Lucknow in the Sepoy Mutiny. Riding alongside was the conqueror of Sind and now Commander-in-Chief in India, General Sir Charles Napier, who happened to be on a visit to Peshawar at the time. Napier was 67, and this was to be one of his last engagements in the field before his death five years later, although here he was again to vindicate his reputation for being 'strict, indeed fierce' with his adversaries.

The Kohat Afridis little suspected the magnitude of the punitive force approaching from the north. The column consisted, amongst other units, of elephant transport, two companies of the King's Royal Rifles back in action, two cavalry columns, infantry of the celebrated Coke's Rifles and 1,600 tribal levies. The Army's might fell first on the village of Akhor at the northern entrance to the Kohat Pass, which was completely flattened on the first day's march. Campbell left behind a squadron of cavalry and some tribal levies to hold the village as the column continued on its march southward, laying waste to every settlement in which resistance was encountered along the way.

The following day they reached their objective, Kohat, which was quickly taken by the 1st Punjab Cavalry.

The Afridis put up a spirited defence in several places, but the expeditionary force had gathered an unstoppable momentum, easily scattering all resistance to the hills. The British losses, of a force of 3,200 men, amounted to nineteen killed and seventy-four wounded. Losses on the tribesmen's side certainly numbered in the hundreds, but this was always more difficult to ascertain, as the Pathans went to great risk to remove their dead and wounded from the battlefield.

Napier was pleased with his men's work, and in particular the loyalty shown by the only native unit that gave a good account of itself. This was a small band of Khyber Afridis who fought most gallantly against their own kinsmen. The Commander-in-Chief ordered the chieftain of this tribal levy and his standard-bearer to precede the column back to Peshawar, mounted on an elephant.

What the Army was pleased to call a conclusive victory over some seditious elements was for the tribesmen nothing more than one round in a cat-and-mouse game that was to carry on for nearly one hundred years. This became apparent within a fortnight of the troops returning to their Peshawar barracks. The freebooters were back on the rampage, staging several daring night-time attacks on the British police post tower above Kohat. The tower was in an untenable position and had to be abandoned, at great embarrassment to the Government, which, short of sending out another column of troops, had no recourse but to negotiate a higher allowance with the Afridis in order to guarantee the peace of the Kohat road. As a longer-term measure, Army engineers were sent to begin construction of Fort Mackeson about 4 miles from the northern entrance to the pass. The fortress was to be garrisoned by a detachment of troops of sufficient strength to deal quickly and effectively with any insurrectionist activity, which was never in short supply. Ironically, the fort's namesake, Lieutenant-Colonel Frederick Mackeson, who was installed as first Commissioner of Peshawar in 1853, was to hold the post for only a few weeks. For in September of that year, while sitting on the veranda of his bungalow, he was approached by a Pathan petitioner who pulled out a dagger and stabbed him in the heart. It emerged that the assassin was from Swat, whose Yusufzai clans were still smarting from the Army's invasion of their territory.

It was like plugging leaks in a dyke. The force of water behind the barrier was so great that no sooner had one hole been filled than another burst open to flood the plains. So it was with the Pathan tribes behind the hill barrier overlooking the British lowland territory of the North-West Frontier. With the Yusufzais of Swat and the Afridis of Kohat temporarily pacified, in 1851 it was the turn of the Mohmand tribe to rise up against the Government. As with the Afridi campaign of the previous year, it was again down to the redoubtable Colin Campbell to don his white plumed helmet and sabre to confront the rebellious tribesmen, who had boldly been attacking posts within British territory.

The Peshawar garrison had only four months of peace to enjoy before fighting broke out with the Mohmands, a tribe that had given the Army some trouble along the Frontier during the march on Kabul in the First Afghan War. The Mohmands, as has been noted, had, more than any of the tribes, kept close links with the Amir of Afghanistan. Their anger over an unwelcome foreign presence in what they held to be sacred Pathan land was inflamed by the preaching of fanatical mullahs, in connivance with the Afghans, who saw the Mohmands as a useful tool for undermining British authority on the Frontier. Raids by Mohmand tribesmen continued almost unchecked for some six months, until, in October 1851, General Campbell took matters in hand and dispatched several columns to destroy the bandits' villages.

The Mohmand *lashkars* were too fired up with fighting zeal to be deterred by these punitive actions, so on 15 April of the following year Campbell went fully on the offensive, with mixed results. 'He immediately moved his troops [some six hundred men] out to try and cut the tribesmen off from the hills,' observes Nevill.

> But the latter perceived the manoeuvre in time to make good their escape and even harass the retirement. Though no serious engagement took place, the moral effect of the presence of Sir Colin Campbell with a strong force was sufficient to secure the dispersal of the hostile gatherings.[5]

Once the marauding tribesmen had been driven back to the hills, the Company of Sappers and Miners was drafted in to shore up the Frontier defences with the construction of another permanent outpost. Michni Fort, which sits on a promontory near the top of the Khyber Pass, was in those days one of the loneliest outposts on the North-West Frontier, where the sentries' faces were lacerated by the ferocious wind that howls up the pass from the Afghan plains. The small fortress, which commanded a strategic position between British India and Afghanistan, is now garrisoned by a detachment of the Khyber Rifles.

The Pathan tribes kept up the pressure that year, affording the Government barely a respite before the Ranizai and Utman Khel of Malakand, living to the north between British territory and the Swat River, rose up, sending raiding parties across the border.

General Campbell put together a force of more than 5,500 native infantry, Royal Artillery, cavalry and Gurkhas for the operation against the two tribes. The column marched northwards from Peshawar, its butcher-and-bolt policy leaving numerous villages and their croplands a smouldering ruin. The tribal *lashkars* showed a reckless bravery in battle, but they were no match for the likes of the 1st Punjab Cavalry, which had marched more than 80 miles in three days, starting from Kohat at 2 a.m., to join General Campbell's attack on the tribal stronghold of Nawadan. The military operations succeeded in putting an end to incursions into British territory by these two tribes. But others lay in wait, ready to lead the Government a merry chase up and down the Frontier, with never a warning of where they would next strike.

Barely a few weeks after settling the Ranizai and Utman Khel campaign, the Army found itself back in the field, this time several hundred miles to the south in Waziristan. Three columns were sent against the Wazirs, the tribe that Nevill dismisses as 'thieves of an extremely daring and bloodthirsty character'.[6] He points out that trouble had arisen with the Wazirs directly after annexation of the Punjab and continued more or less unabated ever since. The frequency and audacity of the raids broke the Government's patience towards the end of 1852. An expeditionary force was put together at the towns of

Bannu and Latammar, in strict secrecy to ensure the advantage of surprise, under one of the North-West Frontier's most charismatic military heroes, Major (later Brigadier-General) John Nicholson.

Nicholson, a legend in his own short lifetime who even inspired a personality cult, called *Nikal Seyn*, gained the respect of the Pathan tribes for his fair-handed conduct and sense of honour. As a soldier, Nicholson achieved something like the status of immortality for his valiant storming of Delhi during the Sepoy Mutiny, an action that cost him his life at the age of 36. Nicholson was also known for his foul temper and ruthlessness. Charles Allen recounts the story of the night during the Mutiny when Nicholson strode into the British mess tent at Jullunder, coughed to attract the attention of the officers, and said, 'I am sorry, gentlemen, to have kept you waiting for your dinner, but I have been hanging your cooks.' Nicholson discovered that the cooks, in league with the mutineers, had poisoned the soup with aconite.[7] With his massive build and sonorous voice, he inspired books, ballads and generations of young Army recruits. As a young, uncompromising major in 1852, Nicholson was chosen as the man to exact revenge from the Wazirs, one of the most hostile of Frontier tribes.

Nicholson organised his 1,500 troops in three columns, divided roughly equally in number, with the 56th Punjabi Infantry in the first, Coke's and Wilde's Rifles in the second, and a third made up of cavalry, mounted police and a police battalion. The Government had identified two Wazir villages, Sapari and Garang, as the raiders' strongholds, and these were singled out as the main objectives of the campaign. A few days before Christmas the three columns, in an almost simultaneous attack, took the villages by complete surprise as planned, sustaining only thirty-one casualties in the entire operation. The rebels had no time to organise an effective resistance: the villages were destroyed and a large number of cattle and sheep were carried off, a tactic designed to ensure that the offenders suffered a devastating winter. The Wazir maliks came forth to tender their submission, and peace was, for a time, achieved with this tribe.

While Nicholson was busy reducing the Wazirs to submission, the ill-fated Frederick Mackeson was engaged in operations against the Yusufzai clans of the Black Mountain region on the border of Hazara, one of the five settled districts. The dark forests of Himalayan fir that cover this range, which stands at 8,000ft above sea level, stretch for about 30 miles between the Indus and Hazara district. The region is bounded on the north and west by the Indus, with remote and little-visited tribal regions forming an enclosure to the south and east. Starting in 1852, but most seriously from 1868, the Black Mountain tribes were to keep Indian Army troops on the move for many years to come.

Nicholson's mistrust of the tribes proved tragically accurate that year. The Deputy Commissioner of Peshawar, which was the post he held at the time, had issued a warning to Government agents to stay clear of the Black Mountain. Disregarding Nicholson's advice, two British officers of the Customs Department, whose job was to prevent the illegal import of salt into the Punjab, had crossed into Black Mountain territory. They were viciously hacked to death in an unprovoked attack by a gang of Hassanzais, a Yusufzai clan inhabiting the western slopes of the range. When the offending clan was threatened with punitive action if it refused to surrender the murderers, its response was to seize two local forts that were in the possession of a friendly chieftain, who had tried to persuade the Hassanzais to comply with the Government's demand.

This was the signal to assemble a force under the command of Lieutenant-Colonel Frederick Mackeson. The Hassanzais' fighting strength was estimated at about 2,500 men, who would come up against some of the most revered British soldiers of the day. The Government dispatched four columns with a total strength of 3,800 men to avenge the murder of the two British customs officials. One column was led by Lieutenant-Colonel Robert Napier, later Lord Napier of Magdala, the conqueror of Abyssinia who was to become Commander-in-Chief in India. A second column was placed under Colonel James Abbott, an immortal of the North-West Frontier who, at the head of a small band of mounted Yusufzai irregulars, had forced the surrender of an entire Sikh army. Captain William Davidson was to lead his 16th Irregulars, along with four mountain gun batteries and two regiments of Kashmir Dogras, while a fourth column of cavalry, sappers and miners, native infantry and the 12th Pioneers was held in reserve.

This was not the most propitious time of year to be marching into Black Mountain country. It was a week before Christmas, the snow already heavy on the ground, threatening supply lines and the evacuation of the wounded, not to mention the progress of hundreds of transport camels. But Mackeson's last-ditch attempts at negotiation had been rebuffed, and so the three columns were deployed for a frontal assault on the hills. Napier's infantry advanced under cover of the mountain guns, in the face of heavy matchlock fire from behind stone breastworks and near-suicidal charges by the tribesmen. Abbott found the enemy in strong force, but he was able to outmanoeuvre the *lashkar*, take the summit and put the enemy to flight. There was no need to call Davidson's men into action and the operation was successfully brought to a close in time to organise New Year celebrations, which for the troops took the form of total destruction of Hassanzai villages, from the mountain slopes all the way to the left bank of the Indus. The expedition served the British as a training ground for mountain warfare, a skill that was to find its usefulness in future campaigns in this part of the Frontier.

By now it was becoming apparent, at least to those with experience in the ways of the North-West Frontier tribes, that some hidden force might be lurking behind these incessant uprisings. The tribes were dominions unto themselves, sharing a code of honour, a language and very little else. There was little if any contact – and scarcely any reason for it to exist – between, say, the Wazirs and the Mohmands, or the Khyber Afridis and the Mahsuds, each of whose lives was conditioned by peculiarities of environment and tradition.

True, the booty to be seized from British outposts – rifles, ammunition, even timber to rebuild the homes that had been flattened in the course of Government punitive expeditions – was a temptation to freebooters of every tribe. But there was something about the methodical, systematic nature of these revolts, which were usually dressed up as a protest against Government demands for tribute, that smacked of some behind-the-scenes orchestration.

Who was galvanising the Pathans into launching these attacks on British outposts? The mastermind behind the plot, according to contemporary as well as modern sources, was the so-called Hindustani

Fanatics movement. The intrigues of these ominous conspirators, who were in league with the Hassanzais, had brought about Mackeson's failure to negotiate a settlement with the tribesmen prior to the Black Mountain campaign. They were the ones who had seized a fort at the village of Kotla, which belonged to a local chieftain known as the Khan of Amb, who was friendly to the British.

The pace now began to quicken, with the outbreak of fresh hostilities coming less than a week after the Hassanzai outlaws had supposedly been dispersed. Mackeson, with his ally the Khan of Amb, moved four regiments of Sikh infantry and Kashmir Dogras along with twelve native guns across the river. Two of the guns were held back, ready to be dragged up the mountain by elephants, if needed. There followed a short engagement in which the fort's three hundred defenders took fright at seeing the mountain guns being moved into place. This was the signal for the Khan's forces to swoop down from a height overlooking the fort, which they retook with relative ease. They then pursued the fleeing tribesmen down the hill, killing thirty in the chase, with no losses on the British side.

There had now surfaced a new and powerful enemy from without, one who would have to be dealt with in the many subsequent campaigns carried out in the Government's struggle to pacify the Frontier. 'Hindustani' should not be confused with 'Hindu', for the term has been used historically to signify the upper Ganges River plateau, or all of northern India, from the Himalaya to the Deccan plateau and from the Punjab to Assam. The subversive agents inciting the Pathan tribes to revolt were zealots of the most fanatical sect of Muslims, known as the Wahhabis. The 'Hindustani fanatics' were a force by now known to the Government, as was their leader, but the roots and true nature of the movement carried on as a riddle until much later.

'The individuals known as the Hindustani fanatics were the followers of a mullah named Ahmad Shah, a native of Bareilly,' writes Nevill in the early twentieth century.

> This man had been to Mecca and returned to India with all the prestige conferred by his pilgrimage by way of Kandahar and Kabul.

> Establishing himself in 1823 on the Peshawar border in what was then the Sikh kingdom, Ahmad Shah proceeded to attract to his side a large following of co-religionists from among the Pathan tribes of the Frontier hills.[8]

This was largely accurate, and the existence of this movement had been detected by intelligence agents in the mid-nineteenth century, even before the annexation of the Punjab. Ahmad Shah and 1,300 of his followers were slain in battle by the Sikhs in 1831. Some three hundred of the Hindustani fanatics managed to escape to the right bank of the Indus, where they regrouped around the banner of one of their fallen leader's lieutenants, the Mullah Sayyid Akbar, who became the standard-bearer and guiding spirit of a cult that was, and is still, rooted in violent bigotry. This is Wahhabism, the movement 'whose adherents saw themselves as engaging in a great religious struggle in defence of Islam but who were [as they still are] profoundly at odds with that same religion', writes Charles Allen. The Hindustani fanatics, or Wahhabis to give them their proper identity, operated a conspiracy that 'worked time and time again to bring the people of the Frontier out in armed revolt, and which in 1857 [the year of the Sepoy Mutiny] played an unacknowledged part in the struggle to overthrow British rule in India'.[9]

Wahhabism was truly the sinister factor behind the tribal disturbances that the Government had to confront during the century of British rule on the North-West Frontier. This fundamentalist movement originated in Saudi Arabia (where, rather disturbingly, Wahhabism is today the established form of Islam in the world's largest oil-producing nation) in the mid-eighteenth century and took roots in Indian soil about a hundred years later. The cult rejects all other forms of Islam and preaches the solemn duty of jihad against all infidels. The Wahhabi cult of warfare and violence took root and flourished among the Pathan tribes of the North-West Frontier, initially as a rallying cry against the Sikh intruders and later to harass the British infidels who had usurped sacred Muslim lands. This argument held relatively little appeal for the tribesmen, for whom Islam has always taken a back seat to Pathan tribal customs, which often have little to do with Koranic teachings. Indeed, a literal interpretation of Wahhabi doctrine would have had the impious Pathans themselves earmarked for a bit of enlightenment by the sword. But this was an alliance of mutual convenience: the Hindustani fanatics punished the infidels by organising and supporting Pathan insurrection, and the Pathans were delighted with whatever weapons and loot they managed to spirit away on their raids. The Wahhabis were not alone in exploiting the warlike propensities of these illiterate tribesmen. There was no shortage of fanatical mullahs, rabble-rousing politicians and assorted subversive agents acting for Indian demagogues and as surrogates of foreign powers, from Afghanistan to Germany. But the Wahhabis were the most deadly, effective challenge to British hegemony on the North-West Frontier, and indeed in all India.

John Nicholson had a razor-sharp intuition for second-guessing the Pathans' intentions. In 1853, when he was serving as deputy commissioner of the district, Nicholson became concerned about the Shiranis, a small tribe living around a peak known as Takht-i-Sulaman, west of Dera Ismail Khan. Nicholson expressed his frustration at the continuous plundering and blackmailing perpetrated in this border region by Shirani raiding parties, who would then make good their escape into the safe haven of Afghan territory. By April, after a few light skirmishes with the tribesmen, there was no longer any doubt that the Shiranis were bent on stepping up their hit-and-run attacks. That was when Nicholson persuaded the Government to take action.

A punitive expeditionary force was raised under the command of Brigadier-General J.S. Hodgson, who was put in command of the Punjab Irregular Force, later to be christened the 'Piffers', a name that was to become synonymous with Frontier gallantry at its most intrepid. The column of nearly three thousand infantry and cavalrymen moved south, laying waste to every village in its path, doubtless with a strong sense of frustration at not having encountered a single Shirani tribesman to engage on the entire march. But there was plenty of action taking place far to the north in

Afridi country, where the Pathan Jowakis of the Kohat Pass had gone on the rampage.

This was very much the flavour of Frontier hostilities, which were not unlike digging a hole in the sand: like the grains that quickly trickle down to fill the hole, no sooner was an insurrection suppressed in one part of the Frontier than another district, often hundreds of miles away, would burst into flames.

General Sir Colin Campbell's efforts to pacify the Kohat Pass in 1850 were now undone, for the Jowakis had taken up the sword, threatening to carry their violent raids into Kohat and even Peshawar. The Army's transport elephants were put on the march, carrying nine-pounder guns and mountain batteries into the Bori Valley, which had been identified as the freebooters' stronghold. In compliance with Government policy, the infantry followed up their attacks by burning the houses in every village, in the hope that this would teach the insurrectionists a lasting lesson. The Jowakis tendered their unconditional surrender three months later, in February 1854, shortly before handing over to the Mohmands their campaign of insurgency.

This fresh Mohmand uprising dealt General Campbell another blow, for he had spent the better part of two years sending his columns to subdue this belligerent border tribe. The tribal maliks, who were responsible for paying tribute to the Government, had steadfastly refused to carry out their sworn obligations. In the summer of 1854 one of the maliks, Rahim Dad, was summoned to Peshawar to make good the arrears. No sooner had he arrived at the Political Agent's office to be confronted with the Government's demands than the tribal leader took flight back to the hills. The Army sent a large detachment of nearly two thousand Sikh infantry, light cavalry, sappers and miners and two companies of the Cheshire Regiment, with native infantry, from Michni Fort in the Khyber Pass to make an example of the tribe's malik. The troops rode off with Rahim Dad's cattle in payment of the sum due, and for good measure they destroyed a few villages on the march back to Peshawar. The score was settled, but the outrages continued unabated.

The authorities were unwilling to undertake another punitive expedition, given the Mohmands' close links with Afghanistan and the tense political situation that existed at the time between the Amir of Kabul and British India. In fact, Major Herbert Edwardes, who succeeded the murdered Mackeson as Commissioner of Peshawar, was determined to improve relations with Afghanistan, and to this end one of his first official acts was to invite the Amir's favourite son, Ghulam Hyder Khan, to Peshawar to negotiate a friendship treaty. The Government went so far as to tender the hand of peace to the Mohmands by offering to forgive past offences, with the exception of murders and other violent crimes. This was a particularly sensitive issue, for it was less than a year since Mackeson's assassination, and the Government was in no mood to negotiate the fate of murderers. Edwardes made this clear in a letter to one of the Mohmand chiefs. 'And as to the prisoners in our gaols, to please you I will release every Mohmand who has been seized merely because he was a Mohmand, on condition that he pay whatever reward was given for his own seizure,' he writes. 'But no highwayman, or murderer, or other criminal will be released. Justice must take its course with such offenders.' Edwardes then goes on to deliver a veiled threat of the consequences should the malik choose to reject the Government's terms. 'My friend, I have spoken my mind out, for it is best to be plain. For the rest, I desire the honour and welfare and strength of you and your family, and I conceive they will be better served by the friendship than by the enmity of the British Government.'[10]

An ongoing bone of contention was a conflict over certain tracts of land, called *jagirs*, that lay within British territory. With the annexation of the Punjab, a number of these *jagirs* had been confiscated from the Mohmands. The *jagir* system dated from the days of the Mughal emperors, who granted these territories on a grace and favour basis to army chieftains in recognition of their military service. The proprietors in turn collected substantial tax income from their landholdings. The *jagirs* of the North-West Frontier, which were found mainly in the fertile plains, were in the hands of tribal notables and maliks. This, in the Government's opinion, was a dangerous state of affairs, for it tended to encourage *jagir* owners sitting in the hills to assume possession of fertile lands in the valleys to which they were not rightfully entitled. Edwardes therefore categorically refused to hand back confiscated Mohmand estates to the tribe. His rationale was to prevent this land being parcelled out under the *jagir* system, which would ultimately tempt the tribesmen into demanding more and more territory from the Government.

The Frontier garrisons had heard little of the Afridis since a British presence had been established west of the Indus in 1849, apart from Colin Campbell's brief campaign against the Kohat section of this tribe a year after the Punjab annexation. This time it was the Aka Khel clan, living south of the Khyber Pass, that came out to attack Government posts in protest over their alleged exclusion from the allowances that other clans received for safeguarding the Kurram Pass. The problem had to be addressed with tact, because the Afridis were one of the tribes whose border was contiguous with the vulnerable settled districts of British India. A series of raids and counter-raids erupted around the Khyber Pass, in which Indian Army units blockaded the Aka Khels from trading with Peshawar, while carrying off large numbers of their cattle as a retaliatory measure. This tit-for-tat warfare continued on a fairly minor scale until the end of 1855, when the Aka Khel, failing to win over support from any of the other seven Afridi clans, threw in the towel and agreed to pay the standard fine the Government imposed on the tribes that caused disturbances.

The Orakzais were thought of as lacking in martial calibre, certainly in contrast to their neighbours the Afridis. This assessment proved itself quite wrong. In 1855 the Government found it necessary to send a 2,500-man force, led by Field Marshal Sir Neville Chamberlain, a much-decorated and much-wounded veteran of both Afghan wars, to bring this tribe to heel. The operation took more than a month to conclude, a reflection of the Orakzais' determined resistance in the face of an overpowering force of field guns, well-trained and equipped Indian Army cavalry and infantry, and detachments of tribal levies. A dawn attack by Government troops scattered the tribesmen for long enough to allow the Army time to level three key villages and round up a large herd of cattle. That year also found Chamberlain at the head of a punitive expedition against the Miranzai tribes who inhabit the valley of the same name, which is found due west of Kohat, extending to the Kurram River. This region was destined to join the Frontier turbulence, for within days of the annexation of the Punjab the Afghans announced their claim to both the Kurram and Miranzai valleys and at one point even sent troops across the border.

The operation was destined to become something of a test case, for many of the men of the 1st and 3rd Punjab Infantry who were part of the column that had families in the very districts that were attacked and destroyed by the Indian Army forces. As was later to be seen with the raising of native militias on the Frontier, the Pathans could be induced to fire on their kith and kin, which after all was a pastime in which they regularly indulged when out of uniform.

The Army inflicted a heavy punishment on the insurgent tribes of Miranzai, but this failed to stop the raiding, which carried on unchecked into the following year. Chamberlain was off once again, this time at the head of the largest force yet assembled on the Frontier, consisting of nearly five thousand men and fourteen guns. Edwardes himself rode with the mounted column against the Turis, the Shi'a tribe that was eventually to seek the Raj's protection against their hostile Sunni neighbours. The tribesmen were no match for so overwhelming a force, and moreover one that was not prepared to accept any terms other than unconditional surrender. The village of Torawari and its surrounding area, which for British India could be taken as the Alsace of the Frontier, was the principal scene of action in this campaign. The headmen were called out to be read the terms of surrender. They were given half an hour to hand over the known criminals being harboured in the village. The maliks were also required to pay a fine for the tribesmen's previous misconduct and give security for future good behaviour. The troops called on the women and children to evacuate the village, but when the deadline had passed and the men refused to send their families to safety, the guns opened up with blank cartridges in the hope of intimidating the inhabitants. A contemporary report gives a graphic account of this engagement, one of the most ruthless waged on the Frontier, which took place in the months leading up to the Sepoy Mutiny.

> At length shells were thrown into the village, and after about thirty rounds, the women were seen rushing out of the village and running towards our position, waving clothes and holding up the Koran.
>
> The fire of the guns was instantly stopped, and the women were sent back to tell the men that they must now come out and lay down their arms, or the batteries would re-open. Slowly and angrily they came out and threw their swords, daggers, pistols and muskets down upon the plain, but only by twos and threes, and still there was no sign of giving up the criminals . . . At last the stacks of winter fodder for the cattle were fired, and the wind carried the flames from house to house, setting off loaded muskets that had been hidden in the straw. Then, one by one, the criminals were brought out, each with protestations that he was the last. But Captain Henderson [the Deputy Commissioner] had the list in his hand, and patiently demanded the remainder.[11]

The search and destroy operation netted thirteen criminals and a cache of 90 matchlocks, 176 swords, 11 pistols, 8 knives and 29 shields. In the first eight years of British rule west of the Indus, the Government had had to dispatch nearly 40,000 troops against the Pathan tribes in seventeen separate punitive expeditions. True, the British took relatively light losses in these operations, with only some four hundred men killed and wounded, fewer than the number of British subjects carried off by cholera in Peshawar and in other Frontier settlements in the same period. The years of constant warfare were nevertheless taking their toll on army morale, as well as the Government's exchequer. Yet the task of keeping the peace among the Pathan tribesmen was to become a lot more arduous, and in very short order. The first threats of trouble coming from far beyond the North-West Frontier were heard in Peshawar in the early part of 1857.

Frederick Roberts, a young Bengal Artillery subaltern, later to become Field Marshal Lord Roberts of Kandahar and 1st Earl Roberts of Kandahar, Pretoria and Waterford, happened at the time to be garrisoned in Peshawar. One restful afternoon while he was sitting at mess, a telegraph signaller rushed in with word of an outbreak of mutinous activity by some sepoy units at a military depot about 100 miles from Calcutta.

'During the months of February, March and April, rumours reached us at Peshawar of mysterious chappatis [unleavened bread] being sent about the country with the object, it was alleged, of preparing the natives for some forthcoming events,' he writes.

> There was also an evident feeling of unrest and dissatisfaction in the minds of the sepoys . . . Bungalows had been burnt in several stations, and the sepoys at the Schools of Musketry had objected to use the cartridges served out with the new rifles because, it was asserted, they were greased with a mixture of cow's fat and lard, the one being as obnoxious to the prejudices of the Hindu as the other is to those of the Mussulman.[12]

Roberts lamented the fact that these warnings of insurrection should have passed almost unheeded, and rightly so, for the British in India had an uncanny ability to ignore calamity staring them in the face, particularly in their dealings with the Pathans on both sides of the border. One of the most scandalous failings of judgement occurred in November 1841, the eve of the ill-fated evacuation of Kabul. The Afghans had stormed the Residency and hacked the agent, Alexander Burnes, to pieces, along with two British officers and all the sepoy guards inside. General Elphinstone, when told of the massacre, took pen in hand and wrote to the British envoy Sir William Macnaghten, 'We must see what morning brings and then think what can be done.' As late as 1919, with all the advances in intelligence procedures of the day, plus the Government's links to an extensive network of informers, Roos-Keppel, who was serving as Chief Commissioner of the North-West Frontier Province, informed the Viceroy Lord Chelmsford in one of his weekly dispatches that he was 'looking forward to a quiet summer'. A few days later, several columns of Afghan troops stormed across the Khyber Pass, touching off the Third Afghan War. In 1857 it was not just the security of the North-West Frontier garrisons that came under threat, but the survival of the British Raj.

A key question was whether the Government would have to deal with pockets of insurrection on the Frontier in sympathy with the rebels or, and this was the unthinkable option, the Pathan tribes could be incited to stage a general revolt. The forces garrisoned at Peshawar, some five thousand Indian and two thousand British troops, were quite inadequate to cope with a widespread uprising. Roberts was confident the two British regiments and artillery would be sufficient to contain any seditious movement by the eight native corps. The fear was of an uprising extending beyond the garrison.

> In the event of any general disturbance amongst the native troops, we had to calculate on the probability of their being joined by the 50,000 inhabitants of the city and, indeed, by the entire population of the Peshawar Valley, not to speak of the tribes all along the border, who were sure to rise. It was an occasion for the gravest anxiety, and the delay of even a few hours in the sepoys becoming aware of the disastrous occurrences at Meerut and Delhi meant a great deal to us.[13]

The disaster to which Roberts refers was of course the outbreak of violence by sepoy units that rocked these two important garrison towns. In 1857 the Government had all of forty thousand British troops stationed in India to hold down the entire subcontinent. It was, moreover, the eve of the Crimean War, with the British garrison in India heavily reduced to provide forces for that conflict. 'As the redcoats marched down to the ports of embarkation, they created the impression among many that the Raj was packing up and moving out, never to return.'[14] Upholding the rule of law under the Raj was the job of three hundred thousand sepoys, but with the events of Sunday 10 May, a terrifying question mark was thrown over the loyalty of these natives under arms. The Meerut garrison was the first to rise, when the men refused to use the new cartridges. The British reaction was predictably unyielding and, in the light of events, wrong. Nearly one hundred of the protesting sepoys were rounded up and sent off to hard labour. The native troops ran wild through the town, slaughtering their officers and every European, women and children no exception, whom they encountered in their path. Later, two hundred British women and children were butchered in the most gruesome fashion in Cawnpore, when the mutineers brought in livestock slaughterers to do the job after the sepoys refused to put these innocents to the sword. The British showed an equal indifference to horror in exacting their revenge. One of the most gruesome punishments was to have captured mutineers lashed to cannon muzzles and blasted into a froth of bone and flesh, 'spraying a solemn warning across the parade ground that not only a hideous death but a profaning of caste and religious burial customs awaited the traitors to the Raj'.[15] In all, some twelve thousand British soldiers and their families lost their lives in the Mutiny. The Indian casualties amounted to many thousands more, though the exact tally has never been established.

The Sepoy Mutiny spread with astonishing rapidity to garrisons in Patna, Lucknow, Delhi and the major stations of Hindustan. There are clear indications that the sinister hand of the Wahhabis, as well as other groups of conspirators, was to be found behind the uprisings. Lord Roberts had good reason to press for urgent action to pre-empt any seditious activity by sepoy units garrisoned on the North-West Frontier. The Army at once raided the Peshawar post office and confiscated all native correspondence. The letters they found showed all too plainly how necessary was this swift action. 'The number of seditious papers seized was alarmingly great,' recounts Roberts. 'They were for the most part couched in figurative and enigmatic language, but it was quite sufficiently clear that every Native regiment in the garrison was more or less implicated and prepared to join the rebel movement.'[16]

The attempt to galvanise the Frontier sepoy units into revolt bore the clear stamp of Wahhabi intrigues. However, these Muslim fanatics had a very specific agenda which in the end, as Charles Allen points out, enabled the British to regain control of the Hindustan posts. 'Theirs was a plan that called for an exclusively Sunni Muslim jihad, and for the strike against the British to come not from a city in Hindustan but from Sittana [a frontier town] and in alliance with the Afghan border tribes.'[17] The Wahhabis, who had a clear-cut plan to crush the British, disdained all alliances with other conspirators and therefore deprived the uprising of a unified command that would almost certainly have destroyed the Raj.

Two, or perhaps even three factors stood in the way of the Pathan tribes joining forces with the sepoy mutineers. First and most important of these was a swift response to the crisis by the rulers of the Punjab and the Frontier, almost all of whom, at astonishingly early ages, were encumbered with the gravest crisis the British ever had to face in India. The Commissioner of Peshawar, Herbert Edwardes, was 37, as was Sir Neville Chamberlain. John Nicholson was all of 33.

These men took immediate steps to disarm any of the native troops among the fifty thousand stationed in the Punjab whose loyalty was in doubt. These sepoys were replaced by reliable Punjabi soldiers and tribal levies who were brought down from the Frontier. The Chief Commissioner, John Lawrence, also in his thirties, negotiated a treaty with the Amir Dost Mohammed Khan, under which the Afghan king assured the British of his neutrality in the Mutiny. Lawrence, the first to be elevated to the ranks of Mutiny Hero, later led the troops that recaptured Delhi, and five years later he received his supreme reward, on being appointed Viceroy of India. In the early days of the Mutiny, however, Lawrence thought there would be little hope of defending Peshawar in the event of a general sepoy uprising. He was the chief advocate of evacuating Peshawar, proposing instead to hold the line at the left bank of the Indus. His colleagues Nicholson, Edwardes and others managed to persuade him that once Peshawar was abandoned, its recapture would require a colossal military operation. 'Not only would it have been followed by a loss of prestige, but it would have been followed by a deluge of Sikhs, Pathans and Afghans upon Delhi,' says Collin Davies. 'Edwardes regarded Peshawar as the anchor of the Punjab, the removal of which would have caused the whole ship to drift to sea. On 7 August, 1857, Lord Canning [the Governor General] telegraphed to Lawrence, "Hold on to Peshawar to the last". India was saved.'[18]

The Pathans cannot easily be persuaded to fight someone else's war, in particular if their enemy's enemy happens to be the despised

Hindus. The Pathan hill tribes nurture a hearty contempt for the effete lowlanders, a people that this martial race considers inferior in every respect. The fact that many of the mutineers were Muslim sepoys made little impression on the tribesmen, who, as we have seen, are Pathans first and foremost. True, the Pathans were successfully recruited into the Frontier militias that were raised by the British from the late nineteenth century onward, but there was a financial incentive for the tribesmen to step forth and take the King's shilling – and it could justly be argued that the Pathans respected the British, as adversaries if not as rulers. There were instances in which Pathans taken prisoner in punitive expeditions would congratulate the British officers on their valour in battle, and even ask their captors how they rated the tribesmen's own fighting skills.

A third reason for the Pathans having held themselves aloof from the Sepoy Mutiny may appear to be tinged with cynicism, yet there were reasons why the tribes could even come to regret a British departure from their homeland. An anecdote that relates to the building of the Khyber Railway will serve to illustrate this point. In 1920, the Afridi maliks flatly refused to sanction a Government project to lay a railway line through their territory up the Khyber Pass. After many frustrating days trying to negotiate with the tribal leaders it was whispered in their ears that the train, laden with goods, would travel slowly up a steep gradient passing close to the maliks' houses. This brought a remarkable change in attitude: the Afridis not only gave the plan their blessing but provided teams of workers to help lay the track. The promise of plentiful supplies of loot cast all scruples of sacred territory out of the window. The Pathans stood to gain a great deal by having the British as neighbours. There was always an opportunity to send a raiding party across the border to scoop up a handful of weapons or, as was often the case, carry off a Hindu merchant or two to be held for ransom.

In the end, the Frontier and its Pathan tribes, whom Caroe considered vital to the stability of the whole subcontinent, failed to respond to the mutineers' call to revolt. General Sydney Cotton, the military commander at Peshawar, acted swiftly to disarm the Indian Army regiments that might have been induced to turn their guns on their officers. Two Frontier regiments did mutiny, and suffered the consequences of their treachery. Their men were pursued and cut down by Nicholson in a running battle. The bulk of the forces not only stayed loyal, but provided troops for the storming of Delhi, nearly 600 miles away. The Corps of Guides distinguished themselves by marching the entire distance in twenty-seven days, campaigning on the road as they went, and were in action within half an hour after striding into Delhi camp.

It was this gallant regiment, garrisoned in Mardan, that held in check an outbreak of Wahhabi-instigated violence west of the Indus in the early months of the Mutiny. The Hindustani fanatics were stirring up trouble in Yusufzai country that required several punitive expeditions to put down. In one of these engagements General Cotton, leading a movable column, observed a strange sight when the last existing stronghold at Sittana was overwhelmed in some desperate hand-to-hand combat. 'The fighting of the Hindustanis was strongly marked with fanaticism,' states a contemporary account. 'They came boldly and doggedly on, going through all the preliminary attitudes of the Indian prize-ring, but in perfect silence, without a shout or a word of any kind. All were dressed in their best for the occasion, mostly in white, but some of the leaders wore velvet cloaks.'[19] In that macabre march into the jaws of death one detects the precursor of the modern suicide bomber: men infected with that rabid fundamentalism which leads them to their destruction with complete serenity, inspired by the unshakeable belief in an eternal reward for their sacrifice.

The heroic march to Delhi was only one of a long string of daring exploits undertaken by the Corps of Guides, known as the 'Piffers', the regiment that more than any other embodied the gallantry of the North-West Frontier.

A stern countenance behind a flowing black beard gave Lieutenant Harry Lumsden a more than usually striking resemblance to an Old Testament prophet. With his imposing demeanour, plus a masterful skill with the sabre and rifle, Lumsden was ideally suited to command the respect of the Pathan tribesmen. In short, just the type of man sought by Sir Henry Lawrence, British Resident at Lahore and brother of John, the Chief Commissioner. In 1846, a few months before the Mutiny, Henry Lawrence handed Lumsden the task of raising a corps of irregulars whose function it was to gather intelligence on tribal movements and act as guides to the troops in the field. Lawrence, in conceiving this unconventional force, appears to have taken his inspiration from Napoleon's elite Guides. Lumsden was the only British officer in this corps, which was formed of one troop of native cavalry and two companies of infantry, about three hundred men in all. The commander had no trouble finding recruits, who were for the most part drawn from the Pathan tribes. Aside from the excitement of soldiering on the Frontier, the Guides received a higher rate of pay than sepoys of the regular Army. Taking into account the rugged terrain that was to be the Guides' regular environment, the Indian climate, and the need to manoeuvre about the countryside while attracting as little attention as possible, one of Lumsden's first measures was to have his men abandon the tight-fitting scarlet uniforms worn by Indian Army troops. Lawrence's creative hand can also be found in this mould-breaking innovation.

> Sir Henry evolved the startling heresy that to get the best work out of troops, and to enable them to take great exertions, it was necessary that the soldier should be loosely, comfortably and suitably clad, that something more substantial than a pill-box with a pocket handkerchief wrapped round it was required as a protection from a tropical sun, and that footgear must be made for marching, and not for parading around a bandstand.[20]

In their place, the Guides were to adopt a style of dress that blended in with the landscape. In doing so, Lumsden set a milestone in military history by outfitting his men in tunics and puttees of a new colour called khaki, an Urdu word of Persian origin meaning 'dusty' or 'dust-coloured'. The Guides' unorthodox and homely appearance quickly earned them the nickname of 'Mudlarks', although it is safe to assume that many a sepoy would have secretly wished for similar clothing to render him a less obvious target for Pathan bullets. In fact, it is surprising that the Army had not acknowledged earlier the need for some suitable bush uniform. Certainly the British soldiers who faced American militiamen in the War of Independence as well as the War of 1812 would have benefited from some type of camouflage. Their red uniforms stood out like beacons for the enemy, who were for the most part clad in homespun garments that blended with the forests and hills.

In the twenty years between the end of the Mutiny and the start of the Second Afghan War in 1878, the Guides fought valiantly in almost every expedition that was sent out against their Pathan brethren. In the novel *The Kite Runner*, by Afghan writer Khaled Hosseini, the hero's father makes this remark about the Pathans: 'We may be hard-headed and I know we're far too proud, but in the hour of need, believe me that there's no one you'd rather have at your side than a Pashtun.'[21] This sentiment was echoed by the British soldiers who fought side by side with the various Pathan levies raised on the Frontier, and there were numerous examples of unwavering loyalty shown by the tribesmen in uniform, who were often put under great duress by having to fire not only on their kinsmen, but quite often on adversaries of their own clan. There were incidents of failures in the system, to be sure, but these were almost invariably brought about by devious mullahs preaching jihad against the British as infidels, not as oppressors or enemies of the Pathan race. Religious rabble-rousing is a powerful weapon for whipping up the ignorant, the illiterate Pathans being no exception. The Hindustani fanatics, that is the Wahhabis, moved with stealth among the tribesmen, knowing how to ignite the fuse of rebellion. It is worth noting that the Guides never suffered any defections or mutinous revolts. As noted, Lumsden offered his recruits a handsome wage and could therefore pick men of high calibre and intelligence. In return, the Guides were expected to act with unstinting valour in the field – and so they did, time and again. No less a soldier than Lord Roberts of Kandahar was indebted to the Guides for riding to his rescue in Afghanistan, when his forces were under siege by a vast army of tribesmen in Sherpur in 1879. A heliograph was received by the Guides at the Lataband Pass 36 miles away. Immediately on receiving the SOS, the men of the Corps leapt into the saddle and tore off through mountainous terrain, carrying only their ammunition. The column rode through the night and crossed the Afghan lines (where the enemy was too preoccupied trying to stay warm to take any notice) to reinforce Sherpur with all speed. 'I was cheered by hearing that the Guides had arrived . . . a most welcome reinforcement, for I knew how thoroughly to be depended upon was every man in the distinguished corps,' exclaimed Roberts.[22]

The Corps of Guides was reinforced by amalgamation with the 1st Punjab Cavalry in 1849, three years after Lumsden's original corps was raised. That was when it officially became the Punjab Irregular Force, or Piffers. The modern incarnation of the Guides is known as the Frontier Force Regiment, the result of an amalgamation in 1957 of the Guides, the Frontier Force Regiment and the Pathan Regiment. The second of these regiments was one of the oldest Frontier units and it recruited veterans of the Sikh wars. The Pathan Regiment was an offshoot of this corps, whose troops consisted of Punjabi Muslims and Pathans in equal proportions.

With the suppression of the Mutiny in 1858 life on the North-West Frontier returned to normal, which is to say a resumption of the cycle of tribal raids, punitive expeditions, the burning of villages and farmland, and the eventual submission of the offending clans, proffering solemn oaths of good behaviour that were usually broken before the dust had settled behind the retreating columns.

The Mutiny also brought an end to the power of the East India Company, which had been the supreme civil and military force for more than a century. The Company rule was abolished and the colony was governed directly by the Crown through a Secretary of State for India with his own department, the India Office. The country was officially at peace, though relations between native troops and their British officers, or indeed between Indians and Englishmen, for that matter, would never be the same. The cruelty shown by both sides during the Mutiny left deep scars of bitterness and mistrust, so that from 1857 onward, until the Union Flag was finally lowered over India exactly one hundred years later, it was as never before a relationship of ruler versus subject.

General Cotton, the senior commander in Peshawar, and the veteran punitive campaigner Neville Chamberlain were called into service on three occasions, in 1858 and 1859, to deal mainly with Mahsud and Wazir raiders. Chamberlain's second expedition against the seditious tribes of the southern part of the Frontier was an especially bloody affair, with Government losses amounting to 100 men killed and a further 261 wounded. Yet these conflicts could be considered a mere warm-up for what was to come in 1863, when Chamberlain took a nine thousand-man force north of the Indus into the state of Swat for another confrontation with the unrelenting Hindustani fanatics, who had been propagating raids and disturbances on both sides of the border. The strategy was to encircle the enemy from the north through the Ambela Pass, which lies four miles along the road south-west of the settlement of Ambela and another twenty from the Corps of Guides' headquarters at Mardan. This was to be the largest expedition to date undertaken on the North-West Frontier, and the costliest in terms of human lives. The Ambela campaign accounted for about half the casualties recorded on Frontier expeditions since the annexation of the Punjab.

The strategic logic looked faultless on paper: the plan was to hit the fanatics in their stronghold at the village of Malka on the northern slopes of the Mahaban range. Once the fanatics and their tribal allies were pushed off the hills and down to the southern flatlands, their escape route would be blocked by army units waiting to pounce on them. It was October, and the column would be moving north and into high and wintry terrain. Chamberlain, whose proposal to hold off from the invasion until the spring was rejected, had misgivings about moving his troops up this road, which he considered littered with logistic obstacles, as he reveals in his diary. 'As a road for troops it certainly presents great difficulties. The track lies up the bed of a stream encumbered with boulders and large masses of rock, and is overgrown with low trees and jungle.'[23] The column hauled its mountain batteries up the pass as far as the horses could carry them. When the path narrowed to a point where the troops could only proceed in single file, the guns were transferred to elephants. Chamberlain also comments on the shortcomings of his force, one of which was the failure to provide a sufficient contingent of sappers and miners to deal with the engineering problems they were to encounter in such tricky terrain.

The British were about to send a huge military force into a remote, mountainous region that was practically terra incognita to Europeans. No one knew for certain the fighting strength of the surrounding tribes, or how they would react to a large body of foreign troops marching through their land. This applied to the main local tribe, the Bunerwals, who were believed to be hostile to the Hindustani fanatics. The Bunerwals were followers of the septuagenarian Sufi spiritual leader Abdul Ghaffar, known as the Akhund of Swat, a man held in great reverence by the Pathan tribes and who was bitterly opposed to the Hindustani fanatics. Ghaffar grew up as a simple shepherd and in his youth he migrated to the Peshawar District as a *talib-ul-ilm*, a seeker after religious knowledge, or taliban. He studied in the shadow of various mullahs and eventually settled down as a hermit in a small village near the Indus, where he stayed for twelve years and acquired a great reputation for sanctity.

In the interests of secrecy, it was decided that the Bunerwals would not be informed of the Army's intentions until the column began to move up the Ambela Pass. Similarly, the Government failed to forewarn any of the chief maliks or headmen of the same Yusufzai clan that inhabited the Chamla Valley, which the force would have to negotiate to reach Ambela. The Bunerwals were not told of the planned attack on Ambela until 19 October, the day before the column crossed the pass. The campaign against the Hindustani fanatics of Swat bore the marks of an ill-considered operation, assembled in great haste and with predictable results. The Government was about to set out into a political quagmire of which it understood little and cared less, a situation cleverly portrayed in the nonsense poem written by Edward Lear after the campaign came to the public eye:

WHO or why, or which, or what,
  Is the Akhund of SWAT?
Is he tall or short, or dark or fair?

Does he sit on a stool or a sofa or chair,
or SQUAT,
  The Akhund of Swat?
Is he wise or foolish, young or old?
Does he drink his soup and his coffee cold,
or HOT,
  The Akhund of Swat?
Does he sing or whistle, jabber or talk,
And when riding abroad does he gallop or walk,
or TROT,
  The Akhund of Swat?

Chamberlain's camp was established in the pass on 22 October. There it came under attack not only from the Hindustani fanatics, but also from a large and unexpected *lashkar* of Bunerwal warriors, who had been tipped off by the fanatics about the impending invasion. A letter to the Bunerwals, found on the body of a battle casualty, warned of the infidels' alleged intention to lay waste their land and annex their territory to British India, and it exhorted the tribesmen to defend their faith. The tribesmen responded with enthusiasm to the Hindustani fanatics' war cry.

The Bunerwals swarmed down on the British encampment from the north, or Chamberlain's left flank. It was learnt that up to twenty-five thousand more of the tribesmen were on their way to join the attack, some from as far away as Dir and Bajaur. Chamberlain's strategy was in disarray and the question now was how to extricate his troops from a pincer movement that threatened to leave the column cut off. Retreat was not an option: never in the history of Frontier warfare had a Government force been routed by the tribes. To allow this to happen now, even if the column was able to fight its way out of the pass without major losses, would be sending a disastrous signal to the Hindustani fanatics and other Koran-waving demagogues. 'Any attempt to follow the original plan of swinging south to attack the fanatics' stronghold or even move forward into the Chamla Valley would imperil his [Chamberlain's] rear and his line of communications through the Ambela Pass,' observes one historian.[24] The troops dug in for a protracted siege, which Chamberlain estimated might leave him pinned down for a month or more until reinforcements could reach him.

The relief column did not arrive until 15 December, by which time Chamberlain himself had taken a bullet in the arm while leading an assault on Crag Piquet, a defensive position perched on a knoll a few hundred yards south overlooking the British camp. This fortified position was the scene of much bloody fighting during the campaign, having changed hands several times in hand-to-hand combat, sometimes in the dead of night, and with severe losses on both sides.

In early December, before the arrival of a relief force that had been mustered at the Nowshera garrison, the tribesmen, whose losses were at least double those on the British side, were beginning to show a loss of appetite for further bloodshed. 'Although fresh reinforcements kept pouring in from Bajaur and other parts, numerous desertions took place, and the Buner and Chamla tribes began to enter into negotiations, the result of which was that the Bunerwals agreed to cooperate in the destruction of Malka and to expel the Hindustani fanatics from their country.'[25] It was not the outcome the tribesmen had fought to achieve, but it was preferable to seeing the British occupy their territory.

An unwelcome turn of events occurred when the Akhund, seemingly against all reason, took the decision to carry on the struggle. At the same time that the Government was negotiating an end to hostilities with the Bunerwals, some six thousand tribesmen were on their way down from Swat to fight with the Akhund, a situation that effectively put his back to the wall. His chief aim was not to destroy the British, for whom he harboured no ill will, but he was under pressure to defend the independence of his beloved Swat, which his followers perceived to be threatened by the continued presence of a foreign military force in their territory.

Chamberlain now had sixteen battalions at Ambela, more than enough seasoned troops to chase this new enemy force into the Chamla Valley at the point of the bayonet, where many were killed, some were taken prisoner, while others simply disappeared into the hills. In all, the Wahhabis lost an estimated seven hundred men in the fighting, with the rest of the fanatics driven from the region.

Chamberlain reached the fortified village of Malka on 21 December, to find the Wahhabis' sanctuary abandoned, though this did not deter his men from firing every building in the settlement. The Ambela campaign had been planned to last three weeks. In the end, the fighting went on for three months, with losses of 238 Government soldiers, a high enough toll for the British, but far fewer than the three thousand casualties the enemy left on the battlefield. The power of the Hindustani fanatics had for the time being been broken and on Christmas Eve Chamberlain's column, elephants, camels and horses in tow, retraced its steps down the Ambela Pass.

It would hardly be accurate to say that, with the conclusion of the Ambela campaign, the North-West Frontier lived in peace in the fifteen years up to the outbreak of the Second Afghan War in 1878. This was never the case, for 'Frontier life' and 'Frontier warfare' were almost synonymous terms. Even as Chamberlain on the Ambela Pass struggled with a situation that was growing more desperate by the hour, the Mohmands of the Khyber Pass area were carrying out hit-and-run raids on the Army garrison of Shabkadr, only 18 miles north of Peshawar. At one point, more than five thousand Mohmand tribesmen, inspired by the Akhund of Swat's defiance of the British forces in the Ambela Pass, launched an all-out assault on the fort. This was swiftly repelled by the 7th Hussars in what was the first action by a British Army cavalry unit on the Frontier. The Mohmands' brief but energetic disturbance ended with the enemy being cut up and scattered by the cavalry charge. It was a memorable fight, distinguished by a most gallant charge of the 13th Bengal Lancers, which has been praised as one of the most brilliant cavalry operations in British military records. This settled matters for the moment, and allowed time for the formation of a punitive Mohmand field force. As one soldier-historian of the period puts it rather quaintly: 'In a very short time the Mohmands were in full flight to the hills, having received a most salutary lesson.'[26]

The British were not to dispose of the Black Mountain Yusufzais in so cavalier a fashion. The various clans of this formidable tribe, always with the manipulative hand of the Hindustani fanatics in the shadows, came out in 1868 to stage the second of four serious uprisings. On each of these occasions the Government had its hands full to prevent the tribes raiding the peaceful district of Hazara in British-administered territory. Trouble began in July 1868, when a *lashkar* of five hundred tribesmen staged a dawn raid on a British police post at Agror, on the western side of the Black Mountain. The tribesmen were driven off, but regrouped on the hillside to come charging back with kettledrums beating and banners waving ahead of the horde. Unit after unit was dispatched from Abbottabad, the nearest Army outpost, which lay 42 miles away. It was clear that these skirmishes were but a prelude to a bigger campaign that would take the Army into the Black Mountain district itself. The situation around Peshawar was too tense to risk weakening that garrison's forces, so manpower was brought in from as far away as Lahore, a distance of 232 miles, which the 20th Punjab Native Infantry covered in a ten-day forced march. The Sappers and Miners achieved an even more impressive feat by marching nearly 600 miles in less than a month to join the force under the command of Brigadier-General A.T. Wilde.

The summer inferno was now over, and on a brisk early October morning, the advance began, with the Gurkhas giving an especially valiant account of themselves as they chased the enemy from one ridge to the next. Within a week all the clans between the Black Mountain and the Indus had offered their unconditional surrender. The Army occupied the key hilltop outpost of Muchai, where the Royal Artillery commanding officer managed to coax two elephants to the summit to demonstrate that, if required, the corps could have put their field guns in place on the spot. Muchai was established as a pivot, in the event with great foresight, for future expeditions into this hostile district.

The Kohat Orakzais, the Dawar of the Tochi Valley and the Jowaki Afridis were the chief troublemakers who kept the Army routinely busy before the outbreak of hostilities with Afghanistan. The Utman Khel, a small tribe occupying the hills north of Peshawar, were the last to bring the troops out of their barracks before the war. In late 1876 a raiding party attacked a group of Government workers who were engaged in building a canal, trapping the men in their tents at night and killing a number of them before the camp was plundered. Reprisals were kept on hold for almost two years while the Government deliberated on its deteriorating relations with the Amir of Kabul. Then, in February 1878, the Guides swung into action under Captain Wigram Battye, a distinguished Frontier officer. The Guides struck at dawn, rushing the village where the Utman Khel leader, Mian Khan, was sheltering. The outlaw was killed in the fighting and the offending tribe was forced to pay compensation to the families of the murdered coolies.

In these three decades of established British presence on the North-West Frontier, the Government had found it necessary to mount more than forty punitive expeditions against the Pathan tribes, while the number of minor skirmishes numbered in the hundreds. The cost in terms of lives on both sides was significant, not to overlook the expense of keeping an army on the move with almost no respite. Over the years, much valuable insight was gained into the tribes and the difficulties they faced in an extremely harsh environment. This was the major factor, apart from their natural warlike proclivities, that drove them to pillage and plunder across the border. It is unfortunate that the Government showed itself incapable of extending a helping hand instead of a mailed fist to these people, a gesture that might have gone some way towards building a more positive relationship between the two sides. With too few exceptions, the imperial attitude towards the Pathans was mirrored in this memorandum, written in 1855 by the Secretary to the Chief Commissioner of the Punjab:

> Now these tribes are savages, noble savages perhaps, and not without some tincture of virtue and generosity, but still absolutely barbarians nevertheless. They have nothing approaching to government or civil institutions. They have, for the most part, no education. They have nominally a religion, but Mahomedanism, as understood by them, is no better, or perhaps is actually worse than the creeds of the wildest race on earth. In their eyes the one great commandment is blood for blood, and fire and sword for all infidels, that is, for all people not Mahomedans.[27]

The tribes were, in the words of one historian, treated by the British like tigers in a national park. 'They could kill what deer they liked in the park. They risked a bullet if they came outside and took the village cattle.'[28] This contempt for the Pathans, born of frustration as well as imperial ignorance, inevitably meant that both sides were destined to endure on a war footing so long as the British occupied the Frontier, and never more so than at the outbreak of the Second Afghan War.

THREE

Poachers Turned Gamekeepers

Four years before Government troops marched across the Khyber Pass, the stage was set for a fresh outbreak of hostilities with Afghanistan. In 1874 the Conservative leader Benjamin Disraeli was returned to power for a second term as prime minister. On matters of empire, Disraeli considered himself a staunch champion of the 'Forward Policy', which favoured the steady expansion of British India. For the Raj, the expansionist school found its justification in the fear, always more prevalent in London than Calcutta, of a Russian menace poised on the doorstep of India. This time, however, Whitehall got it right. The Tsar's General Staff started to draw up an invasion plan in 1877, when the Grand Duke Nicholas marched his army to Constantinople to wage war on the Turks, only to be stopped in his tracks by the British Navy lying at anchor in the Dardanelles. The Russians' next move was to send an alarmingly large embassy, consisting of several hundred soldiers and diplomats, to Kabul to try to persuade the Amir Sher Ali to commit himself to the Tsarist forces, should it come to an invasion of India. Failing that, it was hoped the Afghan ruler would at least agree to a Russian army crossing his territory unmolested.

Sher Ali was in his mid-fifties when war with British India broke out in 1878. The third son of Dost Mohammed was one of Afghanistan's most enlightened rulers. The Amir was responsible for having amalgamated different tribal factions to raise the country's first national army and he laid the groundwork for a system of tax collection. Under his leadership Afghanistan got its first postal system and even a newspaper. He was also a man in harmony with the principles of Victorian modesty. In 1869, the new Amir was invited by the Viceroy to a durbar at Ambala, at which the Government rolled out the full pomp and circumstance of the Raj. On watching a march-past of the Gordon Highlanders in full dress uniform, the normally stern Amir remarked to the Viceroy through an interpreter that 'the dress of the Scots is beautiful, and indeed terrific, but is it decent?'

Sher Ali's chief ambition was to keep his country out of the growing Central Asian power struggle that was festering beneath the surface between Russia and British India. In spite of his father having been ousted by Lord Auckland's Army of the Indus in 1839, Sher Ali was in no way an enemy of the British. He did not have to be reminded of the fate his father had suffered when a British army last marched into Afghanistan, or the bloody fratricidal strife that had accompanied his own ascent to the throne of Kabul, a position he was now unwilling to relinquish. Sher Ali therefore did his best to convince the Russian delegation to turn back, quite rightly fearing a British backlash.

The Viceroy Lord Lytton was a linguist and published poet, a man accustomed to moving in the literary circles of London's Mayfair, and with a marked preference for the company of Charles Dickens to that of the mutton-chop generals under his command. In spite of his genteel upbringing, or perhaps reflecting a poet's mercurial temperament, Lytton flew into a rage when told of the Russian overtures to the Amir. He chose to ignore the fact that Russia and England had just ratified the Berlin Treaty, which brought to an end the stand-off between the two imperial powers.

Within days, Brigadier-General Sir Neville Chamberlain was once more on the march. This time, however, his mission was more extensive than a simple punitive expedition against an unruly tribe. He was on his way to Kabul to demand the Amir accept a British Resident, as it was imagined the Russians had already stationed their own embassy in the city. On 3 September, Chamberlain and his party were stopped in the Khyber Pass by a detachment of Afghan soldiers and told they would not be allowed to enter Afghanistan. Now Disraeli jumped into the fray, handing Sher Ali a 20 November deadline to allow the column to proceed, or face the consequences. Sher Ali wanted to avoid war at all costs and thus, putting his honour on the line, he sent Lytton a letter with his formal acceptance of the British Government's demands. Tragically, the letter arrived too late: on 21 November three Indian Army columns began the invasion of Afghanistan.

The events of the Second Afghan War have been covered in great detail elsewhere, in accounts almost too numerous to mention. The question of that war holds a certain fascination for historians: how, in the space of forty years, Britain, with the memory of the disastrous retreat from Kabul still in living memory, could send its soldiers back into that vipers' nest. In 1839 Lord Auckland had ignored the advice of the Duke of Wellington himself, a man who had never set foot in Afghanistan but who knew a thing or two about warfare. The Iron Duke had cautioned the Governor General that, if he sanctioned an invasion of Afghanistan, the Government would find itself embroiled in perpetual conflict. Auckland chose to ignore this warning, which of course proved to be deadly accurate.

Britain launched its Afghan campaign of 1878 as a far more developed power than the one that had been routed in 1842. British India had by now extended its telegraph and rail network almost to the Afghan border, the Army was equipped with more powerful and accurate rifles, and supply lines had been shortened by sea as well as on land. Moreover, after nearly three decades of skirmishing with the Pathans of the Frontier, who also made up Afghanistan's dominant ethnic group, it was beyond doubt that the British were off to wage war on an enemy who was a familiar face on the battlefield. 'And now the British included the Sikhs within their ranks, a martial people who had been most helpful against Hindus during the Mutiny and who had been familiar with the Afghans for centuries,' comments one writer.

> Finally, among the British troops an air of revenge was still afoot for the events of 1842. Just as the world wars in Europe can be viewed as a two-round bout against the Germans, so can the Second Afghan War be viewed – at least in the minds of young soldiers raised on the tragic tale of Elphinstone – as a second stage of operations by the Army of Retribution.[1]

The invasion force, marching under the command of such Army heavyweights as General Sam Browne and Lord Roberts, fought its way into Afghanistan and drove Sher Ali into a hasty retreat to Mazar-i-Sharif near the country's northern border. There the Amir pleaded for support from the Russians stationed on the frontier under General Antonin Kaufman, who several years before had been making preparations to invade British India. Kaufman at this point was determined to disassociate himself from the Afghan cause, which he considered hopeless. In despair, Sher Ali retired to the half-deserted ruins of Balkh, Afghanistan's oldest city, where in February 1879 he died, broken in spirit. His son, Yakub Khan, acceded to the throne and negotiated a peace treaty at Gandamak acquiescing to British demands to station a permanent resident in Kabul. Furthermore, control of Afghanistan's foreign affairs was placed in the hands of the Government of India. The Amir granted Britain some territorial concessions near Quetta, as well as the Kurram Valley and, most importantly, the strategic Khyber Pass. In exchange, the Amir received a yearly allowance of £60,000 along with a promise of British support against aggression by a foreign power.

It was not quite over. The Afghans, as usual, had a stinger coiled in their tail, waiting for the victorious British forces. Three months later an Afghan mob massacred the British Resident in Kabul and all but a few of his escort. The Army was rushed to Kabul, where Yakub Khan was forced to abdicate and General Roberts took direct charge of the city. The dilemma now was to find a suitable leader to replace the deposed Amir. At that moment Abdur Rahman, a half-nephew of Sher Ali, rode in from exile in Samarkand, having been proclaimed Amir by a tribal grand *jirga*. The British were anxious to wash their hands of a messy situation and readily accepted Abdur Rahman's bona fides, in spite of his barbaric reputation for sadism. The new Amir soon found an effective way to dispose of his opponents, by throwing them down a well in which the bottom layer of victims would already have died, the layer above would be dying and newcomers would in due course sink slowly towards death as those beneath them disintegrated and made more room.

All now seemed well, and Roberts was on the point of withdrawing his forces when news arrived of a British brigade having been dealt a crushing defeat 324 miles away near Kandahar. The force had been attacked by followers of Yakub Khan's brother Ayub Khan, who had just proclaimed himself the only true Amir. Roberts quickly organised a relief force and it was as a result of his heroic forced march that he was invested with the title of Lord Roberts of Kandahar. The diminutive general mobilised ten thousand men and nine thousand pack animals and set off to cover the gruelling trek through burning deserts, arriving in Kandahar in an extraordinary twenty-three days. Ayub Khan was resolutely defeated in a pitched battle outside the city and the last of the Army units in Afghanistan were back in India by the summer of 1881, leaving behind a country engulfed in turmoil. Abdur Rahman spent the next two years of his reign fighting to defend his crown against rebellious tribes.

The Government's 20 November deadline for allowing General Chamberlain's party to cross the Khyber Pass proved to be fateful for Britain's future relations with Afghanistan. Another event took place that day that achieved less notoriety, but which nevertheless had a pivotal impact on the Government's dealings with the North-West Frontier tribes.

The Afghan troops were not the only adversary General Sir Sam Browne had to confront when he led his column through the narrow defiles of the Khyber Pass that November morning. The Khyber tribesmen were out in force, sniping and generally harassing the Army's progress. The Afridis were not going to miss this golden opportunity to pick off Indian Army soldiers, who could thus be relieved of their modern breech-loading rifles. The prime raiders were the notorious Zakka Khel clansmen and it wasn't until a month later, with the Afghan War in full swing, that the Government was able to dispatch five columns from Khyber Pass outposts to subdue the freebooters.

Colonel Sir Robert Warburton, whose name was to become synonymous with the Khyber Pass, was the son of a British Army artillery officer and an Afghan princess. With such a background, Warburton was able to walk amongst the Pathans as an equal, speaking their language and knowing their ways, yet he continued to be a staunch defender of empire, a passionate believer in the need for a stern but benevolent hand with the unruly tribesmen. When he was appointed Political Officer of the Khyber, Warburton's half-caste origins aroused suspicion and mistrust in certain Government circles. The shabby treatment Warburton received from some official quarters even came to the attention of the prime minister, Lord Salisbury, who wrote to Queen Victoria after Warburton's death complaining about this unjust hostility towards a loyal servant of the Raj. 'The racial prejudices under which Sir R. Warburton suffered is deeply regretted, but it is too deeply imbedded in the British official nature to be rooted out,' he wrote.'[2]

Warburton foresaw the need to devise a system by which the Government could rely on the Khyber as a safe point of passage between British India and Afghanistan for troops as well as for the weekly camel caravans that plied their way from the great bazaars of Central Asia to Peshawar and beyond. His idea, quite simply, was to turn poachers into gamekeepers by raising a native Frontier militia and paying the tribesmen to safeguard the Khyber Pass. Warburton's initiative came into force on 20 November, the day the Government's ultimatum to Sher Ali expired. The first recruits were from the Afridi and Mohmand tribes, the ones that had been causing the most trouble in the Khyber Pass. The native levy was christened the Khyber Jezailchis, later to become the Khyber Rifles, taking their name from the *jezail*, the Pathans' elaborately ivory-inlaid musket whose discharge was described by one Frontier officer as 'a rattling and banging, as of a minor train accident'. To the astonishment of nearly everyone except Warburton, once on the payroll the tribesmen turned out to be exceedingly loyal recruits. Lord Roberts himself was one of the most enthusiastic supporters of Warburton's strategy of enlisting the tribesmen as protectors of British interests. He wrote in his memoirs:

> Except in the Khyber itself [where the policy of establishing friendly relations with the Afridis, and utilising them to keep open the Pass, had been most successfully practised by the Political Officer, Lieutenant-Colonel Warburton] we could not depend on

the tribesmen remaining passive, much less helping us if we advanced into Afghanistan.[3]

Elsewhere Roberts recalls an afternoon ride into the Khyber Pass on an inspection tour in the company of Warburton and escorted only by two Khyber Rifles levies, when Roberts' Quartermaster General remarked, 'If this were to be told in England, or to any officer of the old Punjab school, they would never believe it.'[4] The fatal flaw in this strategy was to take for granted the tribesmen's loyalty to the Queen-Empress. This was by no means the case: their devotion was to Warburton, a fact he was to learn in tragic circumstances during the great Pathan Revolt of 1897.

The raising of the Khyber Jezailchis marked a pioneering experiment in enlisting Afridi tribesmen from the hills into the ranks. But it was not the first time a British administrator had successfully worked with the tribes to keep the peace in the border region. In reality, the precedent was not set on the North-West Frontier at all, but in the adjacent tribal land of Baluchistan to the south, which is today one of Pakistan's four provinces.

Colonel Sir Robert Sandeman was Deputy Commissioner of Dera Ghazi Khan, the strip of Baluchistan territory than follows the Indus for 150 miles and whose inhabitants are mostly Baluch, as opposed to Pathan, tribesmen. In 1866, when he took up his appointment, his district was the target of regular raiding parties from Khelat, a khanate that lay to the south of Quetta along the Punjab border. Instead of mounting punitive expeditions, Sandeman devised a system that involved enlisting local support to help settle tribal disputes. At one point he crossed into enemy territory accompanied by a small military escort from the Punjab and supported by a formidable *lashkar* of one thousand Baluch horsemen. The mission was largely successful in making secure the Bolan Pass (the main gateway to Kandahar), settling tribal grievances, obtaining in the process a permanent 'leasehold' for Britain on the strategic city of Quetta, now the capital of Baluchistan province. The Baluch tribes were pacified and Sandeman was rewarded with the appointment as Agent to the Governor General in Baluchistan.

Roberts had words of great praise for Sandeman's work, not least for securing the Bolan Pass for the Army, a passage that was to prove so crucial in the second British invasion of Afghanistan. 'I had never before been to that part of the Frontier [Quetta], and I was greatly impressed by the hold Sandeman had obtained over the country,' writes the Commander-in-Chief. 'He was intimately acquainted with every leading man, and there was not a village, however out of the way, which he had not visited. *Sinniman sahib*, as the Natives called him, had gained the confidence of the lawless Baluchis in a very remarkable manner.'[5] Roberts adds that it was mainly owing to Sandeman's power over these tribes that he was able to arrange with camel contractors to transport to Quetta and Kandahar the huge stocks of winter clothing and materiel he required for his Army in the field.

Unfortunately, what came to be known as the Sandeman System died with its creator. Sandeman had gained an enormous prestige amongst the Baluch tribes, two of which came close to open warfare for the privilege of burying the great peacemaker. Sandeman was, however, mistaken in his belief that this system of friendly persuasion could be extended to the Pathan tribes living north of Baluchistan. It fell to Sandeman's disciple, Richard Isaac Bruce, to carry on his mentor's work north of the Baluchistan border in Waziristan, deep within Mahsud territory.

Sandeman had scored a resounding success in Baluchistan, enabling the Government to put in place roads, forts, cantonments and all the paraphernalia of proper colonial rule in this province, thereby creating a network of tactical support points to bring force to bear where necessary. He was able to accomplish his task mainly by gaining the respect of the tribal chieftains, with whom he established a close working relationship. The Baluchs and other tribes of the region abide by a strictly hierarchical code under which all tribesmen take their orders from the malik or headman. They operate on an oligarchic basis. This is not the case with the Pathans, who uphold their time-honoured system of tribal democracy with the same ferocity as they defend their homeland, and the Mahsuds were having no part of it. Their system of government is the *jirga*, or council of elders and maliks, which sits as judge and jury in matters of tribal law. It has the power to levy fines on offenders, demolish their homes or have them put to death in cases of capital offence such as adultery or murder. But the occasional fanatical mullah notwithstanding, no one man commands the Pathans' allegiance in the way that the maliks in Baluchistan hold sway over their tribes.

The *jirga* forms the backbone of Pathan democracy and as such it merits consideration for the crucial role it has played in Afghan and tribal life over the centuries. The full name, *loya jirga*, derives from the Pashtu words 'grand' and 'council'. The tradition of the tribal assembly is not unlike the public meetings of New England townships, which in early American history were convened to deliberate on most aspects of community life, with the exception of dispensing justice. The earliest records of formal *jirgas* stretch back many centuries. There is documentary evidence of a council of elders having been held in Kandahar as early as 72 BC, called to elect a king, which was the *jirga*'s original role. The British would regularly gather the Frontier tribal leaders in *jirga* to deliberate on matters such as the terms of submission after a punitive expedition or the scale of allowances to be distributed for good behaviour. The *jirga* can comprise anything from a handful to several thousand tribesmen. It was always a formidable sight, the sea of white flowing robes and turbans marching into the barracks parade ground, sometimes after many days on the road, where the men squatted in a semi circle, their rifles stacked in a corner under the watchful eye of the sepoys, while a young officer fresh from Sandhurst and more often than not in baggy shorts fearlessly dictated the order of the day to these grizzled, bearded warriors. The *jirga* has played a pivotal role in contemporary Pathan politics, particularly in Afghanistan. In 2001, shortly after Al Qaeda's terrorist attacks on the USA, the Afghans convened four major *jirgas*, in Rome, Cyprus, Bonn and Pakistan, to decide the post-Taliban future of the country. The following year, some two thousand tribal notables met in Kabul for a week to form a transitional administration under Hamid Karzai, and the following year another grand *jirga* was convened to ratify the Afghan Constitution. It would be a great tactical error, on either side of the border, to disregard this Pathan passion for collective decision-making.

Bruce arrived in Waziristan as Political Agent in 1893, the year in which the Durand Line agreement demarcating the border between Afghanistan and British India came into force. From the very outset, his valiant attempt to impose Sandeman's system of tribal government by maliks began to falter. The case in point was the double murder of a British Public Works Department officer in Zhob, and five Indian soldiers in a separate attack by a gang of five Mahsuds. The tribesmen were forced to surrender and were put up for trial by *jirga*, in which they were given seven years' imprisonment. But some of the more recalcitrant amongst the Mahsuds saw this victory by a British administrator as a threat to their way of life. In short order, three of the maliks responsible for sentencing the killers were themselves assassinated, while the others fled for their lives or went into hiding. Bruce tried to persuade the tribesmen to punish the murderers of the maliks, but to no avail. It was clear that indirect rule through a British agent was not going to be acceptable to the Mahsuds or to any of the great North-West Frontier tribes. In the end, the tribesmen of Baluchistan proved themselves considerably less troublesome than the Pathans. Their tribal culture was not as highly developed and they found British rule less despotic than what they had suffered at the hands of overlords like the Khan of Khelat and the amirs of Sind.

The two colonels, Sandeman and Warburton, held different views on the subject of Frontier administration, but in the end it was the latter's tribal levy system that became the effective template for policing the border area. The first of these irregular corps, the embryonic Khyber Rifles, was a rag-tag bunch of Khyber tribesmen whose only distinguishing feature was a red tag worn by each recruit on his turban, to identify him as being on the Government's payroll. The Khyber Jezailchis and the other native levies that were raised in subsequent years were, dress aside, an irregular corps in all respects. Just as circus tigers do not jump through hoops without a trainer in the cage cracking the whip, the tribal recruits required constant supervision and guidance, lest they slip out of the cage once the trainer's back was turned. The men of the native militias, unlike the trained sepoys of the regular Indian Army, needed to be kept under a watchful eye and it was important that they understood the rationale for every order that was given. As one writer notes, this point was driven home by an event that occurred in 1882, which should have served as a warning for the future. For purely administrative reasons, the Government decided to abandon the small fort of Ali Masjid in the Khyber Pass, which was garrisoned by Afridi levies, and shift the company down to the larger fortress of Jamrud at the eastern entrance to the pass.

> Promptly a Subadar and a Jemadar [corps officers] concluded that the Government was on the run and went round, Koran in hand, urging their men to desert with rifles rather than obey the order. A Havildar [sergeant] defied them and managed to get the company back to Jamrud. The lesson should have been plain. An entire company should not be composed of a single section [Malik Din Khel, in this case] of a tribe like the Afridis, and trans-Frontier Pathans, in their own country, were not reliable when withdrawal was in the wind.[6]

Warburton had hit on a winning formula. The idea of raising tribal levies to police their own kinsmen began to catch on in other parts of the Frontier, coinciding with the roll-out of the system of political agencies. The Khyber came first, with Warburton in charge, and this was followed by Kurram in 1892, and Malakand, Tochi and Wana between 1895 and 1896. The Malakand Agency was placed under the direct control of the Government of India from the outset, with all the other agencies belonging to the Punjab government, which was directly responsible for the North-West Frontier region.

Sandeman himself put together a local militia in 1889, the year the Zhob region was annexed to India. It was called the Zhob Levy Corps, but later became the Zhob Militia, the name it goes by today. Sandeman took Warburton's initiative a step further by arming his men with the latest Army-issue Martini rifles and kitting them out in regimental uniforms. Of course, he was dealing with a softer breed of Pathan, along with some Brahui tribesmen who would be responsive to orders issued by Sandeman through their tribal elders.

Captain (later Colonel Sir) George Roos-Keppel was one of the great benefactors as well as soldiers of the Frontier. He was at that time stationed in the Kurram Valley south of the Khyber Pass, homeland of the Shi'a Turis. Roos-Keppel, with Warburton and Sandeman, was one of the initiators of the native militia system that today continues to play a key role in keeping the peace on the North-West Frontier. Sandeman and Warburton were poles apart in appearance: the uncrowned sovereign of Baluchistan was distinguished for his benevolent, almost jolly countenance, whilst Warburton's cold and haunting grey eyes betrayed a deeply tormented spirit. Roos-Keppel, of Anglo-Dutch descent, answered to Gilbert and Sullivan's 'very model of a modern major-general', with his silk turban and ermine-collared greatcoat, a pair of hooded eyes gazing sternly above a formidable handlebar moustache, in all a man possessed of a Churchillian self-confidence. Roos-Keppel was typical of the many high-calibre British Army officers who found themselves captivated by the Frontier's romance and promise of high adventure. He came to be closely integrated in Pathan culture, at least as far as one could decently expect of a *feringhee* without risking the sort of ostracism Warburton had to endure. Roos-Keppel published a grammar of the Pashtu language, translated arcane Pashtu historical works and co-founded Islamia College, now the undergraduate school of Peshawar University. But, first and foremost, he was a soldier of the Raj.

Roos-Keppel was passionately committed to the strategy of recruiting the Frontier tribesmen into irregular militia corps. As well as serving a tour of duty as Commandant of the Khyber Rifles, he formed the tribesmen into a levy known as the Turi Militia, renamed the Kurram Militia in 1902.

The Kurram Valley was one of the Frontier's most contentious areas, one that Afghanistan has always claimed as its own. In the mid-nineteenth century Afghan troops occupied the valley and even went so far as to install their own governor. This came to an end as a side issue of the Second Afghan War, when the invaders were driven back across the border. Maintaining army units in this remote region was a hugely expensive affair, and the Government had no interest in annexing it to the settled districts. Therefore in 1892 Roos-Keppel decided to make the Turis custodians of their part of the Frontier. After all, the tribe had enjoyed cordial relations with the British and on two occasions, in 1859 and 1879, they had helped the Army rid their country of Wazir raiders.

So it went on through the late nineteenth and early twentieth centuries, as one native militia after another was raised and the tribesmen were successfully induced, against all expectations, to protect British interests on the North-West Frontier. Nineteen of these levies are now under the command of Pakistan's Frontier Corps, headquartered in Peshawar's massive Bala Hissar fortress. Many of the names are synonymous with acts of gallantry, carried out by men who were called upon to fire on fellow clansmen and even neighbours, in defence of a foreign colonial power. The Khyber Rifles are of course the stuff of Frontier legend, a corps whose illustrious name has been emblazoned in works of fiction and Hollywood films. They exemplified this poacher-turned-gamekeeper role as guardians of what is historically the most vulnerable spot on the Frontier. For instance, there was a famous battle in the late nineteenth century in which an Afridi officer, rallying his brothers-in-arms in the defence of a Khyber Pass outpost that was under siege by a tribal *lashkar*, was found to have one son fighting by his side and two others with the attacking force.

There was no shortage of work for the newly raised Frontier militias. The Black Mountain district had been in an unsettled state for years following the Second Afghan War. Sharp skirmishes were fought between rebellious tribesmen, who refused to make payments demanded by the Government for various attacks perpetrated by tribal raiders. In 1884, the tribesmen were routed in a skirmish with Sikh and Gurkha troops. But as usual, sporadic raiding continued once the enemy was given respite to regroup its forces. Disturbances reached boiling point in 1888 with the murder of two British officers and four men of the 5th Gurkhas, an offence that rarely failed to bring the troops out in force. On 17 June a reconnaissance party of sixty Gurkhas and Punjab infantrymen had advanced to a ridge position called Chittabut, to secure an adequate water supply for their camp. This was in the administered district of Hazara – that is, in British territory proper. The tribesmen took them by surprise, pinning the men down under heavy fire, when one of the Gurkhas, Subadar Nagarkoti, shouted to the enemy: 'We have not come to fight but only for a walk.'[7] The severity of the attack mounted, and as the party fell one by one, he tried to coordinate the increasingly futile defence. The two British officers were cut down and only Subadar Nagarkoti and two sepoys survived the attack. Both young sepoys had acted with extreme bravery under fire to defend their commanding officers and were awarded the Indian Order of Merit for conspicuous gallantry. The Army found it particularly galling that one of the murdered British officers happened to be Major Leigh Richmond Battye, a much-decorated officer whose family name was synonymous with Frontier soldiering. There were at least four members of the Battye clan serving in different Indian regiments.

This was the fuse that ignited the 1888 Black Mountain Expedition. The Governor General announced on 29 August that he was 'pleased to direct' Brigadier-General Sir John McQueen to assemble the Hazara Field Force, with thirteen battalions of infantry and one company of sappers and miners to take action against the Yusufzai brigands. The force was to be assembled by 1 October and the Government wanted the job done in no more than three weeks.

The Governor General also wanted to test the reliability of the native levy system in this campaign, to which end he instructed McQueen to include a contingent of 350 men of the Khyber Rifles in the second brigade, under the command of Brigadier-General William Galbraith. The Government was so far happy with the performance of these militia units in their home territories. This would be the first time that one would be brought into action against members of other tribes. Lord Dufferin was impressed by what he had observed of the men during his recent tour of the Khyber Pass with Roberts. The Viceroy decided it was now time to upgrade the Khyber Rifles to a properly equipped corps, using the new breech-loading Snider rifles in place of their antiquated muzzle-loading jezails. McQueen discreetly took steps to ensure that the rifles did not vanish when the campaign was over, as the Pathans were too often known to make off with the weapons of their fallen comrades.

The Khyber Rifles took an active part in the expedition and fought alongside the Seaforth Highlanders in one of the final battles, in which the British regiment and the Pathan levy took the Yusufzai stronghold of Thakot. The two columns marched into the village preceded by a Highland piper, and one wonders what the Pathan tribesmen would have made of the skirls of 'You're owre lang in coming, lads'. A few days later the Khyber Rifles were back in action, this time marching with the Northumberland Fusiliers to subdue the village of Pokal. The offensive was launched at daybreak, after a desperate November night spent on the hillside, in the open and without blankets. The British force advanced in high spirits and eager for a fight the next morning. They overran the village in short order, forcing the tribesmen into submission. This brought to a close the third act in the long-running Black Mountain saga.

The South Waziristan Scouts also stood out as one of the most illustrious of North-West Frontier levies, as well as the one that found itself in the most precarious position. Other corps, such as the Khyber Rifles and the Mohmand Militia, were garrisoned close to regular army units, and these were able to provide support, if needed, when the native levies would come under attack by tribal *lashkars*. The South Waziristan Scouts, on the other hand, were stuck out on a limb in one of the most remote and isolated areas of the Frontier. Moreover, they were up against the Mahsuds, the most hated and lawless of the Pathans, who were dismissed by one British civil servant as 'arrogant, pig-headed and faithless'.

The Scouts, which is the name that eventually took over as a generic designation, be they Rifles, Scouts or Militia, were of course recruited from the very tribes they were eventually to face as enemies in the field. In most cases, this mattered little for men who lived a life of internecine strife and blood feuds. Once uniformed, armed and licensed to engage in their favourite pursuit, they acquired a staunch loyalty to the hand that fed them – that is, the British officers who commanded these irregulars. On one remarkable occasion, a detachment of South Waziristan Scouts was in full downhill retreat after being surprised and overwhelmed by a party of tribesmen hiding behind a ridge. The Mahsud bandits fired straight into the Scouts' backs as they ran for their lives. When one British officer's orderly, also a Mahsud tribesman, saw the bullets begin to kick up dust around them, he pulled off the young Englishman's topi and replaced it with his own turban to draw fire from the trophy their pursuers were trying to bag.

There is an abundance of Frontier lore relating to such incidents that suggests a relationship of respect between sworn enemies. One of the most remarkable incidents took place during the 1908 expedition against the Zakka Khel clan, one of the most bitterly fought campaigns in all of North-West Frontier history. When the Khyber Rifles sent their men into battle, it was discovered that some of the levies were members of the Zakka Khel clan itself. They undoubtedly knew many of the enemy by name and probably came from the same villages. In the end, the troops showed no hesitation in firing on their own clansmen. This was, on the one hand, because they loved a good fight above all else, but it was also a reflection of a spirited faith in their commander, Roos-Keppel.

Accolades of this type appear in numerous Army records and official memos. The British soon discovered these newly-converted game-keepers to be hard as nails, the ideal stuff for *gashting* (patrolling) some of the most inhospitable terrain in all of India. They were ideal soldiers in almost every respect, the fatal flaw being a vulnerability to demagoguery by Koran-waving mullahs. This apart, as one solider notes,

> The Pathan could cover the most difficult hillside at top speed and on his home ground knew every yard of the way. Carrying only a rifle, a knife and perhaps fifty rounds of ammunition [the maximum number issued by the Government], he was virtually tireless, as fresh at the end of a long day as when it started. Brought up in the shadow of the family blood feud, where his life and the prospect of discharging his obligations to his enemy depended on a highly developed sense of caution and cunning, he was a natural tactician, with a keen eye for a fleeting chance.'[8]

The one indispensable factor required for keeping the tribal levies loyal was strong leadership. The Pathans, as has been seen above, are capable of showing respect, even affection, for a strong and just adversary, likewise for a friend. But anything that could be interpreted as weakness or indecision by their superiors was certain to detonate revolt in the ranks, all too often resulting in open mutiny and the murder of commanding officers.

The worst incidence of desertion en masse concerned the most prestigious of these corps, the Khyber Rifles. This took place in 1919 at the outbreak of the Third Afghan War. It was a controversial business and more than one Army officer criticised the Government's decision to disband the corps as a result of these desertions. Those who argued the levies' case pointed out that the men who deserted their posts were not under the command of British officers and therefore lacked a strong hand to impose discipline. The fanatical Afghan mullahs outside the Khyber forts, who harangued these simple recruits with threats of eternal damnation, spread fear and panic in the ranks. Roos-Keppel was one who pleaded for comprehension and leniency. 'In such circumstances, and particularly when there were no regular troops to support them during the Afghan War, the militia men could hardly have been expected to remain loyal to the British Government in the face of the cry of jihad in Afghanistan and of the aggravated anti-British feelings in tribal territory.'[9] The Government turned a deaf ear to this British administrator, who spoke and even thought like a Pathan. The Khyber Rifles were disbanded and not raised again until after the Second World War.

Unfortunately the desertion by Khyber Rifles levies was not the exception to the rule. The Scouts of North and South Waziristan suffered their fair share of attrition through desertion, an offence that was rated as particularly serious if the recruit absconded with his rifle, for it was correctly assumed that sooner rather than later, the weapon would be turned against the Government.

Once the Afghans had been chased out of India, the Government came up with a proposal to raise a back-up or complementary tribal corps to police the border region. This was largely the inspiration of Roos-Keppel and came to be known as the *khassadar* ('police' in

Pashtu) system. This was not a new concept in Pathan society, at least not on the Afghan side of the border, where, during the 1919 war, the Amir Amanullah was able to rely on a force of ten thousand khassadars in his campaign against the British. These tribal police wore no uniform, they carried ancient yet effective breech-loading Snider rifles, and their usefulness consisted largely in taking a portion of the burden off the regular army by providing road protection and general police work. The khassadars were placed under the jurisdiction of the political agent in each district and they were also required to escort him on official tours.

The important factor that set the khassadars apart from the scouts was that these tribal police were servants of the tribe, not of the Government, always carrying out Government duties on behalf of the tribe. They were, in effect, part of the tribe, and if tribal raiders were found penetrating British territory the Government could dismiss the khassadars attached to that tribe, even though they had taken no part in the raids. Companies of khassadars were regularly dismissed en bloc in punishment for tribal hostility or treachery. Similarly, their pay was sometimes stopped or reduced in order to settle or contribute to fines imposed on their tribe by the Government. In a way this resembled the system devised by Sandeman of working directly with the tribes, but it differed in one important respect, in that the levies of Baluchistan were regulated by a contract between the Government and an individual, usually the clan's malik. The khassadar system of the North-West Frontier was founded on a system of collective responsibility.

Frank Leeson, who in 1946 was given command of some two thousand khassadars of North Waziristan to bring them up to scratch before Partition, describes this rag-tag array of tribal police as 'unselected, illiterate, ill-officered, un-uniformed, un-rationed, undisciplined, armed with antique rifles and rusty, home-made ammunition, disaffected by ten years of religious war, subject to periodic mass dismissals, despised and suspected by Military and Scouts alike'.[10] These unruly companies of tribesmen made up the raw material Leeson and his fellow British officers on the Frontier were charged with raising to an acceptable standard of discipline and performance.

The khassadars were recruited, trained and administered entirely under tribal arrangements and this was one of the system's weaknesses: it was impossible to count on their services if things were going badly with the tribesmen. The khassadars were first and foremost Pathans, and only secondly servants of a remote colonial power. There was also the tradition of hereditary employment, which meant that the job and pay could be handed down from father to son regardless of suitability for the position. Moreover, the son or younger brother also inherited the rank of a khassadar who retired or died. This was obviously an inhibiting factor in creating a serious disciplined force. Putting the khassadars' loyalty to the test always entailed a bit of the luck of the draw, with mixed results. In 1937 a seditious Mahsud religious leader called the Faqir of Ipi led thirteen khassadars to desert simply by threatening them with denial of a proper Muslim burial. Later that year a khassadar patrol had no misgivings about shooting up some Mahsuds who were cutting telephone lines, while another unit stood its ground and put up a plucky fight against a Mahsud *lashkar* that was causing trouble in the district. If the khassadars wavered or failed to carry out orders, the scouts would be brought in, and behind them, if all else failed, stood the Indian Army.

After nearly half a century of warfare with the border tribes, in the late 1890s the Government of India decided it was time to do something about defining the border with their troublesome neighbour, Afghanistan. The demarcation of a formal frontier between the two countries, which was non-existent when the British annexed the Punjab, had a twofold rationale. On the one hand, it sent a clear signal to Russia that Britain had established a fixed line of defence of which any violation, directly or through third party manipulation (i.e. the Amir of Afghanistan), would constitute an act of war.

Amir Abdur Rahman, one of Afghanistan's most capable yet ruthless leaders, would now become the ruler of an internationally recognised country rather than the indefinite 'Afghan territory'. This completed Afghanistan's geographical delimitation, as the western border had been set out in an agreement with the Persians in 1857.

Twenty-eight years later the Anglo-Russian Boundary Commission settled the northern frontier along the Oxus, although some areas were under dispute and from time to time were infiltrated by Tsarist agents or army units. But now, with British India exercising jurisdiction over Afghanistan's foreign policy, the Tsar was made aware of how far his territorial writ ran before risking a confrontation with Britain.

A second reason for marking out a formal Anglo-Afghan border was to make it possible to place responsibility for tribal raids on either side of the line, thus helping to clarify a contentious and long-running problem. The agreement that was eventually ratified in Kabul emphasised a commitment by Britain and Afghanistan to refrain from interfering in the internal matters of one another's countries.

The Government was already nervously taking steps to shore up its defences along British India's North-West Frontier. In 1889 the Gilgit Agency, part of the strategic territories of Jammu and Kashmir, was re-established under the jurisdiction of the Resident in Kashmir, eight years after the first British Agent in the territory had been withdrawn. Gilgit was formally brought back under direct British control to fill in a gap of some 50 miles of no man's land between British India and what was nominally Afghan territory, but which fell squarely into the growing Russian sphere of influence in the Pamirs. Colonel Algernon Durand, brother of Sir Mortimer who later negotiated the boundary treaty with Afghanistan, shared the Government's fear of Russian expansion in the region, citing an official dispatch of the day which stated that 'the advance of Russia up to the frontiers of Afghanistan, and great development of her military resources in Asia, had admittedly increased the necessity for strengthening our line of defence . . .'.[11] Durand states elsewhere his conviction that a Russian invasion of India was definitely on the cards. 'The Great Empire . . . is expanding in many directions. Central Asia is now hers. That her soldiers, and the ablest of them, consequently believe in the possibility of conquering India, no one who has had the chance of studying the question can doubt.'[12]

The settlement of some form of boundary was becoming a matter of urgency, and not just because of immediate concerns over Russian expansionism. It was rather the Afghans who were worrying the Government with incursions into Waziristan, the Kurram and the Afridi and Mohmand lands on the British side of the Frontier. These incursions came largely in response to the advance of the British railway line closer to Afghan territory. Therefore it was time to put an end to this cat-and-mouse game and fix a formal border between the two dominions.

Mortimer Durand was a veteran of the Second Afghan War, in which he had served as political secretary to Lord Roberts, and thus had gained a close appreciation of Russian ambitions in Afghanistan. In 1893, when he was serving as Foreign Secretary to the Government of India, the 43-year-old career diplomat was sent to Kabul to negotiate the historic treaty that was to give his name to an international boundary.

The outcome of the British mission was the Durand Line, a 1,200-mile boundary that runs on a south-west axis, from the mountains of Chitral at its northern extreme to the Persian frontier in the inhospitable desert regions beyond the Helmand River. The Government saw in this mission an opportunity to push the dominion of British India right through the tribal areas and, while doing that, obtain some strategic territory west of the Khyber. At 49, Abdur Rahman was only six years Durand's senior. He was, however, a frail man, stricken with gout that rendered him almost helpless and from which he died in 1901. Durand was a forceful negotiator who, in only a few weeks of discussion, persuaded the Amir, under duress, according to several writers, to sign the boundary treaty.

From the outset, Abdur Rahman warned Durand of the consequences of including the Pathan hill tribes within the dominion of British India. In his autobiography the Amir quotes a letter he wrote to the Viceroy, Lord Lansdowne, in which he spells out these misgivings.

> If you should cut them out of my dominions, they will never be of any use to you nor to me. You will always be engaged in fighting or other trouble with them, and they will always go on plundering. As long as your Government is strong and in peace, you will be able to keep them quiet by a strong hand, but if at any time a foreign

> enemy appears on the border of India, these frontier tribes will be your worst enemy. In your cutting away from me these frontier tribes, who are people of my nationality and my religion, you will injure my prestige in the eyes of my subjects, and will make me weak, and my weakness is injurious to your Government.[13]

The progress of events on the Frontier in the ensuing years bore out almost every word of the Amir's prophecy. For one thing, in some places the line was drawn through the middle of villages, sometimes placing farmers living on one side of the border while their fields were on the other. The boundary treaty cut straight through the Mohmand country, leaving the clans of this important Frontier tribe split between two countries. The consequences of this tactical error are in evidence today, in that the Mohmands' political loyalties have always rested more with Kabul than with successive governments on the eastern side of the border, rendering them Pakistan's least reliable Pathan citizens. Kerr Fraser-Tytler, one of the most prominent of Afghan historians, drives home this point that the Durand Line was riddled with defects, from the point of view of ethnography, strategy and geography. 'It cuts across one of the main basins of the Indus watershed, it splits a nation in two, and it even divides tribes.'[14]

For the time being, Sir Mortimer and his retinue could depart Kabul in a jubilant mood. Not only had the Government of India secured a border treaty on their terms; Sir Mortimer had also arm-twisted the Amir into recognising Britain's claim to suzerainty over Waziristan, Chagai, Baluchistan and New Chaman.

There was one more item of business on the Durand Commission's agenda. It would be useful to create a territorial buffer along the northern limits of Chitral and Gilgit, to avoid having a contiguous border with the Russian Empire that was rapidly expanding in that direction. Two years after the treaty had been signed, the British forced upon Abdur Rahman a narrow 200-mile-long strip of mountain country called the Wakhan Corridor. This finger, which today borders Tajikistan on the north and India on the south, extends from Afghanistan in the north-east to the Chinese border. The Amir was not happy about including in his dominions a territory that would place him on the front line in any conflict between Britain and Russia, an easily imaginable scenario given that in some parts of the Wakhan Corridor the two empires were separated by less than 10 miles of rugged glacial territory. This 'gift' from the British, for the Amir a poisoned chalice if ever there was one, was accepted with great reluctance. Indeed, this remote region has often been the source of boundary disputes, and in fact Afghanistan's easternmost border with China was only settled in 1964. The Government of India paid the Amir half a million rupees to meet the cost of administering his new territory. 'It was from their point of view a moderate price to pay to secure the north-eastern end of the Hindu Kush against Russian penetration,' according to Fraser-Tytler.[15] He was right: while the British were in control of India no Russian forces ventured into the Wakhan Corridor, but they did use it as a point of entry in 1980 during the Soviet invasion of Afghanistan.

The Frontier tribesmen lost little time in making known their views on the Durand Line. Barely was the ink dry on the treaty than the British demarcation commission engaged in erecting the boundary pillars in Wana was surprised one morning at dawn by a terrific discharge of firearms, the beating of drums and wild yells and shrieks. A thousand-strong Mahsud *lashkar* swept down on the camp, killing twenty-one officers and men before they were driven off by the Government's military escort. With or without an international boundary, it was obvious that Frontier life was to carry on as normal.

The demarcation of the Durand Line was plagued with ethnic and geographical blunders. For nearly 115 years since the signing of the treaty, Afghanistan has used every opportunity to denounce the agreement as invalid. Afghan rulers from Abdur Rahman onwards have advanced the argument that the Pathan tribes are their people and that the Pathan homeland should form part of the mother country. The Afghan claim is that Abdur Rahman negotiated the treaty under severe internal and foreign constraints. The Amir himself later contended that he yielded to the British terms only under duress. Afghanistan further argues that the treaty was signed with the Government of British India and that the agreement lost its validity when this ceased to exist, with the independence of India in 1947.

Afghanistan has used the UN as a forum, both for opposing Pakistan's membership and also to denounce the existing border treaty. The fact is that no Afghan legislative body has ever ratified the Durand Line agreement. On the contrary, two years after Partition, the treaty was denounced by the Afghan grand *jirga*. So it went on through the second half of the twentieth century. Prime Minister Mohammed Daud Khan, who banished the royal family and founded the Republic of Afghanistan in 1973, called for the repeal of the Durand Line treaty shortly after taking power. The Taliban proved a disappointment on this issue to the Pakistani military who helped put them in power. 'The [Pakistani] military assumed that the Taliban would recognise the Durand Line,' according to the South Asian historian Ahmed Rashid.

> The military also assumed that the Taliban would curb Pashtun nationalism in the NWFP [North-West Frontier Province] and provide an outlet for Pakistan's Islamic radicals, thus forestalling an Islamic movement at home. In fact just the opposite occurred. The Taliban refused to recognise the Durand Line or drop Afghanistan's claims to parts of the NWFP.[16]

The ouster of the Taliban and the creation of an elected regime under President Hamid Karzai has not brought a settlement of the border dispute. As recently as 2005 Karzai showed himself to be of a like mind with many of his predecessors, be they monarchs, military despots or religious fanatics, when he rejected the Durand Line as 'a wall between two brothers'.

The Pakistanis have marshalled a host of counter-arguments in support of the status quo, based mostly on historical precedent and international law. They point out that in 1905 Abdur Rahman's son and successor, Habibullah, signed another treaty with the British undertaking to fulfil his father's commitments. This was ratified in 1919 as part of the peace treaty ending the Third Afghan War, though it can be argued that the Afghan Government was at the time in no position to impose demands on the British victors.

As for the Afghan claim that the treaty was nullified by the emergence of Pakistan and India as separate states, the international law specialist Ijaz Hussain argues that a fundamental change of circumstances cannot be invoked as a ground for terminating a treaty, 'if the treaty establishes a boundary'. Hussain says that Afghanistan 'is not entitled under international law to denounce or withdraw from the Durand Agreement and the action . . . has no validity in international law'.[17]

The Durand Line has been criticised for violating ethnic considerations, but in fact the administrative border that was in existence for more than forty years before the treaty was ratified was no less guilty of this sin, for it left communities split between British India and the tribal areas. As a strategic initiative, it is at best of questionable value, and, as the historian Collin Davies noted in the 1930s, the official border 'possesses no strategic value at all. The Khost salient between Kurram and Waziristan is but one of its many strategic imperfections. This disposes of three possible lines of resistance. The real frontier we are called upon to defend in India is the mountain barrier.'[18]

What then are the benefits of the Durand Line? From the outset it was an ill-defined border and often the boundary pillars were set so far apart that for long distances travellers would not know whether they were in Afghanistan or British-administered tribal territory. However, sovereign nations with contiguous territory require a formal border. In this respect, the Durand Line represented a reasonable attempt to delineate that border. The inclusion of the Frontier tribes in this scheme represented the most contentious issue, one that threatened to open up a veritable can of worms for the Government. Handing the Pathans over to Afghanistan would have been tantamount to a retreat to the Indus. Taking this line of action to its logical conclusion, to accomplish this without disrupting tribal communities meant abandoning Peshawar (thereby capitulating to long-standing Afghan demands) as well as most of the settled areas west of the Indus. This alternative was clearly out of the question. Contrariwise, dragging the many millions of Pathans living on the other side of the border into British dominions was as disastrous a plan as could be imagined. Apart from inviting another war with Afghanistan, it would necessitate the presence of several Army divisions to hold the line against so overwhelming a number of hostile tribesmen. In the end, neither course of action would have mattered a jot to the tribesmen, who treated the Durand Line with supreme indifference and carried on raiding and plundering at their pleasure. To the Pathans, it made absolutely no difference which party claimed sovereignty over either side of their hills. The tribes have never paid allegiance to any government, not to Kabul and certainly not to British India, and they are only vaguely and indirectly touched by the presence of Pakistan. But tribal passions are all too easily inflamed by demagogues, in particular the preachers of hatred and violence who roamed the hills calling for jihad against the infidel. The British were convinced they had carried off a coup with the Durand agreement. The cavalier way in which the Amir was strong-armed into accepting a line drawn through the heart of the Pathan tribal lands proved unworkable from the start. Today it remains the major source of diplomatic friction between Afghanistan and Pakistan.

FOUR

The Hundred Years War

The drawing of the Durand Line, or rather the policy that brought it about, was directly responsible for the worst disaster ever to befall the British on the North-West Frontier. This was the great Pathan uprising of 1897.

The prelude to this revolt, and to a certain extent the event that triggered it, took place two years earlier. This was the Chitral campaign, an episode that swelled the hearts of countless boys of the Victorian era, for this was Frontier warfare at its most heroic. 'In this adventure,' as one historian notes, 'there was danger, there were formidable natural obstacles, remote, romantic-sounding and unexplored territories, and a frantic race against time. If only there had been a blonde, or at least a lady in the fort, the story would have been dramatised and fictionalised ad infinitum.'[1]

Chitral is the largest and northernmost of the North-West Frontier districts, lying some 200 miles north of Peshawar, reached through the remote Malakand and Dir districts. The territory is roughly the size of Wales, whose Snowdonia peaks would be dwarfed by Chitral's towering mountains, such as 25,230ft Trichmir. It is a land of glaciers, fantastic gorges, icy torrents and vast tracts of arid hills, and until the late nineteenth century almost no European had set foot in the territory, whose people are of unknown origin. Chitral is the ideal setting for romantic exploits, a view shared by Rudyard Kipling, who chose it as the setting for *The Man Who Would be King*, his tale of the misadventures of two Englishmen in India. In 1975 the story was made into a grandly entertaining film starring Michael Caine and Sean Connery.

The Chitralis are a non-Pathan, though Muslim, Frontier tribe who may have migrated centuries ago from Wakhan and the Pamir mountains to the north. It has also been suggested that they may be remnants of Mongolian invaders, much as the people of former Kafiristan are said to be descendants of Alexander's soldiers. Algernon Durand was one of the earliest Western visitors. He rode into Chitral in 1885 and took away the impression that these people were predominantly Kho, speaking Khowar, 'and they probably represent the earliest wave of invasion which swept into Chitral from the north over the passes of the Hindu Kush. So remote is their antiquity that they may fairly be considered aboriginal.'[2]

Chitral suddenly acquired a prime strategic value for the British in the 1880s, when war with Russia seemed imminent. Chitral was a protected state under the suzerainty of Kashmir. The territory was important to the British because it lay astride the shortest route between India and Russia, and the local tribes acted as a buffer between the two empires. The area lies at the extreme northern limit of British India's North-West Frontier territory and in 1885 a mission was dispatched to secure the alliance of the Mehtar, or Chitrali ruler, Aman-ul-Mulk. To the Government's relief, the Mehtar turned out to be well disposed to the British and all went well until Aman-ul-Mulk's death in 1892. That was when all hell broke loose in Chitral. The Mehtar was survived by sixteen (some say seventeen) sons, all of whom immediately went for one another's throats to seize their father's throne. Of those who survived this fratricidal struggle, Nizam-ul-Mulk was selected as the British candidate. It was a brief reign, for three years later Nizam-ul-Mulk was slain by his half-brother, Amir-ul-Mulk, who ordered that he be shot in the back as he was returning to camp from a day's falconry. Amir-ul-Mulk persuaded Nizam's followers to change their allegiance on the spot, and his unfortunate half-brother's body was left to rot where it fell. After this event the British quite naturally harboured serious doubts about Amir-ul-Mulk's reliability. In anticipation of trouble ahead, Lieutenant Bertrand Gurdon, a cool, young giant of a man, quickly called for an escort of fifty sepoys to march from his mission headquarters at Mastuj, north-east of Chitral (the capital and district share the same name), to

Chitral town. Surgeon-Major George Robertson, who was Political Agent at Gilgit, was ordered to reinforce Gurdon with four hundred Kashmiri troops.

It was at this point that the Pathans stepped into the fray. Umra Khan, the ruler of the Pathan domain of Jandol, now part of Dir state south-east of Chitral, was at this time basking in the military successes he had achieved over some neighbouring tribes. Surveying the disturbed state of affairs in Chitral, this petty despot now caught the scent of opporutnity and saw a chance to annex this state to his dominions. Umra Khan accordingly assembled a *lashkar* of three thousand tribesmen and marched on Chitral, where he effortlessly occupied the settlement of Kila Drosh, only 24 miles from the capital. The Pathan warlord then sent an ultimatum to Robertson to evacuate Chitral and return to Mastuj. Far from bowing to Khan's demands, Robertson took his column into Chitral Fort, where he thought it prudent to depose the treacherous Amir-ul-Mulk, who was replaced as Mehtar by the much more manageable Shuja-ul-Mulk, a 10-year-old brother affectionately known to the British soldiers as 'Sugar and Milk'.

Robertson dug in for a siege in a fort that was very difficult to defend. It was sited on low ground near the river, from which water for the garrison had to be obtained. The fort was commanded on three sides by hills. The building materials were crude, mostly rough timber laid horizontally, encasing layers of mud and stone, which were built up to make a wall. It was a square structure, of the usual type built by tribal chiefs along the Frontier, with a tower at each corner and a fifth at the end of a gully leading to the river. The towers were built of two wooden cages, all held together by wooden cross supports that stuck out from the walls. Robertson noted that it was no problem for a man to clamber over the protruding supports.

The fort's military commander was Captain Colin Campbell who, in keeping with the tradition of the day, was subordinate to the Political Officer. Campbell had 340 riflemen, with about 300 rounds per man for the Martini-Henry rifle and 280 rounds for the Snider. Umra Khan's strength was estimated at three thousand to five thousand men, counting the force of Chitralis he had won over to his cause. Umra Khan's position was considerably strengthened with the arrival from

Afghanistan of his soldier of fortune uncle, Sher Afzul, who claimed the throne of Chitral.

Robertson could foresee a problem in stocking sufficient food supplies to withstand a protracted siege. He sent reconnaissance parties out to scour the area and bring in all they could confiscate from local villages. The foodstuffs they returned with were deemed sufficient to last the men for three months at most, until the end of April, with a ration of one pound of flour per man each day. There was also some rice in the stores, a few sheep and geese, tea and a small supply of rum to carry them through the bitter winter months.

By the beginning of February Umra Khan had the fort at Drosh in his hands, which brought his tribal army within a few miles of Chitral. He then sent a messenger to the beleaguered Robertson, demanding the withdrawal of the Political Agent and his escort from Chitral Fort. Robertson unceremoniously sent Umra Khan's emissary back with his reply: there would be no surrender. The Pathan chieftain took this as his signal to advance on the garrison.

Fighting broke out on 3 March, when news reached the fort that Sher Afzul was approaching with a large body of tribesmen. Captain Campbell, the senior combatant officer present, rode out of the fort with a party of two hundred Kashmir Infantry to engage the enemy. The engagement did not go well for the British. Campbell and several other officers fell wounded in a furious volley from the Chitralis. With darkness setting in, Campbell was able to remount his horse and order a retreat. The retiring troops were relentlessly harassed by the enemy. This day saw the first of many acts of valour when, in the retreat, Surgeon-General Henry Whitchurch of the Indian Medical Service was awarded the Victoria Cross for gallantly carrying the mortally wounded Captain John Baird into the fort under heavy enemy fire.

Once inside the fort, the men found themselves closed in on all sides by shrieking tribesmen massed several deep outside the walls. The British garrison had taken nearly sixty casualties in this first day's engagement, yet worse was to come in the ensuing forty-seven days that the little garrison was completely cut off from the outside world. The defenders' morale, especially that of the Kashmiri troops, deteriorated rapidly when faced by the prospect of a slow death by starvation and the fact that many of their rifles were rendered unserviceable.

Robertson had realised the need for special preventive measures against fire, given the fort's wooden construction. He gave orders for the water-carriers to sleep with their goat-skins filled and to maintain a state of readiness, night and day. In spite of these precautions, 7 April proved a critical day for the garrison, mainly because of the low state of morale in the fort. The besieging force succeeded in setting fire to one of the wooden towers, thanks to a lack of vigilance on the part of the Kashmiri guard. Nevill relates the details:

> The fire soon assumed alarming proportions, especially as the men were greatly impeded by the severe and accurate fire the Chitralis opened on anyone who ventured to give them a target. Whilst superintending the extinguishing of the flames, the British Agent [Robertson], who had been handicapped by bad health [acute dysentery] throughout the siege, had the further misfortune to receive a bullet wound in the shoulder. Though the injury was severe, he was still able to assist in the defence. At length, however, the fire was brought under control, thanks to a liberal supply of water. But the Chitralis renewed their attempt the next day, when the attention of the sentries was momentarily relaxed at the time of relief.[3]

With a quarter of the men reported ill as outpatients or in the infirmary, Robertson could hardly allow any slipshod discipline. His solution was to replace the Kashmiri sentries with more reliable Sikh troops, changing the relief time each day in order to confuse the enemy.

Life inside the fort was a daily battle not only with the enemy: the garrison was plagued by disease, hunger (pack animals were now being slaughtered for food), filth and anxiety, the exhausted men catching whatever sleep they could between the enemy's unpredictable actions. An air of deep despondency hung over the garrison as the troops faced the prospect of annihilation with no sign of reinforcements. In this they were mistaken, for what none of the defenders knew was that, when large bodies of Chitralis were seen moving off from the fort on 10 April, they were heading to Mastuj to oppose a relief force coming up under Colonel James Kelly, whose exploit recalled the cavalry riding to the rescue in a Wild West film. Kelly had ridden hell-for-leather for a fortnight with a 400-strong column, starting from Gilgit more than 200 miles east of Chitral. His route took him through the treacherous 12,000ft Shandur Pass, marching through knee-deep snow, without tents and carrying minimum baggage.

Kelly was the vanguard of a powerful force of fifteen thousand men mobilised at Peshawar. Three brigades were placed under a high-profile military triumvirate led by Major-General Sir Robert Low, Brigadier-General Sir Bindon Blood and Major Harold Deane, Political Officer, later to be appointed first Chief Commissioner of the North-West Frontier. The British were determined with this show of force to impress upon the Russians that they held firm control of their northern territories.

Meanwhile, the plight of the defenders inside the fort was far from over. The tribesmen had spent two days raising a terrific din at night, shouting and beating their drums till the early hours. Robertson correctly suspected that the Chitralis were planning to tunnel under the walls and that the noise was a subterfuge to drown out the sounds of their picks and shovels. Reconnaissance work confirmed that a mine was being dug within two yards of the wall. Robertson pondered his options and several days later he ordered a sortie of one hundred men, troops he could ill afford to spare, to destroy the mine. With ammunition running dangerously low, the orders were for 'no firing, bayonet only'. The party took with them 110lb of powder to destroy the mine and all the officers were issued with matches. It took one hour for the Sikh and Kashmiri soldiers to rush the house where the digging work was taking place, bayoneting thirty-five Chitralis as the enemy fled in terror, and exploding the mine before retiring to the fort with the loss of eight men.

The following day marked the end of the ordeal for Chitral Fort's gallant defenders. On 18 April the Chitralis broke and ran on the news that Kelly's forces had broken through all resistance and were advancing hard, a day's march from Chitral. The column arrived on 20 April to meet a garrison exhausted by forty-seven days of hunger and illness, but jubilant in victory. General Low's troops marched in a week later and took Sher Afzal prisoner, deporting him and his leading followers to India. Shuja-ul-Mulk was confirmed as Mehtar and all ended on a happy note, the British having only to lament Umra Khan's escape to Afghanistan. The Government ordered a new fort to be built at Chitral. This was a far more prominent affair, held by two infantry battalions, one company of Bengal Sappers and Miners and one section of Mountain Battery with two guns. The message to Russia and the world at large was that there was to be no meddling in India's northern defences, which were firmly under British control.

The Chitral campaign was the costliest blow, in terms both of loss of prestige and of expenditure, the British had been dealt since their arrival on the North-West Frontier. Yet it turned out to be no more than a scene-setter for the next act, a tribal rebellion that was to the Frontier what the Sepoy Mutiny had been to Bengal. It has been said that revolt, 'the theory, practice and fruits of it, was the Pathans' principal contribution to the history of British rule in the north-west corner of India'.[4] The Great Pathan Revolt of 1897 bore out this claim with a vengeance.

The Government's Frontier policy swung to and fro over the years, from aggressive expansion to non-intervention and back, usually in line with the politics of whichever party happened to be in power in Whitehall. The Frontier tribes had watched this penetration of their hitherto independent valleys with growing anxiety. The demarcation of the Durand Line, with its accompanying definition of spheres of influence, the setting up of Political Agencies, and finally the passage of troops through their territories and the garrisoning of these lands, was regarded as part of a deliberate menace to the tribes' freedom.

The years immediately following the Chitral affair were a time of political and natural calamity for India. Native intellectuals had begun to openly question the subservience of India to British policy. Import duties had been imposed to protect the rupee, which was falling in value, and this gave rise to a wave of street protests. The late 1890s saw a devastating outbreak of bubonic plague, followed by the worst famine India had ever known. While the Government, under the liberal-minded politics of the Viceroy Lord Elgin, preoccupied itself with these issues, the first symptoms of insurrection were beginning to fester on the North-West Frontier.

The tribesmen were unhappy about the Government's decision to increase the salt tax in the Frontier region from eight annas (half a rupee) to two rupees per maund, a native weight equivalent to approximately 130lb. Firebrand mullahs were adept in exploiting this grievance to raise tribal passions to boiling point. This was a promising time to be spreading anti-British propaganda, for Britain's prestige as an imperial power was at a low ebb. By 1897 it was easy for simple minds to swallow the line that the soldiers of Islam had put Christianity on the run. Sultan Abdul Hamid II, the last real caliph of the Ottoman Empire and the most revered leader in the Muslim world, had dealt the infidel Greeks a crushing blow. British squares had been broken by Arab hosts in Sudan, where General Charles Gordon was murdered by Arab insurgents, and Christians were being massacred on a vast scale in the Muslim territories of the Middle East and Central Asia. 'In 1897 a spirit of fanaticism was in the air,' writes Collin Davies. 'It would be difficult to state how far these happenings affected the Indian Frontier, but certain letters discovered in Mullah Sayyid Akbar's house in the Warran Valley of Tirah show clearly the wild rumours that were prevalent.'[5] One of these letters was obtained from an informer in Kabul and passed on to this religious rabble-rouser from an Afghan theological conference held in the spring of 1897.

Abdur Rahman's frail but conniving hand lay behind much of the demagoguery that was being spread over the Frontier hills. The Amir was growing worried about the Government of India's stated intention to bring the Pathan tribes increasingly under British control. It was at this gathering of mullahs in Kabul, ostensibly convened at the behest of the Turkish Sultan Abdul Hamid, that the Amir gave them the mission of expelling the infidel from the Frontier. In May reports were circulated at Peshawar that an agent from Constantinople had arrived in Kabul after a fourteen-day camel trek across Persia and Afghanistan, at that time of year a desolate furnace. This mysterious agent was introduced to the assembled mullahs, who were informed that he brought a message from the Sultan in support of their coming jihad. The Amir then took on the exalted title of *Zia-ul-Millat wa ud-Din*, 'Light of the Nation and Religion', and shortly thereafter published what amounted to a manual of jihad, which the mullahs quite correctly received as a declaration of war against the British oppressors. Of course, the Amir cunningly maintained strict neutrality throughout the hostilities of 1897–8. The last thing Abdur Rahman wanted was to have to take on a British punitive expedition against Afghanistan.

The Government cannot be held blameless for what followed. The North-West Frontier had formed part of British India for nearly half a century. The Pathan mind, to which duplicity could be taken as simple expediency, in the Court of Kabul as well as on the Frontier hills, was no longer a mystery to the British. This considered, it is difficult to grasp how the new Viceroy, Lord Dufferin, was not dissuaded from providing the Afghans with the very weapons that within a decade would be handed over to the tribesmen in the Frontier revolt of 1897. A letter to Abdur Rahman contained in the Viceroy's Secret Correspondence file states: 'As a mark of my confidence in your Highness, and of my desire to meet your wishes as far as may be possible, I have given orders that the 5,000 Enfield rifles, which you proposed to buy in England, should be supplied to your agents in Peshawar whenever you are ready to take them. I trust that this gift will be acceptable to your Highness.'[6]

The Mullah Sayyid returned to the Frontier to propagate his fairytales to a following of credulous Pathans. The letter found in his house states, in part:

> Aden, a seaport, which was in possession of the British, has been taken from them by the Sultan. The Suez Canal, through which the British forces could easily reach India in twenty days, has also been taken possession of by the Sultan, and has now been granted on lease to Russia . . . The Sultan, the Germans, the Russians and the French are all in arms against the British at all seaports, and fighting is going on in Egypt too against them. In short, the British are disheartened nowadays.[7]

One supposed holy man, a sinister and bigoted figure known to his acolytes as Sadullah, and to the British as the 'Mad Mullah', boasted to the people of Swat that those who followed his teachings could never be harmed by British bullets, which, he explained, would be turned into water. Sadullah preached jihad against the British, who in the name of God needed be driven out of Swat and Peshawar. This outburst of religious fanaticism, accompanied by an ironclad guarantee of invincibility, coming from a silver-tongued fakir like the Mad Mullah, was all the encouragement required to put the Swati tribesmen on the march.

The Mad Mullah was one of a collection of fire-and-brimstone Muslim fanatics roaming the Frontier to preach the message of jihad. Sadullah was almost certainly in touch with his co-religionists the Hadda Mullah and the Mullah Powindah – to name three of the most celebrated bigots. It was this latter mullah, reviled by the British as 'the evil genius of Waziristan', who touched the match to the fuse.

It didn't help matters that this wave of incendiary agitation was taking place in midsummer, when temperatures on the Frontier soar well above the 100°F mark. The heat acted as a catalyst for the tribesmen's natural proclivity for violent action, and by June the entire border was smouldering. Unsurprisingly, the opening shots of the 1897 revolt were heard in South Waziristan, the stronghold of the intractable Wazir and Mahsud tribes. The previous year a fine of 2,000 rupees had been levied on the Wazir tribe for the unprovoked murder of a Hindu merchant who lived in the settled district and was therefore a British subject. A year later, the inhabitants of a group of villages known as Maizar, 5 miles from the Afghan border in the newly acquired Tochi Valley, were still refusing to pay their share of the fine, which they insisted should be borne by the guilty parties. Henry Gee, the Political Agent at Tochi, made his way to the scene of the dispute with an escort of more than three hundred Sikh and Punjabi infantrymen under the command of Lieutenant-Colonel Arthur Bunny, a 'cheery fellow', in the words of Lord Roberts, who had fought alongside him in the Sepoy Mutiny. The troops were kindly received by the villagers, who even prepared a late breakfast for their guests. Had they been aware that their visit coincided with the Muharram religious festival, when the Wazirs slaughter sheep and which they consider an auspicious time for martyrdom, the troops might have approached with more caution.

The men were enjoying a relaxed meal in the shade of a banyan grove. One Sikh officer even began to entertain the villagers on the regimental pipes. Suddenly a tribesman was observed waving his sword from the top of a tower: this was the signal for the villagers to open fire. The troops had walked into a trap. The firing was directed with deadly accuracy at the British officers. Colonel Bunny took a bullet in the stomach, yet carried on directing the operations until he collapsed and expired on a nearby ridge. Five more British officers were hit in the crossfire, one of them mortally. In all, the force lost seventy-two men in the Maizar ambush.

It was not the best time of year to be mounting a punitive expedition, with the sweltering heat, the lack of drinking water and the Indus swollen with snow-melt, making the river crossing a perilous undertaking. But such was the nature of this outrage – which, incidentally, contravened the Pathan code that demands hospitality even for one's deadliest enemies – that, as soon as the report of what had happened at Maizar reached the Government, two brigades were assembled to march on the Tochi Valley. The 1st Punjab Cavalry rode into the Maizar district on 20 July, to find the villages deserted. They spent the next sixteen days destroying the settlements and towers so as to render the tribesmen homeless and destitute when they reappeared. Sporadic skirmishing went on until November, when the Tochi Field Force was able to consider the valley pacified. The Madda Khel, which was the offending Wazir clan, was finally brought to heel and its maliks made to offer submission to General Bird's force. Though heavily outgunned, the Pathans had put up a stubborn resistance for nearly four months. They were inspired to fight on by news coming in from Malakand and Chakdara forts, where the British garrisons were in a desperate plight, with more than twenty thousand enraged and heavily-armed tribesmen baying for their blood. So unsuspected had been these attacks that the officers at Malakand found themselves busily disputing a chukka of polo when their Pathan scouts galloped up to warn them of the approaching horde.

> In the attack on the Malakand camp all the elements of danger and disorder were displayed. The surprise, the darkness, the confused and broken nature of the ground, the unknown numbers of the enemy, their merciless ferocity, every appalling circumstance was present. But there were men who were equal to the occasion.[8]

This lively description comes from the prolific pen of a young war correspondent who arrived at General Bindon Blood's headquarters in early September. Winston Spencer Churchill, who was 23 at the time, had no doubts about the causes behind the 1897 revolt:

> Here Mohammedanism was threatened and resisted. A vast, but silent agitation was begun. Messengers passed to and fro among the tribes. Whispers of war, a holy war, were breathed to a race intensely passionate and fanatical. Vast and mysterious agencies, the force of which is incomprehensible to rational minds, were employed. More astute brains than the wild valleys of the North produce conducted the preparations. Secret encouragement came from the South – from India itself. Actual support and assistance was given from Kabul.[9]

It is worth keeping in mind that Churchill's employer, the *Daily Telegraph*, paid its war correspondent by the column. What is interesting is Churchill's allusion to 'secret encouragement from the South'. Charles Allen and other historians have singled out the influence of the Wahhabi fanatics in exhorting the tribes to revolt.

> The Mad Fakir's [Mullah's] association with a pretender to the throne of Delhi does suggest links with the Hindustani Fanatics. That he had the support of a significant faction of the Hindustanis at Sittana is beyond question . . . Many young mujahedeen from the Hindustani camp, easily identified by their distinctive black waistcoats and dark blue robes, were spotted among the Fakir's ranks.[10]

James Spain highlights the fact that the timing and places of the attacks at Maizar, Malakand and elsewhere did not emanate from a lone

Aman ul Mulk, ruler of Chitral. His death in 1892 touched off a fratricidal power struggle among his sixteen sons. *(Royal Geographical Society)*

Wali of Swat, 1926. The Wali was the secular ruler of the tribal state. The last Wali was removed by the Pakistani government in 1969. *(Royal Geographical Society)*

Darwesh Khel Wazir tribesmen near Wana. These are some of the fiercest Pathan fighters. *(Royal Geographical Society)*

Malakand fort, the scene of a heroic defence in the 1897 Frontier Revolt. *(Royal Geographical Society)*

Piper George Findlater, shot through both ankles, continues to play as the Gordon Highlanders storm the Dargai Heights in 1897. *(The Gordon Highlanders Museum)*

Afzul ul Mulk and retainers. He murdered three of his brothers to seize the throne of Chitral, and was later killed by his uncle, Sher Afzul, who proclaimed himself ruler. *(Royal Geographical Society)*

British officers dictating terms to Orakzais in 1897 after the Great Pathan Revolt. *(Royal Geographical Society)*

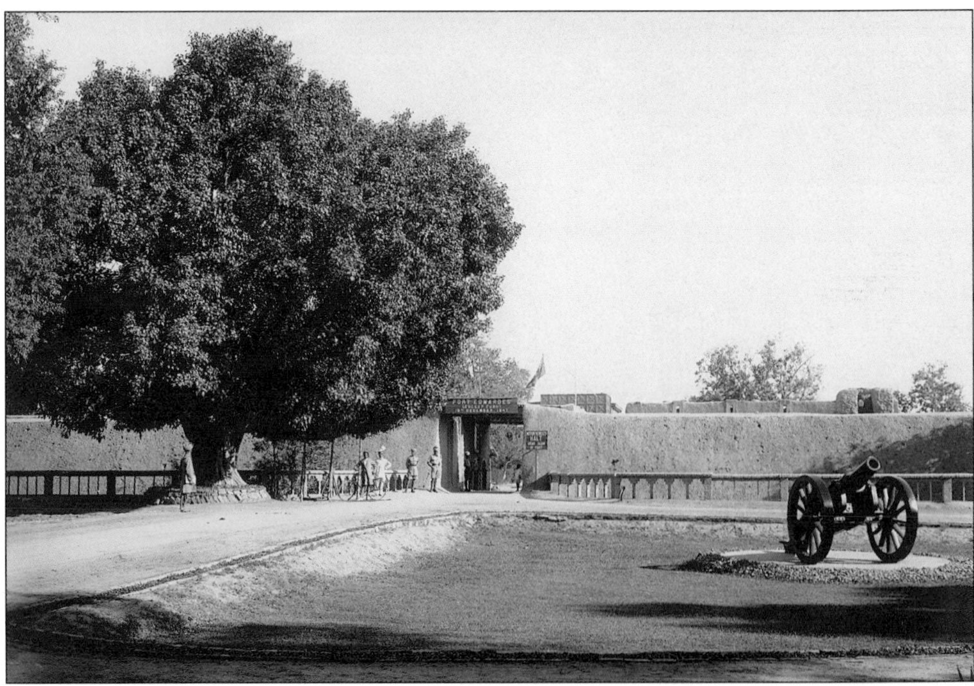

Bannu Fort (Fort Edwardes), built in 1847. This was one of the original five British administered 'settled' districts on the Frontier. *(Douglas Learmond)*

Nowhere to hide: picquet outposts 5 miles from Bannu and the Afghan frontier. Note the graveyard on the left. *(Douglas Learmond)*

A tribal *jirga* at Miranshah, Waziristan, 1937. *(Jonathan Falconer)*

A Mahsud convoy guard, Manzai-Wana, 1937. *(Jonathan Falconer)*

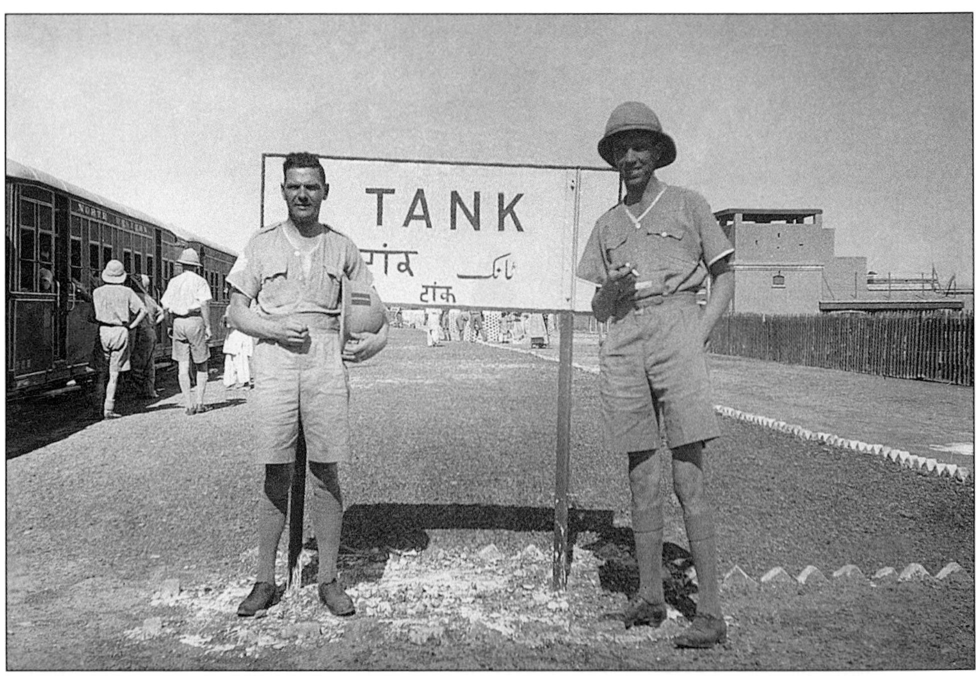

Sergeant Lofty Owen, Royal Air Force, (on the right) poses for the camera with an unidentified RAF comrade at Tank, one of the few outposts of civilisation in the wild Waziristan region of the North-West Frontier Province. *(Jonathan Falconer)*

An RAF soccer trophy of 1930s vintage for matches played between the officers and sergeants at RAF station Ambala. On the cup are the names of the winning teams and the troopships on which they sailed to India. The shirt front bears the signatures of the men from each team. *(Jonathan Falconer)*

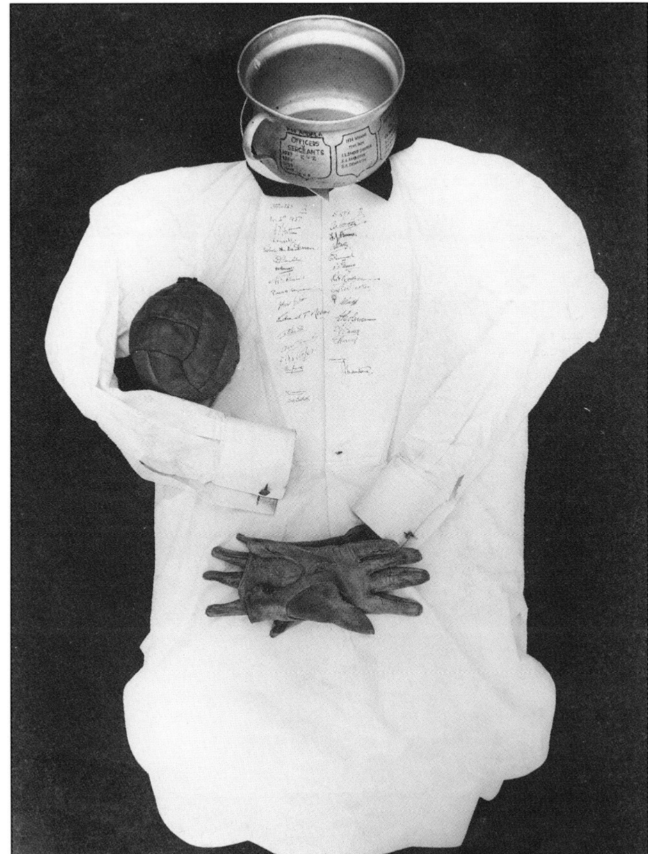

Rolls-Royce armoured cars of the 9th Armoured Car Company, Royal Tank Corps, take part in a military parade on the Waziristan plain. *(Field family collection)*

A sepoy in a delicate bomb-disposal exercise. *(Field family collection)*

A border post between the North-West Frontier and Afghanistan. The notice over the gate advises travellers to 'leave here on the return journey so as to pass Landi Kotal by 4pm and Jamrud by 5pm'. *(Field family collection)*

Bridge construction on the road from Mami Rogha to Lwangi, under the watchful eye of a British Army engineer officer, Lieutenant A.M. Field. The native troops are from the Queen Victoria's Own Sappers and Miners. *(Field family collection)*

A column at rest in Greenwoods Corner, 7,000ft above the Tochi Valley, which was overlooked by the Alexandra Ridge piquet. At 8,500ft, the piquet was the highest permanently occupied outpost in what was the British Empire. *(Field family collection)*

A group of native officers of the Indian Army on the North-West Frontier. *(Field family collection)*

Hawker biplane on a mission over a North-West Frontier outpost. *(Field family collection)*

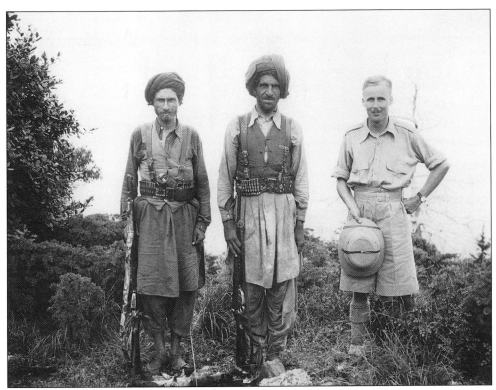

Khassadars, or Frontier tribal police raised and trained by the British. The officer on the right is Lieutenant Skey of the Royal Tank Corps. *(Field family collection)*

Razmak camp situated between Razani in Wazir territory and Makin in Mahsud territory, established after the First World War to keep peace between these two warring tribes. *(Field family collection)*

Messines Lines, part of brigade headquarters in Razmak. *(Field family collection)*

An Army camp at Razani Gardai in Waziristan. *(Field family collection)*

A village tower in Razani, about to be blown up in a punitive expedition. *(Field family collection)*

The job is done. *(Field family collection)*

A sepoy gunner at Spinwam, south-west of Peshawar. *(Field family collection)*

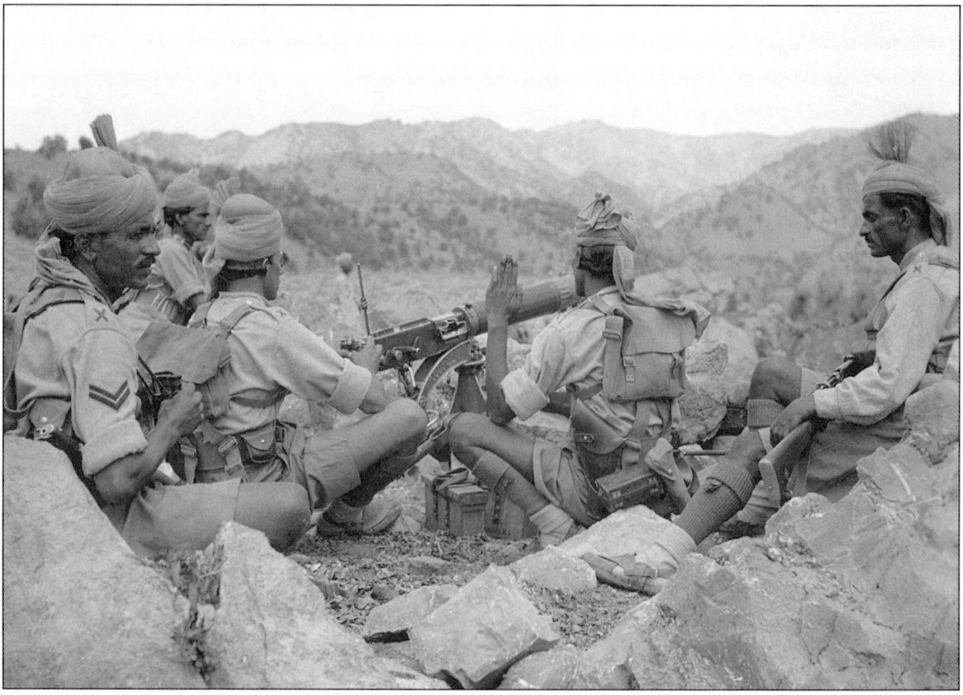

A Vickers machine-gun emplacement in a sangar, or stone breastwork. *(Field family collection)*

The India General Service Medal with bar 'North-West Frontier 1936–37', awarded to British soldiers and airmen for service in the province, which often involved them in action against the Pathan tribes. *(Jonathan Falconer)*

Major John Girling, commanding the Mounted Infantry of the SWS, marches past the first Pakistani Governor of the NWFP on Wana airstrip, where he had just arrived, in 1949. Girling was celebrated for having led the last cavalry charge on the Frontier – by mistake. *(Major John Girling OBE)*

Major John Girling pictured with a group of Pakistani officers, including the APA and the Executive Engineer, 1948. *(Major John Girling OBE)*

The Dhana Shoot was held annually and took place in an area notorious for badmashes (outlaws). Pictured here in 1949, Pakistani officers, including the Subedar Major, with John Girling in the centre. The Dhana Valley was the scene of Girling's epic cavalry charge. *(Major John Girling OBE)*

The Piffers (Punjab Frontier Force) Chapel, at St Luke's Church in Chelsea, London. *(Nick Smith and Chris Edwards)*

agitator, religious or otherwise. 'The call to battle was not given by one leader but by dozens of local figures each acting on his own, although some of these, mostly mullahs, were in communication with each other and with reverend colleagues in India, and possibly in Turkey.'[11]

The Malakand and Chakdara outposts had been built on the line of communication with Chitral and in defiance of strong opposition from the Swati tribesmen. The two garrisons formed part of the Frontier strategy to safeguard road links between Army headquarters in Peshawar and Dir district to the north, a section of which shares a border with Afghanistan and could therefore be used as an invasion route into British territory through the Shingara Pass.

The attacks on the Swat outposts caught the Government as well as the garrisons by surprise. The battles that took place with the besieging tribesmen were intense but brief, thanks to the swift arrival of reinforcements from other Frontier units. Hardly had news of this fresh insurrection reached Lord Elgin at his summer residence in Simla, than local commanders were on their way to relieve the beleaguered troops. When the Viceroy grasped the seriousness of the threat to the Swat garrisons, he instructed General Blood to put together a punitive expeditionary force of three brigades to deal with the seditious tribes. The column consisted of ten thousand men, a massive body of soldiers for a North-West Frontier operation. This, however, represented only a fraction of the seventy-five thousand troops that were eventually mobilised in the course of the Pathan Revolt, which took more than two years to put down and required punitive operations against most of the major tribes, in particular the Mohmands, Orakzai, Afridis and Wazirs. British India had not known such an outburst of rebellion since the Sepoy Mutiny forty years before, and Churchill was hardly overstating the threat when he wrote, 'The whole British Raj seemed passing away in a single cataclysm.'[12]

The tribesmen launched their attack on 26 July, when the preacher who was known to the British as the 'Mad Mullah' emerged from his encampment at daybreak in the company of six young followers, preaching jihad as he headed towards Malakand outpost, only 8 miles away. By late afternoon he had gathered a *lashkar* of several thousand in his wake, which began severely pressing the garrisons at Malakand and Chakdara.

There were moments when it looked as if the sepoys might not be able to hold off the waves of fanatics who threw themselves against the walls. It was fortunate for the defenders that the native troops, and these included many Pathan levies, did not hesitate to rally round their officers. During lulls in the fighting, the Mad Mullah and his followers assailed the native troops with religious harangues, attempting to induce them to shoot their officers and desert with their weapons. At one point, a group of tribesmen who were dug in a few yards from some Afridis of the Punjab Infantry – who were holding a defensive position outside the fort – shouted across to their brother Pathans to rise up and defend the cause of Islam. The Afridis, to the consternation of their fellow sepoys, cried out that they were ready to join the sacking of the fort. But once they had the tribesmen off-guard, they instantly shot dead those who had raised their heads above the parapet.

The garrison was only a few days into the siege, but food and ammunition were already running low and the situation was starting to look desperate. Only hours before the enemy cut the telegraph wire, a message was cabled from Malakand to the one force that could be relied on to mount a rapid relief operation, the Corps of Guides. The officers of the Guides were sitting down to dinner in their Mardan mess when an orderly rushed in carrying the SOS. The Guides immediately swung into action. Within three hours the baggage and supplies were assembled and the cavalry went dashing off to the relief of Malakand, followed closely behind by the Guides' infantry. It was 36 miles to Malakand, with a gruelling 2,000ft climb to the pass. The first relief detachment pulled up at the gates of the fort sixteen hours after riding out of Mardan, a truly prodigious feat for a heavily laden column moving under the blazing July sun. Even more remarkable was the fact that not a man was lost on the march, in spite of the heat and lack of sleep. There was no respite for the Guides: no sooner had the troops reached the fort than they found themselves engaged in ferocious hand-to-hand combat that lasted the better part of the night. The enemy was driven off with heavy losses, and the next attack, which came on the following night, was delivered with the tribesmen much diminished in numbers and spirit. The unexpected appearance of the rough and ready Guides, for the most part men of the enemy's own blood, had badly dented the morale of the attackers.

On 31 July a relief column under Colonel A.J. Reid fought its way through the woods to Malakand with 700 men and 190,000 rounds of ammunition. Reid's force and the Guides together made short work of the remnants of the Swati tribesmen who were still at large, and with this, the relief of the Malakand garrison was achieved.

Less than 10 miles away, Chakdara fort was manned by two companies of Sikhs whose water supply was now depleted. The situation was alarming but not yet desperate, thanks to the valiant endeavours of Gunga Din (who gave his name to one of Rudyard Kipling's most celebrated war poems), for he was the native who carried water to the soldiers, right under the gun-sights of the enemy. It would be a sad soul indeed who failed to be stirred by the power of Kipling's tribute to the little water-carrier. In the battle, Gunga Din is shot by a Pathan bullet that 'drilled the beggar clean', yet before he expires the boy loyally continues rushing about with water for the wounded British soldiers. The subaltern who narrates the poem cries out in agony, 'For Gawd's sake git the water, Gunga Din!' The mortally wounded servant wordlessly obeys, and the soldier tells us of the boy's pathetic end: ''E put me safe inside, An' just before 'e died, "I hope you liked your drink," says Gunga Din.' The epic of Gunga Din was made into a Hollywood film in 1939, with Cary Grant and Douglas Fairbanks Jnr in the lead roles.

More was to come on this day of vintage North-West Frontier valour. The Chakdara defenders were putting up a determined fight against a howling mob of ten thousand tribesmen. Most of them were by now barely able to stand on their feet, and ammunition was running low, when there occurred an incident that could have gone straight onto the cinema screen. Having lost telegraphic communication with the outside world, a Sikh signaller displayed an extraordinary burst of heroism under fire by crawling up onto the roof to send a two-word heliograph message to Malakand: 'Help us!'

Darkness had now fallen and the enemy began closing in for an all-out attack with scaling ladders and bundles of grass to set alight, and with complete disregard for their own casualties. The battle raged all night, and just as dawn was breaking a cheer went up on the parapets. The oncoming waves of Swati attackers were pressing the exhausted troops to the point of exhaustion when the flash of a heliograph from the nearby Amandara ridge announced that help was on its way.

Churchill was again on the scene to report the action:

> Then suddenly, as matters were approaching a crisis, the cavalry of the relieving column [the 11th Bengal Lancers who formed part of Bindon Blood's column] appeared over the Amandara ridge. The strong horsemen mercilessly pursued and cut down all who opposed them. When they reached the bridgehead on the side of the river remote from the fort, the enemy began to turn and run.[13]

The Malakand fort had taken the brunt in this phase of the Pathan Revolt. The defenders suffered 173 killed and wounded in roughly a week of fighting, far outweighing the twenty losses Chakdara suffered over the same days. The reason for the disparity in casualties was that the attack on Malakand had taken the troops completely by surprise. Another factor was that the Pathans, in an uncharacteristic display of chivalry, had allowed the Chakdara officers who were surprised on the polo field to ride straight through the *lashkar*'s ranks and return to their fort unmolested. The losses on the tribesmen's side were far more severe. The Mad Mullah and his followers had incited about twelve thousand tribesmen to join the assaults on the two garrisons, four times the number that the Government believed the fanatics were capable of raising. Of these, seven hundred had been killed in the siege of Malakand, while at Chakdara, where the open ground allowed the troops to bring their Maxim guns into play, more than two thousand had fallen. Taking into account the several hundreds of fleeing tribesmen who were cut down in the cavalry pursuit, the Pathans lost at least a quarter of their force.

General Blood now turned his attention to the offending tribes. The Malakand Field Force was fully assembled and ready for action on

7 August. The columns of cavalry and infantry, with the support of thousands of pack animals to transport their 'British and native' field hospitals, mountain guns, provisions and ammunition, advanced, undeterred by a monsoon downpour, into the Swat Valley and swiftly obtained the submission of the lower Swati tribesmen. The more stubborn fighters of the Upper Swat Valley had established a defensive position on some high ground at Landakai, where, under the command of their firebrand mullahs, they made a stand against General Blood's troops. A squadron of the 11th Bengal Lancers was dispatched ahead to reconnoitre the terrain, where they spotted a number of stone breastworks festooned with tribal banners. The stone sangars were manned by some five thousand Bunerwal Yusufzais, the followers of the Akhund of Swat who had put up such a ferocious resistance in the Ambela campaign.

Bindon Blood himself rode forward to survey the field of the approaching battle. He decided on a flanking action, sending the Royal West Kent Regiment straight at the sangars to distract the enemy's attention, while the Punjabi and Sikh infantry would move up from the left and cut off the tribesmen's retreat route. The attack was a total success, not only in dislodging a panic-stricken enemy from the ridge, but also in forcing what was known as the 'Gate of Swat', thereby opening the way to the region's upper reaches. As was to be expected, there were acts of gallantry by the Guides Cavalry on that day. The horses could not negotiate a narrow pathway beyond the ridge that had been partially blocked by the tribesmen, who were fleeing by the hundreds in the direction of the Buner hills. Before the Sappers and Miners reached the broken path, ten cavalrymen – five British officers and five sepoys – leapt from the saddle to pursue the enemy on foot. They came under a heavy fusillade from the retreating Swati tribesmen. Within seconds, two British officers lay dead and two others wounded at the foot of a hill. The Pathans closed in with their swords and began hacking at the men on the ground. Once more, it was the cavalry to the rescue: Lieutenant-Colonel Robert Bellew Adams and Lord Fincastle (who happened to be covering the campaign for *The Times*) dashed in with a handful of native troops to rescue their fallen comrades. In spite of heavy fire and with a horse shot out from under the newspaper reporter cum cavalry officer, the two Englishmen were able to carry the wounded officers and the body of another to safety behind a clump of trees. For this act of bravery, they were awarded the Victoria Cross, the highest military distinction for valour. The tribal leaders were badly shaken by the pounding they had taken from the Army's heavy artillery. They had lost almost four thousand fighters and had seen many of their villages and croplands put to the torch. One by one, the maliks came forth to submit to Bindon Blood, and on 26 August the operation was at an end, a little more than a month after the first attacks had been launched on Malakand and Chakdara.

The Waziristan uprising inspired by the Powindah Mullah had been quelled and the Government had disposed of the Mad Mullah. But now the ranting of another fanatic, the Hadda Mullah, was fanning the flames of revolt. While General Blood was putting together his expeditionary columns at Nowshera, the Mohmands had sent their warriors to attack a Border Police fort at Shabkadr, a scant 15 miles north of Peshawar. The siege lasted for twelve hours and was only lifted with the arrival of a force consisting of four guns of the 51st Field Battery Royal Artillery, 151 men of the 13th Bengal Lancers, two companies of the Somerset Light Infantry and 400 men of the 20th Punjab Infantry. The Government was bent on nipping the uprising in the bud, before the unthinkable happened and the *lashkars* managed to fight their way into the Frontier's main command post. The 800-strong column came under attack from an enemy estimated at up to seven thousand Mohmands and for a moment it looked as if the only alternative to wholesale massacre would be a hasty and humiliating withdrawal. The Peshawar garrison then rushed a further four companies of the 30th Punjab Infantry to the police post, supported by a small force under Brigadier-General Edmund Elles, who was in command of the Peshawar District. The 13th Bengal Lancers decided the outcome of the day with a charge that scattered the tribesmen into the hills. The British casualties had been heavy, with four officers and nine other ranks killed and sixty-one wounded.

General Blood was instructed to move his column westward to Bajaur, the Hadda Mullah's stronghold, where he was to join up with the Mohmand Field Force under Elles, who was marching northwards deep into Mohmand country to meet the Malakand Field Force. This territory had been the scene of some fierce engagements with the Swati tribesmen in the 1863 Ambela campaign. Together, the two powerful columns pressed home their pursuit of the Mohmand rebels. The fighting reached desperate proportions as the Mohmands were driven to a fever pitch, not only by the Hadda Mullah, but also by the burning of their villages.

The march into Mohmand territory took the troops through the mouth of the Mamund Valley, home of the Mamunds, one of the four clans of the Tarkani tribe of Bajaur. The British had no particular quarrel with these tribesmen, who owned villages on both sides of the Durand Line. However, the sight of hundreds of rifles neatly stacked outside the tents of the British encampment, right in the middle of their valley, was too great a temptation for the Mamunds to ignore. The tribesmen would bide their time, in the Pathan way, and furtively stalk their prey. Under the watchful eye of the Mamund warriors concealed behind boulders along the ridges, three columns led by Brigadier-General P.D. Jeffreys advanced through Bajaur. Once the Mamunds were satisfied that the columns were too far separated to provide support for one another, they seized the moment and swarmed down on the British troops.

Churchill was caught up in this action, one of his first battles in the Frontier campaign. While other chroniclers limit themselves to giving a tally of battle casualties, the young war correspondent spares no graphic detail in recounting the sight of battlefield carnage from a close-range perspective. 'A soldier . . . sprang into the air, and falling, began to bleed with strange and terrible rapidity from his mouth and chest. Another turned on his back, kicking and twisting. The [sepoys] caught hold of the injured and began dragging them roughly over the sharp rocks in spite of their screams and groans.'[14]

The day was starting to turn against the badly outnumbered troops when one of the officers, taking the decision that any course of action was preferable to standing their ground and being butchered on the spot, ordered the bugler to sound the 'charge'. The effect on the men's morale was instantaneous: the officers waved their swords to urge the Sikh infantry forward – and to great effect, for a counter-offensive was the last thing the tribesmen expected. Stunned by the sudden attack, the Pathans turned tail and fled, pursued by the soldiers, who maintained a steady fire as they gave chase. Meanwhile another *lashkar* of some two thousand Mamunds unleashed an attack along the column's flank. The Guides Cavalry arrived in time to check this advance and send the remnants of the enemy stumbling back to the hills. A few more successful engagements took place that day, 17 September, with the Guides in the forefront, fighting all the while under a driving rain.

The Army was occupied for the next seven days in conducting systematic operations in the Mamund Valley to punish the guilty clans. After burning the tribesmen's villages, the sepoys carried off enough forage to feed the entire brigade's transport animals for a month. Bindon Blood, along with other commanders of the expeditionary force, had a few more clashes with the Mamunds in several places across the valley, but by December the Government was satisfied that the tribe had received proper punishment.

The Bunerwal Yusufzais were the only Frontier tribe north of Peshawar that had yet to be pacified. General Blood was called in again, this time as Commander of the Buner Field Force, which was made up of two British battalions, Bengal and Punjabi infantry and the Corps of Guides. The Army had given an ultimatum to the tribes that dwelt between Buner and the Indus, offering them a final chance to save their country from invasion and a rerun of the punishment they had been dealt by generals Cotton and Chamberlain in the Sepoy Mutiny. All the tribes of this region lost no time in tendering their submission, with the exception of the Bunerwals. So there was to be more action before this stage of the Pathan Revolt was brought to an end.

It was New Year's Day 1898 when the column moved out, riding eastward towards the Buner border. Blood ordered his troops to clear the way into Buner country proper through two high passes, and this was accomplished with the help of two mountain batteries that opened fire on the tribesmen, who fled in terror. Once across the boundary, the problem was to bring up supplies quickly enough to keep the rapidly advancing troops on the move. The hill paths were in such poor condition that Blood found it necessary to round up five hundred local porters to transport the troops' rations and equipment.

By mid-January the force had crossed the Ambela Pass, marching past Guides headquarters at Mardan and from there on to Malakand and Chakdara, with the aim of strengthening the defences of these two strategic outposts. Blood was now in full control of the Buner district and he was able to traverse the country at will, encountering little or no resistance from the tribesmen, none of whom relished the prospect of seeing their villages burnt and their crops destroyed in the depths of winter. In this operation, the Army had pacified 300 square miles of rugged mountainous terrain.

The Bunerwal and adjacent Yusufzai maliks were brought in and heard Blood's peace terms, which they duly accepted, but the Government's worries were far from over. In fact, the worst was yet to come, and this was to take place in the most dangerous of all Frontier theatres of operations. Even as the campaigns against the followers of the Mad Mullah and Hadda Mullah were in progress, the Government's attention was drawn to the south, where Mullah Sayyid Akbar was spreading the doctrine of jihad in the Khyber region. Fired by the mullah's rhetoric, the Afridis and Orakzais of the forbidden land of Tirah, only a few miles distant from the outlying districts of Peshawar, had risen in revolt. This zealot, along with several of his colleagues, had in the preceding months been in close touch with the Afghan military. Their chief contact was Amir Abdur Rahman's son, General Ghulam Haidar Khan. These meetings took place early in 1897, and in the ensuing months more than one thousand Afghan mullahs were sent across the border to stir up trouble for the British.

It was the year of Queen Victoria's Diamond Jubilee, but in Simla, the summer capital of the Raj, the mood was anything but celebratory. Lord Elgin spent most of August firing off frantic telegrams to the Secretary of State, giving a blow-by-blow update on the alarming developments that were unfolding in the Khyber district. The dispatches arriving from the Army's commanders in the field were sketchy and contradictory. On 19 August reports were received of 10,000 Afridi warriors and 1,500 mullahs advancing on the forts held by the Khyber Rifles. A week later, disastrous news came in of the fall of Landi Kotal, the key outpost in the Khyber Pass. By the following week Elgin was reassuring London that the Government was firmly on top of the crisis. Then, in the second week of September, the *lashkars* were back on the rampage, with heavy fighting reported in the Kohat district.

The first warnings of the impending attack came on the morning of 17 August. The military situation in the Peshawar Valley that day could have been accurately described as turbulent, and so it was in the official report. 'The Bunerwals were openly hostile, fighting was going on in Swat, the Hadda Mullah . . . was endeavouring to induce the Mohmands to renew the attack, and it was sufficiently probable that he would succeed. The Tirah Afridis were moving to the attack and the attitude of the Kohat Pass Afridis and Jawakis was most doubtful.'[15]

The Jawakis' involvement in the uprising took the Government by surprise. It was twenty years since a punitive expedition had been mounted against this section of the Adam Khel Afridis, whose maliks had duly settled their fine with the Government and were living in peace along the Kohat Pass district. It was here that the Sayyid Mullah's sinister powers of persuasion came into play. This bearded demagogue, acting with the connivance of Kabul, found willing converts in the Orakzais south of the Khyber. The Afridis, on the whole, professed little love for the British, but they possessed a few areas of rich farmland and were in receipt of handsome allowances by virtue of their strategic position in the territory, which lies adjacent to the Khyber Pass, the key military and commercial trade route between India and Central Asia. There was good cause for the Afridis' reluctance to commit themselves to the Frontier uprising. Colonel Sir Thomas Holdich, as a survey officer with the Russo-Afghan Border Commission as well as the Durand Line delegation, had gained extensive first-hand knowledge of the Frontier tribes. Holdich cites other reasons for the Afridis' turning a deaf ear to Sayyid Mullah's summons to jihad.

> A very large number [of Afridis] had served at one time or another in the ranks of the British Army, so that there were pensions to lose – besides the subsidies granted to the Afridi militia who garrisoned the Khyber Pass for us, and whose large allowances would certainly perish if they mutinied. As for the grievances of the Swatis or Mohmands, the Afridi cared no more for them than for the grievances of so many Red Indians. Neither did he possess that spirit of fanaticism which has carried many a better Mussulman to the Gates of Paradise.'[16]

About quarter of a million Afridis inhabit roughly 1,000 square miles of hilly country south and west of Peshawar Valley in the Sofed Koh range. Tribal solidarity is an alien concept to the eight clans that make up this grouping, and in fact it is quite common for blood feuds to erupt between clans, and even families of the same clan. Like many of the Pathan tribes the Afridis are migratory, and they are still on the move today, for the Afridis have become the lorry drivers of the North-West Frontier, transporting goods, smuggled and otherwise, between Peshawar and Afghanistan. Like the Sikhs of India, the Afridis possess an uncanny talent for motor mechanics and they are capable of prolonging almost indefinitely the life of the most decrepit of vehicles.

The one Afridi clan that consistently rejected the hand of conciliation and which wreaked more havoc on British settlements than any of the others was, of course, the Zakka Khel. The Sayyid Mullah had no difficulty finding devotees to his cause among these clansmen, treating them as one fanatic to another. The Zakka Khel held great influence over the other clans by virtue of their extensive land holdings in the Khyber region. When it came to recruiting the Pathan tribesmen for military service, the Zakka Khel were considered untrustworthy in the ranks and few of their men served in the Army or the Khyber Rifles. In this sense, they had no state pensions to lose by their misbehaviour. They were, in Holdich's words, 'the traffickers in salt and (it is said) in slaves with Afghanistan, the wolves of the community'.[17] Hence the Zakka Khel were willing converts to the cause of jihad. And once they had come out fighting, no Afridi could afford to stand on the sidelines and risk losing face – or worse – with his brother jihadists.

The first objective the Afridi *lashkars* placed in their sights was Fort Maude, one of only three forts in the Khyber Pass capable of putting up a fight. The morning of 23 August saw the opening of hostilities, with fewer than three hundred men of the Khyber Rifles behind the battlements, facing an enemy that numbered in the thousands. The fighting commenced with a desultory exchange of fire between the levies and the tribesmen sheltering behind clumps of trees and crudely assembled stone sangars. It took only a few hours for the garrison to realise they had no hope of holding their position. The commanding officer gave orders for the troops to evacuate the fort and beat a retreat down the Khyber to Jamrud, the main stronghold on the road to Peshawar. This left a large section of the pass in the hands of the insurrectionists, who wasted no time in rushing up to their next objective, Ali Masjid, to the beat of drums and wild cheering. About eighty Khyber Rifles levies were garrisoned inside the fort when the mullahs pitched up at the head of the mob and began bellowing to the troops to abandon their posts or be branded traitors to Islam.

The reply was a swift volley of fire from behind the walls. The fighting raged throughout the day, and when darkness cast its shadow over the Khyber Pass, the weary defenders were startled to see a fiery orange glow light up the sky several miles to the east. This was Fort Maude, or what was left of the outpost after it had been fired by the *lashkar*. The garrison at Ali Masjid was running low on ammunition, and with Maude gone the defenders had lost their relay point of contact with Peshawar. The terrified militiamen knew only too well that the attackers would show little mercy to anyone taken alive inside the fort. As Afridi tribesmen, they were also aware of how their cousins were wont to dispose of battlefield casualties. That was when they decided to risk a swift breakout under cover of night, hoping to follow the twisting dry *nullahs* down the road to safety at Jamrud. So far their losses had been light, with one man killed and another wounded. It made no sense to risk a massacre at the hands of the frenzied *lashkar* outside the gates. The troops swung open the large wooden doors and made their getaway without much difficulty, letting the tribesmen swarm inside to unleash an orgy of looting and burn the fort to the ground. The breakout was a success, and by dawn the column of exhausted and demoralised levies, having spent the night picking their way across broken ground and along the dry river channels, came straggling into Jamrud.

On 26 August, the day that General Blood put an end to hostilities in Malakand, the 10,000-strong Afridi *lashkar*, intoxicated by their victories and spurred on by their banner-waving mullahs, turned their attention to their principal objective, the chief Khyber outpost of Landi Kotal. This massive fortress, which sits on the summit of the Pass, was the only one where a protracted defence could be organised – or so the Government would have liked to believe. The outposts of Maude and Ali Masjid suffered from fatal shortcomings: the former lacked an adequate supply of water, while the latter was surrounded on all sides by hills, making it a sniper's dream.

Unbeknownst to the enemy, Landi Kotal's fate had actually been sealed a week before the fort came under siege. On 18 August Captain (later Sir) William Barton, the Khyber Rifles Commandant, telegraphed Peshawar begging the Government to release whatever troops could be spared to strengthen the fort's defences in preparation for the coming attack. There were almost twelve thousand British and native troops stationed in and around the city. The reply came in the form of a perplexing order to report with haste to Jamrud for urgent 'consultations'. Barton set off for Jamrud, certain that he was on a time-wasting strategy review, or some trivial administrative matter, at a time when he needed to be with his troops to conduct the defence of this last bastion of British control of the Khyber Pass. What he could not have imagined, and what left the Khyber Rifles Commandant dumbstruck when he arrived at Staff Headquarters, was to find himself virtually under house arrest. Barton was told to stay put, and that far from reinforcing Landi Kotal, the Army was to withdraw its troops from Jamrud – which was tantamount to abandoning the Khyber Pass to its fate.

While Barton was digesting this inexplicable order, the Afridi horde marched up the Khyber behind a stream of banners and war drums, their numbers swelling at each village along the road. The command of Landi Kotal had been left to Subadar Major Mirsal Akbar Khan, a much-decorated sepoy whose plight reached tragic proportions when he learnt that, apart from having one son fighting alongside him inside the fort, two others stood outside with the massed besiegers. Mirsal Akbar Khan hadn't much time to indulge in remorse, however, for he was cut down in desperate hand-to-hand fighting on the day the outpost was stormed. The Landi Kotal detachment of 370 Khyber Rifles levies was forced to abandon the fort, but to their credit they retreated in an orderly fashion, with their arms, to Fort Jamrud at the mouth of the Pass. The Khyber Pass was lost, and the key outpost of British India's North-West Frontier was to remain in hostile hands for the next four months.

The Political Officer Robert Warburton, the one man who might have prevailed on the Afridis to put down their arms, was at the time of the storming of Landi Kotal in Lahore on leave, preparing to return to England on mandatory retirement. A telegram from Simla persuaded Warburton to return to the Khyber, but by then it was too late. 'What they [the Government] expected us to do, or what they hoped might be done, to avert the catastrophe that followed, and to save them from a war with a Power whose might they know only too well, must be left to the regions of imagination,' he wrote in his autobiography. 'We were in for what I had laboured all my years and by every means in my power to avert – a great Afridi war.'[18] It was very quickly to escalate into more than an Afridi war. After the destruction in swift succession of Maude, Ali Masjid and Landi Kotal, Warburton's dreaded 'Khyber debacle' was followed by the rising of the Orakzai tribe, who came out for the Sayyid Mullah, striking first in their homeland of Kohat District and then further west in the Kurram Valley. By mid-August the Khyber uprising had escalated into a war against the combined *lashkars* of Afridis and Orakzais.

The Government now called upon the services of one of the most highly regarded soldiers to have served on the North-West Frontier. General Sir William Lockhart, a man of stern countenance, rimless spectacles and bristly moustache, looked every inch the son of the Lanarkshire clergyman that he was. In some ways Lockhart and

Warburton, who was to serve under Lockhart in the coming Tirah operation, led parallel lives. They were of the same age, they had served in a variety of theatres, from Bengal to Abyssinia, and they were both esteemed worthy adversaries by the Pathans. Lockhart came to acquire the sobriquet of 'Amir Sahib' among the tribesmen. The General's career was no doubt the more distinguished of the two, for after Lockhart had put down the Pathan Revolt he went on to become Commander-in-Chief in India. Warburton, by contrast, went home a broken man. Yet the hand of Fate caught up with both men almost simultaneously, for they died within weeks of one another in 1900.

After the disaster at Landi Kotal, Lockhart was hastily summoned from home leave in England to organise the Tirah Field Force. The General made clear his objective of accepting nothing short of unconditional surrender. 'The British Government has determined to despatch a force under my command to march through the country of the Orakzais and Afridis and to announce from the heart of their country the final terms that will be imposed,' Lockhart announced in a statement read to a deputation of the insurrectionist mullahs. And to his own men he issued this warning:

> It must be remembered that the Force is opposed to perhaps the best skirmishers and best natural rifle shots in the world, and that the country they inhabit is probably the most difficult on the face of the globe. The enemy's strength lies in his knowledge of the country, which enables him to watch our movements unperceived by us, and to take advantage of every rise in the ground and every ravine.[19]

The Tirah Field Force was composed of two divisions, made up of six mountain batteries, two companies of sappers with two printing sections of the Bombay Sappers and Miners to distribute the battle orders, four British and four native field hospitals, a machine gun detachment, three battalions of light infantry, one regiment of infantry, two cavalry units and an artillery battalion. In all, 34,500 fighting men and 20,000 non-combatants, plus 72,000 pack animals with attendant vets and blacksmiths. It was the largest army raised in India since the Sepoy Mutiny, and with good cause: there was no doubt in the Government's mind that the threat to British rule was now as serious as in 1857. A host of legendary regimental names of the Indian and British armies were thrown into the campaign, from the Gordon Highlanders and King's Own Scottish Borderers to the Bengal Lancers, Hodson's Horse and the Gurkhas. It was an expeditionary force worthy of Empire.

Lockhart's objective was to penetrate and pacify Tirah, the 900-square-mile forbidden sanctuary shared by sections of the Afridi and Orakzai tribes, which is found about midway between the Khyber and Kurram valleys. The British – and, for that matter, every previous invader since Alexander – had never entered this upland territory that begins south of Peshawar, from which it is cut off by the great Sofed Koh range. The Army was about to embark on a march into the unknown to confront an enemy force estimated at 40,000–50,000 rifles, in an unmapped territory and with no safe lines of communication. The view shared in the ranks, however, was that this was the critical campaign that would determine the outcome of the North-West Frontier revolt. 'One of the greatest difficulties felt at the outset of the Tirah campaign was the lack of topographical information,' writes Captain Nevill. 'Many of the parts about to be invaded had never been visited before by Europeans, and native sources of intelligence have always to be looked upon with suspicion.'[20] All the approaches to Tirah are encircled by formidable logistic obstacles. From the north and south, the routes bristle with physical barriers, from the altitude and roughness of the passes to be negotiated to the steep defiles along the river routes, which make the construction of roads passable even for mules a daunting and time-consuming task.

Lockhart was confident that his success depended on being able to deliver a swift and definitive blow to the Orakzais, who inhabited the lower reaches of Tirah, in order to open a reliable line of communication for supplies and reinforcements. Therefore, military considerations dictated this as his invasion route.

Robert Warburton was called back to active service on 29 September. He was appointed to Lockhart's political staff, with Sir Richard Udny, Commissioner of Peshawar District, acting as chief political officer. By 18 October, Lockhart's column had marched into Tirah. Warburton was at the village of Kahi on the day hostilities opened with an attack on the Samana Ridge. This rocky outcrop, which lies at the southernmost limit of Tirah, was, as the troops were about to find out, all too easy too defend.

Early that morning a detachment of British troops was ordered to take the hill, but the assault ended in failure, as the men were unable to cross the exposed zone of fire laid down by the tribesmen on the ridges. Many of the Orakzais were armed with stolen or captured breech-loading Snider and Martini-Henry rifles, which rarely missed their target in the hands of marksmen like the Pathans. Lockhart called for the Gordon Highlanders to charge the hilltop. The battalion commander, Lieutenant-Colonel Mathias, rallied his men with the cry, 'The General says this hill must be taken at all costs. The Gordon Highlanders will take it!' With this, the men surged forward through a hail of bullets, determined at all costs to dislodge the enemy from the Dargai Heights. This 5,000ft-high summit on the Samana Ridge was a crucial objective that commanded a strategic mountain pass. The Scots stormed up the hill, sweeping away all resistance as they charged, and in less than forty minutes the regimental colours were flying from the summit. The Gordon Highlanders gave three cheers for Colonel Mathias and, as he came over the last ascent, the Colonel rather breathlessly commented to a colour-sergeant, 'Stiff climb, eh, Mackie?'

The charge of this historic Scottish regiment set the tone for an act of gallantry that is commemorated in the Gordon Highlanders' regimental museum in Aberdeen, where Piper George Findlater's VC stands on display. Findlater took bullets in both ankles in the charge. In spite of his wounds, he continued encouraging his comrades onward to the strains of 'Cock o' the North' and 'The Haughs o' Cromdale' before he passed out from loss of blood. Queen Victoria herself visited Findlater in hospital to award him the VC. He was, of course, unfit for further military service, but such was his celebrity that he was able to command considerable fees playing his pipes in music halls.

This heroic feat was immortalised in William McGonagall's outrageously uplifting poem 'The Storming of Dargai Heights'. To the Colonel's exhortation, the Scottish bard dedicates the lines:

'Men of the Gordon Highlanders,' Colonel Mathias said,
'Now, my brave lads, who never were afraid,
Our General says ye must take Dargai heights to-day;
So, forward, and charge them with your bayonets without dismay!'

while Piper Findlater receives his tribute a few stanzas further along:

In that famous charge it was a most beautiful sight
To see the regimental pipers playing with all their might;
But, alas! one of them was shot through both ankles, and fell to the ground,
But still he played away while bullets fell on every side around.

Another episode on the Samana Ridge was destined to join the annals of Frontier lore. This was the defence of Saragarhi, which has become one of eight tales of collective bravery published by UNESCO. Saragarhi was a makeshift fortified tower of stone and mud walls, garrisoned by twenty-one sepoys of the 36th Sikhs, who held out for seven and a half hours against an overwhelming Orakzai *lashkar*. Rather than retreat to safety, the sepoys chose to defend the position to the last man. One of the defenders, Sepoy Gurmukh Singh, gained everlasting fame in regimental history for having kept up a running account of the battle by heliograph with Fort Lockhart a few miles away. His signals continued flashing until the enemy rushed the gate, at which point the Sikhs engaged the attackers in a fierce hand-to-hand battle, until the last of the defenders fell. Some captured tribesmen later admitted to having lost 180 men in the siege. The Sikhs were given a posthumous Indian Order of Merit and their families were each allotted 50 acres of land and 500 rupees. A plaque erected on the spot by the Indian Government attests to 'the heroism shown by these gallant soldiers who died at their posts . . . thus proving their loyalty and devotion to their sovereign, the Queen Empress of India, and gloriously maintaining the reputation of the Sikhs for unflinching courage on the field of battle.'

The first victorious battle of the Tirah campaign ended on a hiccup. After a very brief time on the summit the troops were forced to withdraw from the Dargai Heights for lack of adequate stocks of food and ammunition. This caused the force to be stalled for two precious days, awaiting fresh supplies to be transported up the line, in order to allow the men to consolidate their position. During that time, the British regiments had to endure the frustration of looking up from their camp to contemplate the tribesmen back in control of the summit, defiantly waving their war banners at the British below. This went on until 20 August, and it required a bombardment by nine-pounder mountain batteries and a five-hour battle with a very stubborn enemy to recapture the position, with a loss of 199 killed and wounded.

Warburton witnessed the engagement and spoke of 'a figure in white' standing on the ridge for a long time, rallying the tribesmen to resist the British attackers. 'My own opinion was that this figure in white was a mullah, who had placed himself in a prominent position to watch our advance and give warning when the rushes were made,' he writes.[21] This would almost certainly have been none other than the Mullah Sayyid Akbar, leading a last-ditch attempt to expel the British heathens from the sacred land of Tirah.

The Army's next offensive took place on 29 October when the 1st Division set off at dawn to capture the Sampagha Pass. It took a four-hour barrage by the mountain batteries to dislodge the Afridis from their stronghold on the pass. The Tirah operation was virtually wound up two days later with the crossing of another summit, the 7,050ft-high Arhanga Pass, whose northern flank drops into a broad, terraced valley called Maidan. This took the Force out of Orakzai territory and into the heart of Afridi country. The Pass itself was not an insurmountable obstacle to the nomadic tribesmen, who herded their flocks across its summit twice a year. But it turned into something of a nightmare for an army corps with almost twenty thousand baggage animals in tow, advancing in single file, where every hold-up to secure a shifting load or pick up a fallen animal caused a 15-mile tailback. The massed guns of two divisions were brought up and began pounding the enemy position on the Arhanga Pass, which was eventually taken.

The rest of the campaign was a series of protracted and desultory skirmishes, as by now the tribesmen's fighting spirit was broken. By the end of October, three brigades of the Tirah Expeditionary Force were encamped in the Maidan of Tirah. The Army spread out across the valley on its traditional butcher and bolt mission. Fully twenty thousand men were sent to traverse Tirah in all directions, destroying every fortified hamlet they encountered in their path. Among the buildings to be demolished was the Mullah Sayyid's palatial home, which, as Warburton recounts, had taken three years to build. It was a moment of great satisfaction for the founder of the Khyber Rifles, who was devastated by the Pathan Revolt, which he alone, had he been on the spot before the first shots were fired, could have prevented. As he contemplated the remnants of the mullah's house, Warburton wondered why no one had taken it upon himself to shoot down this fanatic before he had caused so much tragedy in the Khyber.

Having penetrated Tirah for the first time, the troops now faced the task of extracting themselves from the valley. For a while it looked as though the operation might get mired in a replay of the disastrous 1842 retreat from Kabul. The Afridis were wily enough to know that a frontal assault on Lockhart's well-equipped, massive force was hopeless. The tribesmen, however, were skilled practitioners of guerrilla warfare. Their specialities were night raids and the harassment of retreating troops passing through the defiles and *nullahs* of the mountain territory they knew so well. The raids were so frequent that in every encampment a sentry was posted near the latrine – which had to be sited just outside the perimeter – and any man using the facilities was obliged to leave his rifle with the sentry to avoid it being stolen by a Pathan lurking behind the bushes. It was the Pathans' second guerrilla speciality that threatened to bring disaster on the retiring Tirah Field Force. On 16 November, for instance, one retiring regiment lost seventy-two of its rearguard during a punitive operation in the Waran Valley, while five days later another suffered twenty-three casualties in its retirement from the nearby Rajgul Valley.

The Army's return march to Peshawar began on 9 December 1897, under severe winter conditions that alternated between snow and freezing rain, with temperatures dropping as low as 11°F. On the second day of the march, the Force lost about twenty men and another fifty or sixty fell the day after, most of them from exposure. The column halted to allow the men a chance to recover. Two days later, the weather showed signs of improvement so General Lockhart ordered the Army back on the march, although the cold was still intense. All the while the tribesmen continued to launch sporadic attacks on the rearguard, causing the loss of about sixty men on that stage of the retreat. Fighting continued the following day, but the two main columns that were marching back to Peshawar met at a junction and together they fought their way through to the Khyber, where they retook the captured forts almost without opposition.

The operation had been a success but, as far as Lockhart was concerned, the campaign was not yet over. No sooner had the two divisions under his command arrived wearily back in Peshawar than the General began preparations to dispatch one of the divisions to the Zakka Khel stronghold of the Bazar Valley, and another column up the Khyber Pass. His objective was to ensure that every inch of Afridi and Orakzai territory stayed pacified. Both columns marched out of Peshawar on Christmas morning and within twenty-four hours their objectives had been reached. The tribesmen were in so demoralised a state, due to the wholesale destruction of their homes and land, that by New Year's Day three British brigades were in possession of the Khyber Pass, from its entry point at Jamrud to the summit at Landi Kotal, where the road begins to trail down to the Afghan border.

The mopping-up operations continued on an ad hoc basis for another five months and it wasn't until 2 April 1898 that the Pathan maliks of the offending tribes came to tender their submission to 'Amir Sahib'. True to his word, Lockhart forced the rebels to their knees. Under the terms of surrender the offending Afridi and Orakzai clans were made to guarantee the safety of the Khyber Pass, deliver all the weapons stolen in their pillage of the Khyber Rifles garrisons, hand over for trial twelve mullahs who had taken a prominent role in inciting the tribes to revolt, and pay a fine of 50,000 rupees. One detail not to be omitted: the tribesmen were to return the regimental silver stolen from Captain Barton's quarters in the storming of the Landi Kotal garrison.

The Government of India had emerged victorious from its most testing confrontation yet with the Pathan tribes, at a cost of 1,150 British and Indian casualties. Officially, peace had been restored to the Frontier. In fact, 'truce' would be a more accurate description of the situation that prevailed at the conclusion of the 1897–8 Pathan Revolt, for on the North-West Frontier, periods of 'peace' could never be taken as anything but a lull between hostilities.

The campaigns in Tirah and adjacent Pathan lands of the Frontier achieved more than a military victory. The penetration of this area also enabled the Government to expand its topographical surveys along the newly-demarcated Afghan border. Until then, the hostility of the tribes and the inaccessible nature of this region had acted as a check on border survey work, to the extent that the Government possessed a more detailed geographical knowledge of most of Afghanistan, Persia and certainly Baluchistan. In the past, surveyors could only carry out their work under cover of a military expedition. After 1898, Boner, Swat, the Mohmand country, the Tochi Valley and Tirah became fertile territory for the Great Trigonometrical Survey of India. This was a crucial prerequisite for safeguarding British interests on the Frontier, as it provided detailed knowledge of defensive positions, water supplies and communications.

FIVE

A Most Superior Person

One morning in December 1899, George Nathaniel Curzon strutted down the red-carpeted gangplank of an Indiaman steamer that had just docked at Bombay, after the customary month-long crossing from England. Lord Curzon landed in India in his usual state of acute pain, the result of a curvature of the spine that had plagued him since he was 19, and which was to torment him his entire life. The ruler of Britain's proudest colonial possession was only 39 and he already stood at the zenith of his career. The ramrod erect posture he adopted on the landing stage as he surveyed the Gate of India was, some would say, the result of the corset he wore to relieve his spinal torment. Others attributed his imperious bearing to an aristocratic upbringing, for 'Curzon was an aristocrat by birth and conviction, intellectually one of the most unswerving authoritarians that ever walked. His sense of his high office was matched only by his sense of duty. Nothing was too much trouble but nothing could be left to anyone else, because no one could be trusted to do it as well as Lord Curzon himself.'[1]

The Viceroy, who was to have a greater impact on the North-West Frontier than anyone else, before or after, had been brought up in a magnificent Derbyshire country mansion and park, and received an exquisite education at Eton and Balliol College, Oxford, where his fellow undergraduates were inspired to compose the famous doggerel:

> My name is George Nathaniel Curzon,
> I am a most superior person.
> My cheek is pink, my hair is sleek,
> I dine at Blenheim once a week.

As was customary, the new Viceroy's arrival was celebrated with the pomp usually reserved for visiting royalty, a tribute which he himself might have considered appropriate to a man of his eminence, for Curzon could never be faulted for an excess of humility. 'That night there was a dinner for a hundred people and a reception for 1,400 more, and this time the Curzons stood on a carpet of gold,' writes one of his biographers.

> The next morning the Viceregal train which was to take them to Calcutta was painted white. On their arrival at the capital of the Indian Empire (on 3 January), they found that 200,000 people lined the route, and their escort to Government House was a squadron of cavalry, a company of infantry, and a Viceregal bodyguard of 120 lancers. The cannons sounded a salute.[2]

The Queen-Empress's representative was of the staunchly imperialist school of the Conservative Party led by the Marquess of Salisbury, who was serving his third term as prime minister. Curzon had already been on four trips to India and was well acquainted with the North-West Frontier, having visited Peshawar and the Khyber Pass ten years before his appointment as Viceroy. He was a passionate traveller with wide experience in the Far East, Central Asia, Persia and the Pamirs.

Curzon was also a champion, with reservations, of the Forward Policy, one of several strategies adopted over the years by Britain to deal with the Frontier problem. He considered the North-West Frontier to be India's principal military concern, and took very seriously the threat of Russian intervention from across the Afghan border. Early on, the Viceroy dispatched the explorer and spy Sir Percy Sykes, founder of the South Persia Rifles, to explore Kerman province in the south-eastern region of Persia and adjacent parts of Baluchistan, and to establish a British presence there to discourage Russian encroachment southwards towards India. Later in his career, and with the same objective in mind, he sanctioned and supported Colonel Francis Younghusband's invasion of Tibet in 1904.

A digression would be useful here to look at the various policies that shaped the Government's relationship with the North-West Frontier and its Pathan tribesmen. Olaf Caroe, one of the Frontier's leading historians, takes the view that official Frontier strategy, for the fifty-odd years from the annexation of the Punjab to Curzon's arrival at Calcutta, can be divided roughly into two periods. The first would be the first thirty years, to the outbreak of the Second Afghan War in 1878, and the second the following period of almost marathon conflict with the tribes, culminating in the Pathan Revolt of 1897. 'On a broad view the first thirty years represent the testing time of the so-called Close Border policy,' he writes. 'During those years there were innumerable military promenades through one or other part of tribal territory but no permanent occupation, and the most favoured tribal regions had not even been seen.'[3]

The objective pursued by the Close Border policy was, in a word, to 'hold the line' against tribal raids into the Government's settled districts. This idea was closely modelled on the Sandeman experiment in Baluchistan, though it never achieved the same degree of success. Where Sandeman succeeded in securing the Bolan Pass and Quetta, while pacifying the Baluch tribes in the vicinity, the civil and military authorities in Peshawar found it a constant struggle to keep the Khyber Pass safe for the passage of camel caravans and columns of troops. Peshawar continued to be the target of numerous attacks by tribal raiders well into the twentieth century, and the Pathan tribes were as ungovernable on the day the British quit the Frontier as when they first crossed tribal territory in 1839, en route to invade Afghanistan.

The most extreme interpretation of the Close Border concept involved a retreat to the east bank of the Indus, a tactic that was never put into practice. A distinguished advocate of this policy was the Duke of Wellington, who at one point argued that the most effective way to meet an enemy was on the banks of the Indus, at least as a temporary expedient. The Iron Duke later qualified his views, as can be seen in his private papers: 'The art of crossing rivers is now so well understood, and has been so frequently practised . . . in the late wars in Europe, that we cannot hope to defend the Indus as a barrier.'[4]

It was noted earlier that John Lawrence, who served as Chief Commissioner of the Punjab during the Sepoy Mutiny, was for evacuating Peshawar and pulling the British garrison back to the Indus, a policy which higher authorities persuaded him to abandon. Lawrence's hawkish detractors referred to his vigorous non-interventionism as the policy of 'Masterly Inactivity'. The Close Border policy was in essence one of non-intervention. To this end, the Government tried to keep a line of contact open with the tribesmen by distributing annual allowances for good behaviour, and also through middlemen of the Peshawar border known as *Arbabs*, who were first used by the Sikhs to conduct their dealings with the Afridis. This system proved unreliable and many of these *Arbabs* would as a matter of course exploit their position of power to stir up tribal unrest, by which they aimed to make themselves indispensable to the British. For Warburton, the intrigues of these would-be mediators constituted the greatest failing of the Close Border system. The father of the Khyber Rifles went even further, to assert that with the benefit of having served twenty-nine years in the Peshawar district he had no doubt that the majority of the wars and fights between the British Government and the tribes 'were due entirely to the evil intrigues and of machinations of the *Arbabs*'.[5]

Warburton's future successor William Barton was another vigorous opponent of the Close Border system:

> Even before the Afghan War of 1878 it had become obvious that the policy of Close Border had been a hopeless failure. The tribes felt that they had no part or lot in the *Pax Britannica* of the administered territory, that the British Government had no use for them. Such political predilections as they had were towards Kabul rather than towards India. To have expected any display of loyalty from them would have been absurd.[6]

Disenchantment with the Close Border experiment served as a contributing factor to a second invasion of Afghanistan. Behind every shift in strategy there lurked the menacing claws of the Russian bear, and the Government's Frontier policies were shaped primarily by considerations of border defence. When reports began landing in Calcutta about Russian agents making overtures to the Amir in Kabul, it was time to revamp the Frontier plan of action and go on the offensive.

The events of 1878–80 in Afghanistan, and in particular the shock of the Great Pathan Revolt and its aftermath, engendered a plethora of supporters of a vigorous Frontier Forward Policy. One might have expected to find Churchill in the vanguard of the most forceful proponents of Frontier expansion, and the young subaltern of the 4th Hussars does not disappoint. 'The "full steam ahead" method would be undoubtedly the most desirable,"' he writes in his summary of the Malakand campaign. 'This is the military view. Mobilise, it is urged, a nice field force, and operate at leisure in the Frontier valleys, until they are as safe and civilised as Hyde Park. Nor need this course necessarily involve the extermination of the inhabitants. Military rule is the rule best suited to the character and comprehension of the tribesmen.'[7] Churchill acknowledged the Government's lack of resources to implement a quick-march Forward Policy. The alternative he proposed was a 'sure and strong gradual advance to the Frontier, which above all must be consistently pursued. Dynamite in the hands of a child is not more dangerous than a strong policy weakly carried out.'[8]

Lord Roberts, who spent a good part of his career campaigning on the Frontier and in Afghanistan, was another staunch believer in moving the line forward from the administrative border to the Durand Line. In his opinion, all strategic points needed to be connected with the Indian rail system to enable the rapid dispatch of troops to the scene of action. To Roberts, fixing the administrative boundary of the settled districts as the line of defence was unthinkable. 'A Frontier more than one thousand miles in length, with a belt of huge mountains in its front, inhabited by thousands of warlike men . . . seemed to me then, as it does now, an impossible Frontier, and one on which no scheme for the defence of India could be safely based.'[9] Roberts was especially concerned with the spectre of Russian armies pouring through Afghanistan to the weakly defended gates of India. 'The Forward Policy . . . is necessitated by the incontrovertible fact that a great Military Power [Russia] is now within striking distance of our Indian possessions, and in immediate contact with a State [Afghanistan] for the integrity of which we have made ourselves responsible.'[10]

There were also apostles of an extremist wing of the Forward Policy, men who tried to drum up support for a 'Scientific Frontier' that would supposedly resolve at one stroke all the ethnological, political and military issues confronting the Government. This 'ideal' line of defence against a Russian invasion would require the annexation of a sizeable chunk of eastern Afghanistan, boldly running a line on a north–south axis through Kabul and Ghazni to Kandahar, and calling everything east of that line British territory. The pro-Scientific Frontier lobby argued that the northern flank of this line was defended by the Hindu Kush, and the southern tip by hundreds of miles of trackless desert. The Government never gave this plan any serious consideration, for it would have required an exorbitant and constant supply of men and materiel to accomplish the task, all of which could not be spared.

The Viceroyalty of Lord Curzon marked the apogee of an imperial system that had been built by the Marquess of Dalhousie, who presided over the Sikh defeat, and his post-Mutiny successors. At the time of his appointment Curzon was the rising hope of the imperialist wing of the Conservative Party, thus his arrival at Government House brought comfort to the champions of the Forward School. The new Viceroy was hailed as 'the greatest of all the Russophobists, the arch-disciple of [the avowed foe of Russian expansion] Sir Henry Rawlinson'.[11] Curzon's mind was deeply rooted in the problem of frontiers: there is no record of how long he spoke on the subject in a lecture he gave at Oxford in 1907, but the text of the speech runs to nearly twenty thousand words, so a conservative estimate would have had him standing at the lectern, back pain and all, for a good three hours.

Throughout history, frontiers have been inextricably linked with warfare, Curzon told his audience. This, he insisted, is why the problem of the North-West Frontier of India and the 'Power' that lurked beyond must be treated as a matter of maximum strategic importance. 'To take the experience of the past half century [nineteenth] alone,' he told his audience,

> the Franco-German War was a war for a Frontier, and it was the inevitable sequel of the Austro-Prussian campaign of 1866 . . . The Russo-Turkish War originated in a revolt of the Frontier States, and every Greek war is waged for the recovery of a national Frontier. We were ourselves at war with Afghanistan in 1839, and again in 1878, we were on the verge of war with Russia in 1878, and again in 1885, over Frontier incidents in Asia. The most arduous struggle in which we have engaged in India in modern times was waged with Frontier tribes.[12]

After decades of expansion and conquest, the Government of India found itself with its military resources severely stretched and 6,000 miles of border to defend. Curzon plunged straight into the challenge of overhauling the whole Indian administration, with special attention on the Frontier problem. He was unhappy with the deployment of British troops near the Afghan border. This placed a crucial reform on the new viceroy's agenda: the reorganisation of military dispositions along the North-West Frontier. More than ten thousand troops were stationed across the administrative border and nothing had been done to link them up by lateral communications. There were proposals on the table to build more fortified garrisons, which would have put the supply chain under even more stress than it was now experiencing. This would also have increased the danger of losing the odd post to tribal raiders, which could easily have sent the Frontier up in flames. Curzon's aim was the withdrawal of British forces from these advanced positions, concentrating the troops in British territory behind the lines as a safeguard and support for tribal levies to be deployed along the front line. It was a daring policy and an effective one, so successful in fact that it was one of the first actions taken by the newly formed Government of Pakistan after Partition. A second objective was to improve the system of communications behind the lines, to enable the rapid deployment of troops to support the native militias in the event of invasion. To this end, within a year of taking up his post Curzon had extended the railway system from Nowshera to Dargai, in order to strengthen the British position at Malakand. Peshawar became the hub of a frenzy of rail and road-building activity. The broad-gauge railway line was extended from the Frontier capital to Jamrud at the entrance to the Khyber Pass. An alternative road link to Landi Kotal was built through Mullagori territory, while communications between Peshawar and Kohat to the south were improved with the construction of a cart road through the Kohat Pass.

Curzon was particularly concerned about the defence of the Khyber, which he had visited before becoming Viceroy and which he considered to be of primordial strategic importance. One of his first official visits was to Peshawar, where he hosted an impressive durbar to assure the local maliks and village headmen that he had no intention of interfering with their religion or independence. Curzon was prepared to pay them allowances, if they could offer assurances that roads and passes would be kept open and guarded by local militiamen. The Khyber garrisons had been swept away in a few days by a mob of Pathan tribesmen during the Great Revolt, and Curzon was determined to avoid a repetition of this disaster.

He found a strong ally in General Lockhart, who three years previously had emerged from his bitter campaign in the Khyber region. 'The Khyber Pass has to be kept open to us,' Lockhart declared after the Tirah campaign. The General argued that the Pass played a dual role, not only as the likeliest invasion route into India but also serving as a strategic corridor in the event of having to dispatch British troops to Afghanistan. While the Pass was the main trade route between the Punjab and Afghanistan, its commercial value was far outweighed by considerations of military strategy, 'in the event of military intervention in that country [Afghanistan] becoming necessary', as had twice been the case in the past and was to occur again in about twenty years' time. Lockhart agreed with Curzon's decision to retire British and Indian Army troops from the area and replace them with native levies. 'The defile of the Khyber Pass should be guarded by irregular troops raised locally,' Lockhart said. 'It must be remembered that, in undertaking military operations in Afghanistan, the friendly attitude of the Frontier tribes would be of much greater moment than the absolute safety of any single pass, however important. If the attitude were friendly, the pass would be secure in any case.'[13]

Under Curzon's reorganisation of the Frontier defence system, the Khyber Jezailchis were officially re-raised as the Khyber Rifles and their fighting strength was increased to two battalions of six hundred men each, with a higher scale of pay. The levy was placed under British officers and supported by a movable column kept in readiness in Peshawar. Once this was done, all regular troops were boldly withdrawn from British India's most vulnerable invasion point.

As the Pakistani Frontier historian Lal Baha points out, it was in the Khyber that the most important communication projects were undertaken, Curzon's policy being to secure the Pass against external threats, while not disregarding the ever-present menace of the Afridis on the British side of the Durand Line. 'Within two months of his taking over as Viceroy, Curzon considered the feasibility of constructing a railway through the Khyber Pass with the object of linking Peshawar with Jalalabad, and later with Kabul,' she writes.[14] In fairness, the idea for a Khyber railway did not originate with Curzon. It was his predecessor, Lord Elgin, who in 1898 had proposed a narrow-gauge railway linking Peshawar with Landi Kotal. The project met with Government approval but was placed on the back burner when Elgin left India, and the railway did not become a reality until the 1920s, many years after Curzon's departure. Baha argues that to be of any positive military value the line would have needed to be extended to Dakka or Jalalabad, both of which lie to the west of the Durand Line. Abdur Rahman was not having it and the Amir made his displeasure at such a project known to Curzon, stating that he was not prepared to allow 'even a single span' of track to pass through Afghan territory. This left the Government with the options of either occupying the two Afghan cities in question, which would have brought on another costly war, or trying to win over the Amir by peaceful means, mainly through improving relations with Kabul. This would have amounted to a stopgap strategy at best, for Abdul Rahman died shortly afterward and was succeeded by his son Habibullah. Curzon plumped for a third option, which was to abandon the plan.

The policy of removing British troops and sepoys from advanced positions on the Frontier was extended north to Chitral and south to the Kurram Valley, encompassing some of the most turbulent sectors of the Frontier. 'South of Kohat, a force of tribal militia, 450 strong, called the Samana Rifles was raised under British officers,' says Baha. 'It was largely recruited from the Orakzai tribesmen and formed part of the Border Military Police.' The Samana Rifles replaced the regular garrison of the Samana Ridge region, which had been the scene of much desperate fighting in the Tirah campaign.

> In the Kurram Valley, the Kurram Militia was augmented and reorganised in two battalions, 1,250 strong, on the model of the Khyber Rifles. Both the Samana and the Kurram positions were to be supported by a light railway to be constructed from Kohat to Thal. Further to the south, two battalions of the Waziristan Militia (the future South and North Waziristan Scouts), 800 strong each, were raised, one being for the Tochi Valley, or North Waziristan, and the other for the Gomal Valley, in the Mahsud territory of South Waziristan.[15]

The raising of the Waziristan militias coincided with an outbreak of raiding by the Mahsuds, who in 1900 launched a series of audacious attacks on Government police posts in their territory. The resumption of hostilities with these defiant tribesmen was a painful reminder that every conflict with the Frontier tribes, like the Pathan Revolt, invariably ended in stalemate. The Government might congratulate itself on having achieved a military victory over its foe. But once the dust had settled on the battlefield and both sides had collected their dead and wounded, the hills belonged to the Pathans. The British were able to hold out because of their superiority of arms, but the Pathans were not to be vanquished.

The torch of insurgency was passed to the Mahsuds after the 1897 revolt, while the rest of the Frontier basked in a rare peace for about a decade, thanks in large measure to Curzon's intelligent policies. The

Mahsuds were never in a conciliatory humour, and to keep the tribesmen from raiding across the administrative border was a considerable achievement. But as a Government analysis of the problem contended, this could not be a final end of policy.

> What is the final end? Possibilities, so far as can be seen, are three. The old welter may continue, or Mahsud country may become part of Afghanistan and the Mahsud throw in his lot with the inhabitants of that country, or he must be trained to take his place in the federation of India. To that, as to Tipperary, is a long, long way to go, but it is the only one of the three to which our officers can worthily address themselves.[16]

Before this could become a reality, the Government was obliged to take retaliatory measures.

By November 1900, the cumulative fines levied on the Mahsuds for outrages committed across the border amounted to 200,000 rupees, a small fortune, of which absolutely nothing had been paid. The tribesmen were called to a *jirga* where they were given until the end of the month to settle 50,000 rupees of their debt or face the consequences. The Mahsud maliks acknowledged the warning with a nod, picked themselves off the ground and returned to their villages unimpressed by the Government's threats. On 1 December the Army began ringing the Mahsuds' homeland with a series of police posts, backed by movable columns of regular troops, effectively to cut the tribe off from contact with the outside world. Now it was the Mahsuds' turn to respond to the blockade, which they did in their inimitable style by handing over 50,000 rupees to the Government, while simultaneously sending further raiding parties into villages in the settled district, thereby raising fresh demands for compensation. More strident measures were needed to bring the tribesmen to heel. Four mobile columns were raised in Waziristan, each carrying out search-and-destroy missions that resulted in the destruction of many villages and inflicting nearly four hundred casualties on the Mahsuds. It was not a cheaply won victory, for casualties on the British side numbered 146 killed and wounded, a testimony to the ferocity of the tribesmen's resistance. Finally, after further sharp skirmishes on 10 March the maliks came into the British camp to offer their submission, and the blockade was lifted.

As was usually the case, this was not the last time the Government would hear from the refractory tribes of Waziristan. Before the end of the year Major-General C.C. Egerton, who had commanded the Mahsud operations, found it necessary to organise another four columns in Bannu to halt the raiding activities of the Kabul Khel Wazir clan. After eight days of intense fighting the clansmen took to the hills, suffering the loss of several villages, five thousand head of cattle captured and three hundred of their people taken prisoner. The Mahsud blockade brought to an end the Government's major military operations south of Kohat until 1908, when the Army was sent back into the field in response to a notorious outbreak of raiding on Peshawar by the Zakka Khel Afridis.

The sinister figure of the Mullah Powindah made his appearance in Waziristan in the years immediately following the Frontier uprising. The spark that triggered the blockade and subsequent punitive expedition was the brutal murder, in October of that year, of a British officer on the orders of the Mullah Powindah, 'that pestilential priest', in the words of Lord Kitchener, Commander-in-Chief in India. The incident took place at a Border Military Police headquarters at the village of Kot Nasran, which was attacked and looted by a Mahsud gang. This was followed by the murder of two more British officers by the Mullah Powindah's men. The Government set in motion a manhunt for one Pashakai, a Mahsud who was said to have killed one of the officers with the Mullah's blessings. As a reprisal, the Government first retained 10,000 rupees, the balance of the half-yearly allowances, 'until the tribe kill or surrender Pashakai – failing this the forfeiture of this sum to Government'. The memos that flowed from this incident accurately mirrored the Pathans' ability to keep the Government on the hop.

'The Mullah Powindah has sent in several letters saying that he has done his best to arrest Pashakai, but that the latter is now out of his reach', says a report issued at the beginning of May 1906. Then on 12 May, 'The whereabouts of Pashakai are very mysterious', followed a week later by, 'There seems to be little doubt that Pashakai is in Mahsud country'. On 2 June: 'The Mahsuds held a full *jirga* at Kaniguram on the 28th and all sections agreed that Pashakai must be given up to Government.' But alas, 'Everyone, however, disclaimed knowledge of his whereabouts.' At last the Mullah Powindah put in an appearance on 9 June: 'At the second Mahsud *jirga* at Kaniguram, the tribe made the Mullah Powindah take an oath on seven Korans that he had not helped to conceal Pashakai since the Jandola *jirga*, and that he did not know where he was.' Finally, on 16 June came news of great cheer from the Mahsud maliks: 'The Mahsuds have burnt Pashakai's house, destroyed his crops, and heaped stones all over his fields. The Mullah Powindah was present at the destruction. The hope of a settlement with Government has caused great joy in Mahsud country. Alms have been distributed to celebrate the occasion and sermons preached in the mosques.' The Mahsuds, in an apparent show of contrition, surrendered four of the five men wanted by Government and paid a fine of 25,000 rupees. They also issued the following syrupy proclamation: 'In the above case the Sublime Government has imposed upon the Mahsud tribe a fine of 25,000 rupees. We have paid the fine without the least objection, the amount having been cut from our usual allowance, and we have surrendered the first four men out of the five demanded.' But sadly, they concluded, 'Pashakai is the only man remaining and we have not yet been able to hand him up to Government.'[17] The tribesmen claimed to be thoroughly ashamed of their failings and lamented the fate that awaited them, begging only for their faults to be pardoned. On 19 July, the tribal allowances having been restored, the Mahsuds were back in action. A *lashkar* of two hundred freebooters attacked a village across the British border and carried off all the cattle they could round up, and then retired with beating of drums, as was their custom in a successful raid.

By 1904 the defence of the entire North-West Frontier between the administrative border and the Durand Line was in the hands of the tribal levies, albeit under the command of British officers. Curzon was dismayed by the Government's vast military expenditure in combating the Pathan Revolt. The cost of Frontier defence had risen far out of proportion to the relatively small number of tribesmen involved. The Government of India benefited from this military reform in other ways – for instance, in being able to hold taxes at their customary low level. In the past, street riots had been a regular response to Government tax hikes, and previous viceroys had gone to great lengths, sacrificing all sorts of social programmes, to keep the tax burden low. The cost of maintaining several corps of tribal irregulars in the field was infinitely less onerous than paying regular Army wages to thousands of frontline troops. Moreover, Curzon believed that providing the militiamen's families with a cash income would make them less inclined to join raiding parties.

Several military leaders thought the system a risky gamble and that having units of armed Pathans, operating on the border beyond regular Army control, was asking for trouble. Even Lockhart, now Commander-in-Chief in India and a supporter of the Khyber levy system, expressed concern that militiamen could turn against the Government and revert from gamekeepers to poachers, their Army issue arms and training making them all the more dangerous as enemies. Curzon bridled at the Army's scepticism and retaliated by accusing his critics of misunderstanding his policy. 'He rapidly made plans to visit the Frontier and talk to people on the spot,' writes Thomas D. Farrell. 'He toured the Frontier from the Khyber to Baluchistan in April [1900] and talked with administrators, soldiers and tribal maliks. Curzon was pleased when the maliks assured him that they would be proud to have their young men serving in the militias.'[18] Curzon then set out a list of the basic duties of the militias, which involved holding the Frontier posts, picqueting the roads, pursuing raiders, escorting officers, the protection of contractors, and furnishing guards over prisoners; and with that the Viceroy considered the matter settled.

Curzon now shifted his attention from the field of defence to that of civil administration. The plan he put in place in 1901 brought about the most radical shake-up in government the Frontier had ever known. In that year the tribal territory and the administered districts were jointly severed from the Government of the Punjab to form the

North-West Frontier Province, known to the initial-obsessed inhabitants of the Indian subcontinent as NWFP. Except for the interval in which West Pakistan was in existence, this continues as one of Pakistan's four provinces.

This was not an original project. A proposal to give the central Government more direct control over Frontier administration and policy was put forward in 1877 during Lord Lytton's viceroyalty, but the plan was shelved with the outbreak of the Second Afghan War. The creation of some sort of separate Frontier unit had been mooted under successive viceroys, with the backing of veteran frontiersmen such as Warburton, Sandeman, Lockhart and Durand, to name a few of the scheme's most illustrious supporters. On the other hand, a few Government officials stood vehemently opposed to the plan. The reaction in some circles was one of amazement that Curzon would even consider the Frontier, with its savage tribesmen, as worthy of sharing the same status as citizens of the Punjab and other Indian states. Curzon had the ability to make things happen and, like all men of greatness, he swept aside the opposition to his ideas and forged ahead, undeterred by what others might see as insurmountable obstacles. Curzon stuck to his guns, and on 9 November 1901 the Pathan territory up to the Durand Line became a separate province of British India.

Before coming to India, Curzon had followed with great consternation the near debacle of the 1897 tribal uprising. This event brought home the fact that the North-West Frontier could not be effectively governed by men sitting behind desks in Lahore, hundreds of miles from the Pathan reality. The Frontier had to be placed under the direct control of the Government of India. Therefore, Curzon began to put together his plan even before taking up his post and had discussed the proposed Frontier restructuring with his predecessor Lord Elgin.

The administration of this new province was delegated initially to a Chief Commissioner, and later transferred to an all-powerful Governor General, with the Chief Commissioner acting as his agent. Each of the five settled districts was placed under the control of a Deputy Commissioner, who would invariably be someone with many years of experience in Frontier affairs under his belt. Such a man was Sir Harold Deane, who had served as Political Officer in the Malakand Agency during the 1897 uprising. Prior to that, Deane had spent ten years as Deputy Commissioner of the Peshawar District. Curzon took a bold step in appointing this relatively junior official to what was one of the most demanding jobs in the Indian Civil Service. The Viceroy was confident of Deane's ability to work effectively with the tribes, with whom he was on good terms – so much so, in fact, as to incur the tongue-in-cheek wrath of Winston Churchill. 'We had with us a very brilliant Political Officer, a Major Deane, who was much disliked because he always stopped military operations,' Churchill remarked in his memoirs of the Malakand campaign.

> Just when we were looking forward to having a splendid fight and all the guns were loaded and everyone keyed up, this Major Deane – and why was he a Major anyhow? So we said – being in truth nothing better than an ordinary politician – would come along and put a stop to it all. Apparently all these savage chiefs were his old friends and almost his blood relations. Nothing disturbed their friendship. In between the fights, they talked as man to man and as pal to pal.'[19]

Churchill's jibe aside, along with Roos-Keppel and Warburton, Deane was accepted by the Pathans almost as one of their own, and he ranked as one of the most influential and respected of frontiersmen. For the maliks, to be seen walking alongside the tall, blue-eyed, statesmanlike figure of Harold Deane was a mark of pride.

The great merit of Curzon's work was that, in creating the new province, he displayed an understanding of existing tribal boundaries. Unlike the Durand Line, which attempted to demarcate a border that completely disregarded the region's ethnic realities, the five original political agencies of the North-West Frontier Province caused little disruption among tribal groupings. The tribes of Malakand, Khyber, Kurram and North and South Waziristan were situated comfortably within the boundaries of their ancestral homelands. Curzon's arrangement of the Frontier province persisted untouched for half a century, until the creation of the Mohmand Agency in 1951, followed by Orakzai and Bajaur in 1973, which amounted to a bit of fine-tuning of the tribal territories. Except for Malakand, the tribal regions now comprise what is known as the Federally Administered Tribal Areas, or FATA, a territory about the size of Belgium, with 5.7 million inhabitants. The Malakand Protected Area, on the other hand, along with Dir, Swat, Chitral and the former states of Amb, make up another administrative unit known as PATA, the Provincially Administered Tribal Areas. Outside these two entities, which are administered under a special legislative framework, lie the six Frontier Regions, or settled districts, of Peshawar, Mardan, Kohat, Bannu, Dera Ismail Khan and Tank.

The need for a special legal structure to govern the tribal territory was recognised as early as 1872, under the viceroyalty of Lord Mayo, who travelled around India more than any of his predecessors had done. It was Mayo who introduced the system of provincial administration that later gave a great impetus to local government, from which Curzon took part of his inspiration for the North-West Frontier reforms. In a twist of tragic irony, in the same year that the new code of Frontier administration was enacted, Mayo was assassinated by an Afghan Pathan convict while on a visit to a penal colony in the Andaman Islands.

The Frontier Crimes Regulation (FCR) was enacted by Mayo in 1872 and revised in 1887 under Lord Dufferin, one of a handful of viceroys who possessed first-hand knowledge of the Frontier, having toured the Khyber district with Roberts. The Frontier Crimes Regulation, a draconian statute which, to the irritation of numerous Pakistani politicians and lawmakers, still stands as the governing law of the tribal territory, was given its current form by Curzon in 1901. This special code, which pertains only to Pathan tribal territory, recognises the doctrine of collective responsibility. Under the law, the authorities are empowered to detain the fellow members of an outlaw's tribe or to blockade his village until such time as the fugitive surrenders or is acceptably punished by his own tribe in accordance with local tradition. The 1901 law is an instrument of rough justice, conceived to regulate the lives of people on the fringes of society. This was, of course, the status of the Pathan tribes living outside the administrative border more than a century ago. The objective was to place a tight control on the tribesmen's activities and impose heavy penalties on those who took to raiding or committing other outrages in the settled districts.

The code invests the Political Agent in the agency under his jurisdiction with despotic powers. Under Section 21 of the law, once the Deputy Commissioner has determined that a person or tribe has acted in 'a hostile or unfriendly manner towards the British Government or towards persons residing within British India', he may draw on a number of punishments. He can order the arrest of all suspects and the seizure of their property, and debar any member of the tribe from access into British India. This is now construed as referring to all provinces of Pakistan. Fines are imposed on communities that are suspected of having acted as accessories to a crime, and these can be levied in the form of land revenue tax or retention of tribal allowances. The law also prohibits the construction of 'new villages or towers' within 5 miles of the frontier of British India, which is now also taken to mean the provinces of Pakistan. 'Where it is expedient on military grounds, the [Government] may . . . direct the removal of any village situated in close proximity to the frontier'.[20] The law also provides for arrest and preventive detention without warrant. Suspects may be required to post a bond for good behaviour or for keeping the peace, and failure to do so can result in imprisonment for up to three years.

A number of unorthodox regulations came into being within the context of the FCR, the aim of which was to provide safeguards for British citizens travelling through tribal territory. One of the most celebrated is the law that establishes the sanctity of the road, which was considered British territory, similar to the status of diplomatic legations on foreign soil. The Government more or less let it be known to the tribesmen that they were free to settle their blood feuds in any manner they saw fit. However, the right of way was sacrosanct, and firing across the road would be considered a criminal act punishable by a 2,000 rupee fine, a small fortune in those days. There was one famous case of an Afridi tribesman arrested after a gun battle with a member of a rival family. He was charged under this act, and it later emerged that as well as violating the sanctity of the road, his bullets were flying across the camel track and the railway line. Accordingly, he was fined 6,000 rupees.

The Frontier Crimes Regulation has been denounced as unjust and inhuman, and numerous committees of jurists and politicians have been convened to study its reform and eventual abolition. 'Unjust arrests, derogatory trials, inhuman prison conditions and human rights abuses are some of the common attributes of retributive justice in the [tribal] areas,' writes Mumtaz A. Bangash, a noted Pakistani jurist. 'During the past fifty years, numerous houses, *hujras* [meeting halls], shops and markets had been bulldozed and vehicles impounded, and huge fines were levied on various tribes which even resulted in armed clashes . . . [The FCR] violates basic human and democratic rights of the people.'[21]

The Federal Shariah Court of Pakistan, the country's supreme council of mullahs, has itself denounced the FCR as un-Islamic, although this ruling seems a touch ironic, for the Pathans are less concerned about the law's violation of their religious practices than of their tribal code of honour. Pakhtunwali, which was mentioned in reference to the Turis and their conflicts with neighbouring Sunni tribes, merits some discussion, for it is one of the features that sets the Pathans sharply apart from other Muslim societies.

The concept of Pakhtunwali, and the Pathans' resolute adherence to their tribal code, make a nonsense of the term 'lawless', with which the western media regularly characterise any reference to the North-West Frontier. The code of Pakhtunwali is no less severe than the Frontier Crimes Regulation in its system of punishing offenders. On the other hand, it provides for the maximum amount of law and order in a society of warrior tribes.

'Pakhtunwali is fundamentally an honour code,' says Khalid Aziz, who served as Political Officer in Khyber, North Waziristan and Orakzai agencies. 'It is a code which has succeeded in curbing the strong individualism of the Pathan. It enforces a rigid standard of behaviour on individuals and the tribe. It is a mixture of Islamic principles and *riwaj* [tradition]. In the case of inheritance, *riwaj* supersedes the Islamic injunctions.'[22] The *riwaj* precept is in fact a loose collection of ancient customs governing all aspects of the tribal people's lives. Under the FCR, a defendant has the right to plead his case in court before a *jirga* of three tribal elders or maliks. The Political Agent's job, acting as magistrate, is to ensure that the *jirga*'s findings comply with *riwaj*, which may vary from one tribe to another.

The basic principle of Pakhtunwali is *badal*, which translates as 'revenge'. This is the tenet that leads to blood feuds, some of which may last for generations. There was a case in the 1950s of a Pathan, educated in Britain and a practising barrister in London, who was called back to the Frontier to settle a blood feud, since he was the last surviving male member of his family. Revenge is the obligation placed on an individual or the family that has been insulted or injured. Since the insulted party also belongs to a clan, and then to a sub-tribe, the insult thus becomes an obligation to be redeemed individually or collectively, and the result can be the annihilation of entire families or small tribes. *Badal* permits no limitation in time or space, and the obligation holds as long as a single member of the clan survives. Murder cases that had their origin in some remote village of the Khyber have been reported in places as distant from the Frontier as Saudi Arabia. The Frontier doctor Thomas Pennell was once visiting some patients in a village of the Kurram Valley. His host told him that the houses on the opposite side of the street were once the stronghold of a rival family, and he pointed to the spots where his brother and uncle had been shot in a gun battle. To Pennell's astonishment, the man then introduced him to an Afghan who had just entered the room and who turned out to be his brother's killer. 'Yes, we are good friends now,' his host remarked, 'because the debt is even on both sides. I have killed the same number in his family.'[23] After a blood feud, the fatalities are added up and if they are found to be equal, this satisfies both sides that they can make peace without sacrificing their honour.

There is a second important component of Pakhtunwali and that is *melmastia*, which can be interpreted as a gesture of courtesy, from simple hospitality to friends to sanctuary for a person seeking refuge under a Pathan roof. Anyone can claim asylum in a Pathan house, regardless of the relationship between host and fugitive. There have been incidents in which a Pathan sheltering an outlaw under his roof has died defending his guest. Equally, as soon as a guest who is in disfavour with his host has set foot outside the house he becomes fair game, a fact of Pathan life that some Government agents and soldiers have learnt the hard way. The principle of *melmastia* always posed a major headache for the Frontier authorities whenever they were in pursuit of freebooters who had committed outrages in an administered district. Once these criminals were ensconced within the walls of a Pathan's home, there was little the Government forces could do to dislodge them without provoking their hosts into violent action.

Linked to *melmastia*, or more properly an extension of the principle of sanctuary, is *nanawati*, the third tenet of the Pakhtunwali code of honour. This carries with it the principles of humility and submission, for a Pathan seeking *nanawati* is in fact asking forgiveness of his enemy. A tribesman may have provoked a blood feud with a neighbouring family or clan, yet he is not prepared to accept the consequences of his actions. He will approach his enemy, throwing himself upon his adversary's mercy. For a martial people like the Pathans, begging for *nanawati* is obviously an act of great shame. The offended party is under no obligation to accept his enemy's penitence, but if he is in a benevolent mood he may receive a sheep as a token of goodwill. This is a very rare occurrence, and when it happens it is usually the tribal *jirga* that orders the lifting of *badal*.

The American diplomat James Spain, who lived among the Pathans, defines other violent crimes that were in the past, and to an extent today are still, common on the Frontier. One of these is *meerata*. 'This is a murder accomplished for the specific purpose of removing the victim from the line of inheritance, so that property will pass to the murderer or to someone more favoured by the murderer,' he writes.[24] There are situations that often result in killings and which involve relations between the sexes. These are known as *jhagh* and *tor*. The first concerns a man's fear that he may lose the girl he fancies to another suitor. He therefore 'stakes his claim', announcing to any would-be comer that he will have to deal with him first. *Tor* refers to illicit love affairs. In the case of adultery, the man usually forfeits his life and the wife, if she is lucky, only her nose, although it is quite common for both parties to be hunted down and murdered by the aggrieved husband.

For the Pathans, Curzon's radical shake-up of the Frontier – the elevation of their homeland to provincial status and the special legal system that was enacted to govern the region – amounted to nothing more than a case of *plus ça change*. There is a story, celebrated among Frontier officers of the day, which superbly illustrates the tribesmen's indifference to the British Raj and the great political events taking place outside their hills. A Political Officer was on a tour of his Frontier district in the company of an escort of village headmen. Over lunch, he asked one of the chief maliks whose side, in the event of war between Britain and Russia, his people were likely to take in the conflict. 'Do you wish me to tell you what would please you, or to tell you the truth?' the malik was reported to have asked. The British official, bracing himself for the worst, assured his host that he wished only to hear the truth. 'Then I shall tell you,' chuckled the old greybeard. 'We would just sit here in our hills watching you fight until we saw one or the other side utterly defeated. Then we would come down and loot the vanquished to the last mule! God be praised!'

Curzon's supporters would point to the relative calm that reigned on the North-West Frontier from 1899 to 1905 as proof of the success of his reforms. More sceptical Frontier veterans might argue that this was a mere coincidence: that the tribes called a truce when and where they pleased, and reverted to raiding on the same basis. What is certain is that Curzon's tenure coincided with the demise of a different and far greater threat to peace and stability in India. The final years of his viceroyalty saw the winding down of the Great Game as imperial Russia, smarting from a humiliating defeat at the hands of the Japanese and worried about the growing power of Germany, sought to mend its fences with England. The end result was the St Petersburg Convention of 1907, which at least on paper put an end to the rivalries between the two imperial powers regarding Tibet, Persia and Afghanistan. Most importantly, the Russians renounced all claims to Afghan territory and agreed to conduct their dealings with the

Amir through the British Government, while Persia was broken up into spheres of influence. London and Calcutta heaved a sigh of relief, but in Peshawar it was business as usual, as the garrison braced itself for an onslaught by the dreaded Zakka Khel.

The opening years of the twentieth century found a steady stream of Zakka Khel Afridis journeying between their homeland in the Bazar Valley and Afghanistan. In 1904, large numbers of these tribesmen visited Kabul and were warmly received by the Amir. A former Zakka Khel malik by the name of Khwas Khan acted as the middleman who cemented relations between the tribal bandits and Habibullah, who succeeded to the throne in 1901 on the death of his father, Abdur Rahman. Khwas Khan held a messianic sway over the tribesmen and he was able to gradually work them up to a war footing, holding out the promise of a recaptured Peshawar as a treasure chest of unimaginable booty and restored Pathan pride.

The momentum toward a full-scale outbreak of lawlessness started building in 1905, the year Curzon left for England. By March of that year no fewer than ten serious attacks had been carried out on British interests by gangs of marauders from Hazarnao, an Afghan town 11 miles from Dakka, who were in league with outlaws from British territory, mostly members of the Zakka Khel clan. There were swift and daring raids on villages within the administered districts, Border Police posts came under attack and British subjects, including police officers, were abducted by these gangs.

The Government retaliated by withholding allowances for the whole Afridi tribe. Once the payments were renewed, the Zakka Khel found, to their outrage, that they were denied any share of the money. This only reinforced their determination to line their pockets by raiding villages and holding abducted British citizens to ransom.

In the six months from August 1907 to January 1908, the Zakka Khel carried out eleven attacks on the Peshawar district. On 8 January 1908 they perpetrated their most daring raid on Peshawar city itself and penetrated to within 200 yards of the main police station. The nearest city gates were held with great difficulty, but the raiders fled through the famous Mohabbat Khan mosque and by the aid of ladders escaped over the wall. The Border Military Police arrived too late to be of any assistance, and three constables were shot dead by the Zakka Khel brigands. The Army and Border Military Police were sent to hold the railway line and picquet the Grand Trunk Road, leaving the city's defence force reduced to very low numbers, which made it impossible to risk a sortie to pursue the raiders.

Military patrols were stepped up along the border region in an attempt to intercept the raiding parties before they could reach any parts of the settled district. The main imperative was to safeguard the streets of Peshawar, which had become the scene of frequent armed robberies symptomatic of the spread of lawlessness. Losing control of the Frontier capital, apart from the obvious military humiliation, would amount to a disaster of major proportions in terms of loss of prestige and credibility with the tribesmen. The tribal marauders could rely on several advantages that militated against a successful border patrol policy. For one thing, they possessed a superior knowledge of the ground and were able to avoid fortified positions, while their spy networks proved efficient in tipping them off to the whereabouts of Army patrols. They traversed the gullies and defiles of the border with an unrivalled expertise, and could avail themselves of a speedy line of retreat to their hideouts in the hills. The Zakka Khel were only too aware that the Government had ordered the disarming of all villagers near the border in 1900, so their incursion met with virtually no armed resistance.

Not only were the cards stacked in the tribesmen's favour in terms of logistics, but to place the Government even more on the defensive, the Zakka Khel were better armed than the Frontier militia, and even some regular Army units. The extent of Afghan duplicity in this campaign of hit-and-run violence was evident in the quality of the rifles carried by the tribesmen. From 1906 onwards the number of weapons smuggled into tribal territory through Afghanistan grew at an astonishing rate, rising from fifteen thousand in 1907 to almost forty thousand by the time the Army, by now wholly fed up with this mischief, was making preparations to launch a punitive expedition against the Zakka Khel. During the 1897–8 Tirah Expedition only one Afridi in every ten was armed with a Martini-Henry rifle. By 1908, these weapons were the rule, not the exception. The significance of the volume of trade is reflected in the price of one of these prized rifles, which dropped from 500 rupees to 130 rupees between 1906 and 1908. Armed with the Martini-Henry, the Zakka Khel were able to keep their pursuers, who carried the less powerful Snider and Lee Metford rifles, at a safe distance, and invariably make good their swift escape into the hills.

The Ghilzai traders of Afghanistan were responsible for running guns by sea from Muscat through the Persian Gulf, then by camel caravan across Afghanistan to Kandahar and Ghazni, where the weapons were picked up by agents acting for the Zakka Khel insurgents. The Ghilzais gradually acquired a monopoly on gun-running in the Persian Gulf and this became a flourishing enterprise until the Government sent a Gurkha regiment to the region to intercept the shipments. A squadron of Royal Navy cruisers was also dispatched to the Gulf to engage the dhows, whose fear-struck Arab skippers eventually refused to transport weapons. This soon ceased to be a cost-effective business, with payment from the Afghan traders having fallen to a third of the value of their sailing vessels, which were frequently confiscated or blown out of the water by British warships. The Ghilzais also encountered growing hostility from the tribes of Kerman that lay on their main trade route in eastern Iran. The Sultan of Muscat took a hand in stopping the arms dealers of his kingdom from supplying the Ghilzais, for fear of provoking reprisals from the British, who provided help in keeping at bay hostile Bedouin tribes of the Omani hinterland.

This enabled the British to eventually set up an effective blockade of the Gulf to halt the arms traffic, but not in time to avoid having to mount a full-scale punitive expedition against the Zakka Khel. Roos-Keppel was convinced that the spread of these outrages was a deliberate act of defiance aimed at undermining British authority on the Frontier. 'Every man, woman and child in the [Zakka Khel] clan looks upon those who commit raids, murders and robberies in Peshawar or Kohat as heroes and champions,' he complained to the Government. 'They are the crusaders of the nation. They depart with the good wishes and prayers of all, and are received on their return after a successful raid with universal rejoicing and congratulations.'[25]

By the beginning of 1908 Harold Deane's patience was exhausted. After careful consideration, he could see no alternative but to petition Calcutta for permission to take punitive action. The Secretary of State for India advised Curzon's successor, Lord Minto, that the Government was prepared to sanction a strike against the Zakka Khel, but under no circumstances was the Army to occupy or annex any part of tribal territory, for a blockade of the Zakka Khel country would have required the troops to temporarily occupy land belonging to other Afridi clans. The Government had no wish to provoke the Pathans into staging a replay of 1897.

In early February Major-General Sir James Willcocks was ordered to mobilise two brigades from the 1st Peshawar Division to march on the Bazar Valley. The Zakka Khel Field Force left Peshawar on 13 February. The column moved with remarkable speed and within twenty-four hours the troops had picqueted all strategic points on the Khyber Pass road up to Landi Kotal. The advance went so swiftly that the tribesmen had no time to organise their defences. By the next day, all the main entrances to the Bazar Valley were in Willcocks's hands. The following morning Roos-Keppel himself took a column of Khyber Rifles and Gurkhas into the valley unopposed, thanks to a ruse devised by Willcocks, who had detailed a road-building party to carry out repairs on a different route from the one he planned to take.

Willcocks began a relentless bombardment of the Bazar Valley with the Army's four new 10-pounder guns, whose devastating power the tribesmen had not yet experienced. Before the month was out the Zakka Khel maliks, pressed by the other Afridi clans, presented themselves in Willcocks's tent to tender their unconditional submission. On 1 March the whole force was ready to commence the march back to Jamrud. 'No Frontier tribe had ever been punished so effectively or so rapidly before,' writes Collin Davies, 'and their casualties were so heavy that they exceeded those sustained by the whole Afridi tribe during the Tirah campaign of 1897–8.'[26] So ended what the satirical magazine *Punch* lampooned as 'The Weekend War'.

Hardly had the echoes of conflict died out across the Bazar Valley than disquieting reports reached Peshawar of a rising by Mohmand tribesmen to the north, who were threatening Shabkadr Fort.

Willcocks moved out from Landi Kotal with two columns and, after some skirmishing in the Khyber Pass, the Army quickly threw the rebel tribesmen back to the Afghan border. The wisdom of Curzon's Frontier reforms was put to the test and emerged with full marks in the Zakka Khel affair. The tribal levies stationed in the Frontier battle zone gave an exemplary account of themselves. Not a man deserted his post when called on to fire at his fellow Pathans, as a number of officials had feared would be the case. The Khyber Rifles came under attack during the engagement with the Mohmands and in one instance a detachment of sixty levies holding Michni blockhouse, near the top of the pass, found themselves besieged by a 4,000-strong *lashkar*. It was touch and go for seventeen hours – the enemy even managed to plant a scaling ladder on the wall. The only officer in the garrison was a Pathan subadar, who rallied his men to stay at their stations all night, until at daybreak the attackers finally broke off the siege. The scaling ladder is now in possession of the Khyber Rifles as a trophy of war.

By the end of May 1908, the Frontier was enjoying one of its rare periods of calm. To the Government's annoyance the campaign had one important side effect, in that it highlighted Kabul's complicity in the conflict. A month before the final shots were fired Pathan spies had informed Roos-Keppel, as Political Officer, along with his colleagues, that the whole country between Kabul and Gandamak was up in arms, with transport, food and ammunition for a *lashkar* of ten thousand men being supplied by the Commandant of Kahi, an Afghan garrison in Ningrahar. One Colonel Ali Ahmed, an Afghan Brigadier-General commanding at Kahi, who was in league with several fanatical mullahs, had plotted an attack on Landi Kotal for 30 April or 1 May. In fact, the intelligence report was out only by one day, as the assault took place on 2 May.

There was no doubt as to Afghanistan's involvement, not only in encouraging the tribes to rise against the British, but also in providing the raiders with sanctuary in Afghan territory. Even as the Zakka Khel were perpetrating their raids around Peshawar, an indignant Viceroy voiced his anger to the Amir on the eve of the King's proposed official visit to the Khyber on the first stage of an official tour of British India.

'I am desired to inform you that the Zakka Khel section of the Afridis have been giving a great deal of trouble during the past few months, and that quite recently they have committed two very serious raids in the Peshawar district,' wrote Lord Minto. This was in the wake of a raid on a town 8 miles from Peshawar, in which the Zakka Khel carried off two sepoys of the Border Military Police, four Hindus, one Mohammedan, fourteen camels, two tonga ponies and some bullocks and donkeys. 'I am also to instruct you to inform His Highness that His Excellency the Viceroy will regard it as a friendly act if His Highness will cause the immediate restitution of the Police sepoys and others who have been carried off, as well as the stolen animals.'[27] The British subjects were eventually returned to India, though there is no information on the fate of the abducted animals.

The Government of India experienced some anxious moments at the outbreak of war in Europe in 1914. A renewal of Afghan-inspired disturbances on the North-West Frontier would have required the dispatch of troops that were badly needed in other theatres of operation. There was also the fear that Turkey, who had entered the conflict on Germany's side, would coerce Habibullah into sending his mullahs to the border to stir up a wave of religious fanaticism among the tribes. The Amir did in fact entertain German as well as Turkish agents in Kabul during the First World War, but he wisely withheld support for a possible invasion of British India. Had Afghanistan declared war against Britain, this would almost certainly have aroused the Pathan tribes and touched off another general conflagration on the Frontier. The Amir's avowed neutrality was a signal to the tribes to hold back in this particular conflict. Another deterrent to trouble-making was the fact that many young Pathans were serving in the Indian Army as well as the native militias and khassadar units. The poor villagers of the Frontier had no wish to jeopardise the monthly remittances they received from their sons who were fighting for the Raj.

The British had in Habibullah, if not an ally, at least a man of reason with whom they could maintain friendly relations. This in itself rendered him fair game for ultra-nationalists conspiring in the bazaars and tea houses of Kabul. Thus it was almost a foregone conclusion that the most peaceful transition of power in Afghanistan's modern history should end in tragedy. One night in February 1919, while Habibullah was on a shooting trip in the Laghman Valley near Jalalabad, a gunman crept into the Amir's tent and blew off the top of his head with a rifle. The killer's identity remains a mystery to this day, but at the time the finger was pointed at the British, the Russians and a raft of domestic rivals. The public outrage somehow had to be placated, therefore one unpopular Afghan colonel was charged with the murder, tried and convicted on the flimsiest of evidence, and hanged. Almost immediately a proclamation was issued in Jalalabad appointing Nasrullah, who was not unduly disturbed at his brother Habibullah's assassination, the new amir. At the same time Habibullah's third son, Amanullah, seized power in Kabul and, with the backing of the Army, declared himself Amir. Nasrullah withdrew from the power struggle, following which Amanullah, neatly tying up loose ends, uncovered enough 'evidence' to implicate his uncle in Habibullah's murder and have him sentenced to life imprisonment. The new ruler of Afghanistan was 27 years old. He was thought by the British to be conceited, arrogant and somewhat dim, and a man very much on the defensive. Powerful elements within the Afghan Army suspected the Amir of complicity in his father's murder. Amanullah attempted to purchase their loyalty, as well as time for himself, by granting the officer corps a substantial pay rise. Pressure was mounting on him to appease his increasingly nationalistic generals, many of whom were demanding action against the British. The anti-British party was led by the powerful Nadir Shah, Commander-in-Chief of the armed forces, and the dowager Queen, Amanullah's mother. The argument in favour of a military strike was that the Raj was in a weakened state after four years of warfare in Europe. Indian nationalists had taken to the streets to stage pro-independence riots in major cities across the subcontinent. Was this not the ideal moment to rid India of the infidel and reclaim Peshawar, the jewel in the Afghan crown?

On 11 April 1919, Amanullah was handed the answer to his problem on a silver platter. That day, Gurkha troops, acting on orders from their British commanders, opened fire on a public assembly at

Amritsar. The exact number of people who fell in the atrocity is still a subject of heated debate. However, the Indians put the death toll at 379, with some 1,200 wounded. Two days later, Amanullah called for a jihad against the British, the irony being that very few Muslims were among the victims of the Amritsar massacre. Within a fortnight the Afghan Commander-in-Chief, Saleh Mohammed, led his troops across the border in an attack on Bagh in the Khyber Pass, a village of no strategic value, though vital to the five hundred sepoys of the Khyber Rifles at Landi Kotal, for the settlement was the source of the garrison's water supply. The Government of India moved swiftly to counter the Afghan offensive and a general mobilisation was called on 6 May. The Third Afghan War had begun.

A battalion of Somerset Light Infantry was rushed to the front to reinforce the Landi Kotal garrison. A convoy of sixty-seven lorries, with their canopies down to conceal their contents from the tribesmen, raced up the Khyber Pass transporting supplies and ammunition, as well as three truckloads of beer. Meanwhile, a bizarre plot to incite an uprising in Peshawar was foiled when it was discovered that the city's postmaster was also employed as an Afghan agent. This civil servant, who was an Afghan national, was caught in possession of inflammatory pamphlets calling on all Muslims to rise up against the British masters. The spy had been handed the seditious pamphlets, signed by Amanullah, while on a visit to Kabul. Roos-Keppel quickly threw a cordon of troops around the city and had the postmaster and his accomplices put under arrest. By the next morning it was business as usual in the city's bazaars.

From the Army's perspective, the border situation was looking ugly. The Afghans had 50,000 men under arms and could muster the support of another 80,000 well-armed tribesmen. The Afghans were capable of putting some 280 breech-loading guns in the field, and an equal number of muzzle-loaders. The British forces available for service on the entire North-West Frontier consisted only of two Indian Army divisions and cavalry brigades, with one division and another cavalry unit in reserve.

The Khyber Rifles outposts bore the brunt of the Afghan assault, and what transpired there over the next few days might appear to cast doubt on Curzon's strategy of shifting responsibility for border defence to the Pathan militias. There is no denying that it was a cut-and-dried case of desertion en masse by native levies in the face of enemy fire. Whole units of Khyber Rifles abandoned their posts and fled to the countryside, many taking their weapons with them. However, it is important to understand the native levies in the context of Pathan tribesmen. Without British officers to bolster their morale and keep them at their posts, abandoned to the mercy of frenzied mullahs outside the gates threatening the recruits with eternal damnation, confused by false tales of the fall of Peshawar and the defeat of British troops, it is no wonder that these simple tribesmen in uniform panicked and deserted their posts. Roos-Keppel was taking no chances, and with deep regret he ordered the Khyber Rifles to be disbanded. 'I am afraid it will be the end of what was a fine corps, which in the Zakka Khel expedition did not lose a man or a rifle, although we had three companies of Zakka Khels with us,' he later wrote to the Viceroy.

> The militia outposts were located far off in tribal areas, and miles of hostile and dangerous country separated them from the nearest posts of regular troops. In such circumstances, and particularly when there were no regular troops to support them during the Afghan War, the militia men could not reasonably have been expected to remain loyal to the British Government in the face of the cry of jihad in Afghanistan and of the aggravated anti-British feelings in tribal territory.[28]

That was the end of the first native militia raised on the Frontier, and it was only after the Second World War, twenty-five years later, that the corps was raised anew. This was done as a reward for the tribesmen's loyalty during the European war, in which hundreds of Pathan youths of the Peshawar district volunteered for overseas service in the locally-raised 1st Afridi Battalion.

Roos-Keppel, who had succeeded Deane as Chief Commissioner in 1908, went on the offensive. The first attempt to retake Bagh faltered when the troops encountered huge gatherings of hostile tribesmen on the crags surrounding the village. On 9 May the Royal Air Force was called into action against the Afghan forces. The RAF had previously taken part in raids against the tribesmen during localised disturbances in Baluchistan and Waziristan, in 1916–17. Aerial bombardment was a tactic that the Pathans despised and considered 'unsporting'.

The RAF in India came to play a key role in policing the North-West Frontier Province. Air power historian David Omissi makes the point that border security was the most important active military problem for British India in the 1920s. With the outbreak of the Third Afghan War, the RAF was often in the forefront of dealing with incursions by Afghan militants or raids by local tribesmen, as an alternative to marching a punitive column into the troubled district. 'The Air Staff argued that the RAF could replace these costly military expeditions,' writes Omissi.

> Aircraft could strike swiftly and cheaply into the mountains, with (they claimed) very little risk to the pilots. Air operations could save a lot of time, effort and money in controlling the Frontier. After initial hostility to these ideas, Sir Henry Rawlinson [the Commander-in-Chief in India, 1920–5] said he was prepared to give the RAF an extended hand in Frontier operations.[29]

As the Bagh relief operation progressed, the British troops managed to hold what ground they had gained while three BE2C Bristol Fighter aircraft began strafing a *lashkar* of Afghan tribesmen in a camp at Dakka, where Afghan officers were distributing rifles, ammunition, blankets and other stores to Pathan tribesmen. 'When the RAF aircraft appeared, the Afghan officers ran for cover – to emerge when the planes had gone to find the Pathans had taken all the rifles and other materials and disappeared into the hills,' writes former Indian Army officer Edgar O'Ballance. 'In this raid, one and a half tons of bombs were dropped and 1,151 rounds of ammunition fired. Enemy casualties were estimated to number about 600 men. The Afghan GOC (Naib Salar Khan), Governor of the Jalalabad Military District, was wounded, losing a foot, and his brother, the Malik, was amongst the dead.' The Bristol Fighter was a slow mover, with a maximum speed of 72mph at 6,500ft, which made it easy prey for Pathan marksmen. 'Due to the plane's slow rate of climb after take-off, RAF pilots soon had the unusual experience of being shot at by Afghan rifle fire from mountain crest lines above them.'[30] Bagh was retaken on 11 May, when six infantry battalions launched a dawn offensive with the support of eighteen field guns and twenty-two machine guns. The well-entrenched Afghans were driven from their position in a bayonet charge, and as retreating troops fled to the border they came under a heavy RAF bombardment.

Amanullah had little heart for this war, knowing that his army would be in a hopeless position once the British were able to muster reinforcements from other Indian garrisons. But with his general staff fully committed to jihad, the Amir had no choice but to play the game. Amanullah reasoned that his best strategy was to keep all his options open. While he called a Grand Assembly of tribal maliks and mullahs, to whom he promised victory and, with it, Karachi as an Afghan port, he simultaneously sent a letter to Lord Chelmsford declaring that the whole incident had been a sad misunderstanding. The British, the Amir tried to explain, had misconstrued the attack on the Khyber, which in reality was only a precautionary measure. The Afghan troop mobilisation had been ordered simply to protect the border against British internal security problems spilling over into Afghanistan. The Government of India wasn't having it. Roos-Keppel would accept nothing short of a definitive Afghan defeat, which was to serve as an example to the Frontier tribes that had thrown in their lot with the enemy.

The Afghan battle plan called for a three-pronged offensive across the Durand Line. The Khyber attack had already been launched, and the next advances would be into the Kurram Valley, south of Peshawar, with the movement of another army group against Quetta in Baluchistan. The British had rushed about nineteen thousand troops up from the Punjab, men who, for the most part, were battle weary from fighting in Europe and anxious for demobilisation. Morale was instantly boosted when the soldiers were told that the bulk of the Afghan invaders had converged at Thal, a small cantonment 50 miles south of Peshawar in British territory, where the Government force was badly outnumbered and under heavy attack. The Army had thirteen guns mounted on lorries at its disposal. Once the gunners reached Thal and began hammering the Afghan positions, it was only a matter of hours before a messenger arrived at the British lines with a message from General Nadir Shah, saying that the Amir had ordered a ceasefire.

> Dyer's [the British commander] response was, 'My guns will give an immediate reply'. The sight of advancing forces was regarded with dismay by the Afghans, and General Nadir Shah said, 'My God, we have the whole artillery of India coming up against us'. He immediately gave the order to withdraw and, harassed by cavalry, armoured cars and RAF aircraft, the Afghan force rapidly moved away, halting some three miles distant to make camp.[31]

General Dyer (not to be confused with the General Dyer who ordered the massacre at Amritsar) was all for pursuing the enemy back to the border and beyond, but in the midst of the bombardment he unexpectedly received an order to halt the advance, for the Amir had thrown in the towel. By that time, Afghanistan was facing a British force that had swollen to 340,000 men, many of them battle-hardened troops who had fought in the trenches of Europe.

The severe pounding the RAF had inflicted on Dakka and Jalalabad on the Afghan side of the border was a sobering lesson. The *coup de grâce* was given when, on 24 May, Empire Day, 'Jock' Halley, reputed to be the smallest pilot in the RAF, took his gigantic Handley-Page V/1500 on a raid over Kabul. The world's largest bomber circled the Afghan capital and dropped a bomb near the Amir's residence. Amanullah decided that the game was over – but not lost.

The two belligerent powers agreed to convene a peace conference in Rawalpindi on 26 July. Once at the negotiating table, Amanullah began playing for time by making unrealistic demands for concessions, such as the transfer of Waziristan to Afghan sovereignty and an increase in the Government of India's annual subsidy to Afghanistan. After a few days of acrimonious debate the British lost patience and threatened to resume hostilities. The Afghans knew exactly what they were doing and how to play the risks. By whittling down their adversary's resistance, they were able to extract terms that eventually made it look – at least to Amanullah's subjects, which was the crucial factor – as if the Afghans had walked away victorious from the peace talks.

'It has sometimes been argued that Amanullah and the Afghans were the real victors of the war despite their total military defeat,' says military historian Brian Robson.

> The peace terms signed at Rawalpindi in August 1919 imposed no territorial losses or financial repatriations on Afghanistan, and the only obvious gain on either side was the abandonment of British control of Afghanistan's external relations. To that extent, Amanullah had gained what he set out to achieve, and the victory celebrations in Kabul, if they seemed hollow to British eyes, were not entirely without foundation.[32]

After all, Amanullah had achieved independence for his country, something that his father and grandfather had in vain demanded of the British. The Amir erected a triumphal pillar in Kabul and distributed medals to his defeated generals to commemorate their victory over 'the greatest Empire in the world'. The British refused to renew their subsidies to Afghanistan, as well as the licence to import arms. This, however, was a trifling matter, for the Amir well knew to whom he could turn for assistance. Within a few weeks of ratification of the peace treaty an Afghan mission arrived in Moscow on a friendship visit, thus stoking the Government of India's smouldering fears of Russian, and now Bolshevik, intrigues in Central Asia.

The Amir could not count on his subjects' gratitude for long. In 1928 Amanullah embarked on a tour of Europe, which started off with a small hitch that could be taken as an omen of things to come. On his rail journey to Karachi, whence he was to sail to Southampton, the Amir pulled the emergency cord instead of the lavatory chain as the train was climbing a gradient in the Khojak tunnel. A few months later, Amanullah returned from his royal progress to find the Afghans in a sullen mood, with many grumbling about public exchequer money that had been squandered on their leader's trip. The Amir, perhaps rather tactlessly, tried to silence the grumbling by pointing out that the many valuable presents he had brought back far outweighed the cost of the journey. The European experience opened Amanullah's eyes to the enlightenment of Western civilisation. However, an attempt to initiate reforms in his own country, such as the education of women and the introduction of European dress, only served to further enrage his fundamentalist opponents. By January 1929 the writing was on the wall: Amanullah was forced to abdicate, fortunately escaping the fate that had awaited many of his predecessors who had fallen into disfavour. He fled up the Khyber Pass in a Rolls-Royce, clutching his beloved caged canary, with his erstwhile loyal subjects in hot pursuit. The rebels had chosen Habibullah Ghazi, known as Bacha Saqao ('water carrier's son'), as their new Amir. Not everyone was pleased with this development. General Nadir Khan, for instance, the officer who had surrendered to the British in 1919 and was now enjoying a peaceful retirement on the French Riviera, saw this as a chance to redeem his honour. He returned to Afghanistan to lead an army of 2,500 Wazirs and Mahsuds against Kabul, where he had the Bacha Saqao hanged and proclaimed himself Amir.

Amanullah found temporary sanctuary with his former enemies in British India. Fortunately for the ex-Amir and his descendants, during his trip through Europe he had received from the King of Italy a decoration that carried with it the right to claim kinship with the Italian royal house. Amanullah sailed to Europe to remind the Italian monarch of his kind gesture, and the ex-Amir soon found himself living in gilded exile in Rome, where he stayed until his death in 1960.

There is a curious twist to the uprising that toppled Amanullah from power. In September 1928, three months before the Amir was ousted from his Bala Hissar palace, rumours began to circulate about a British RAF officer, one T.E. Shaw, who was purported to be on a spying mission for the British in Afghanistan disguised as a *pir*, or Muslim holy man. Newspaper reports had this secret agent fomenting unrest among rival factions, which eventually touched off the revolt against the Amir. The agitator in question was T.E. Lawrence, known to the world as 'Lawrence of Arabia'. Lawrence was stationed in the border town of Miranshah in North Waziristan, where he claimed to be working on a new translation of Homer's *Odyssey* and completing the final draft of *The Mint*, his book about life in the RAF. Once the rumours reached Fleet Street, the British press began to have a field day with the hottest story of the season. The Indian press quickly picked up on the reports of Lawrence's alleged spying activities. Then the French and Russian papers sprang into action. It was gold dust for the press: the famous adventurer who had raised the Arabs to revolt was perceived to be just the man to rid Afghanistan of an untrustworthy Amir. The Government did its best to quash the stories, but it was too late: the uprising in Afghanistan and Amanullah's hasty departure made Lawrence's presence in the area too much of an embarrassment. He was pulled out of India and what, if anything, might have been lurking behind Lawrence's activities in Waziristan is shrouded in mystery.

SIX

The Red Shirts are Coming

Waziristan was ever a running sore for British officialdom on the North-West Frontier. The Government would from time to time be obliged to take action against the Shinwaris, Afridis or other tribes, whenever acts of brigandry and sabotage overtook what had come to be considered the limits of acceptable misbehaviour. The standard punishments ranged from withholding tribal allowances to mounting an all-out punitive expedition, after which the offenders would retire to the hills to tend their goats and rebuild their demolished homes. It was a different matter with Waziristan: for the Mahsuds and Wazirs, raiding was a way of life.

'No area of the Frontier has been more turbulent than Waziristan and no tribes more aggressive or dangerous than the Wazirs and Mahsuds who inhabit it,' writes Brian Robson.[1] Even after the Amir had sued for peace in May 1919, the two main tribes of this largely desolate region continued to rampage across the administrative border, keeping up the pressure on British India in the vain expectation that the Afghan Army would soon return to the battlefield. The South and North Waziristan militias had also suffered desertions during the Third Afghan War, though not on the scale of the Khyber Rifles. Many of the levies had run off with their rifles and joined forces with the Mahsuds. Taking advantage of the confusion that reigned in the border region during the Afghan conflict, these brigands carried out nearly two hundred raids from the outbreak of hostilities until November 1919. In that month, Major-General Sir Skipton Hill Climo's Waziristan Force, with a strength of some thirty thousand combat troops, was ready to move on the insurgents. Once the Army's tactical objective was fixed, the striking force was renamed the Tochi Column, for Tochi was to be its first area of operations. It was a highly modern unit for a Frontier force, comprising an armoured car battery, 4.5in howitzers, and eighteen RAF Bristol fighters held in reserve. This was the first time in Frontier history that aircraft were used as support for ground troops and it proved to be an effective tool of war. The RAF extended to the enemy on the ground the gentlemanly gesture of dropping leaflets to warn the tribesmen of what was coming their way, albeit ignoring the fact that their readers were illiterate almost to a man. Then, on the morning of 18 November, before the desert heat whipped up air turbulence to a dangerous level, the bombing raids began. It took only a few hours of persuasion for the maliks to come out and offer their submission. The Tochi Wazirs had been brought to heel with remarkable ease and it was clear that from May 1919, when the Government introduced warfare from the air, the face of Frontier conflict had taken a radical turn.

The column now turned south to Derajat, the area made up of the two districts of Dera Ghazi Khan and Dera Ismail Khan, to confront the Mahsuds, who were always a harder nut to crack. Major-General Sir Andrew Skeen, a veteran of the Pathan Revolt, was the man chosen to lead the troops in the Mahsud campaign. The death in 1914 of the Powindah Mullah, who for years had acted as the prime instigator of Mahsud mischief, failed to dampen the tribesmen's lust for pillaging British territory. More than any of the Pathan tribes, the Mahsuds were disposed to committing atrocities on a grand scale. Their outrages ranged from burning to the ground the town of Tank in a demonstration of support for the Amir, to a devastating attack on the Wana Column during the Third Afghan War, in which they used every trick in the book, from forging evacuation orders, to massacring the Government troops and making off with their guns and ammunition. The Wana Column's desperate retreat from Moghal Kot to the safety of the Zhob Militia post at Mir Ali Khel, 13 miles to the south, cost the lives of five out of eight British officers, with at least forty casualties among the other ranks. It was one of the great sagas of Frontier warfare, which the official report hailed as 'a stirring example of the height to which the devotion of the British officer can rise'.[2]

The accumulation of Mahsud transgressions over the years was not to go unpunished. The tribesmen were invited to a *jirga* on 3 November, at which they were given a week to accept the terms of submission that had been forced upon their Wazir brethren. If the tribesmen failed to comply, they could expect operations against them to commence with an aerial bombardment. Major-General Skeen estimated that since the start of war with Afghanistan in May 1919, the Mahsuds had managed to steal about 7,500 modern rifles from the troops and were in possession of about one million rounds of ammunition. The Mahsuds were glowing with self-confidence after the success of their recent attacks on Government columns. When no reply was received by 11 November, the RAF was called in to bomb three Mahsud villages. By now the tribesmen were adept at taking to the hills in advance of these aerial attacks, so the bombardment failed to inflict major casualties.

With winter setting in, Skeen set as his priority a rapid advance in order to achieve his military objectives in the shortest possible time. He decided on an advance to Wana, the Mahsud stronghold, to commence no later than mid-February. The next phase of the Mahsud campaign involved some of the toughest and costliest soldiering the British forces had ever encountered on the North-West Frontier. In less than a month, from the end of December 1919 to 20 January 1920, the Army had fought twenty actions at brigade level and still the Mahsuds refused to surrender. Now the Derajat Column, having cleared the road from the settlements of Jandola to Kotkai, marched on a gorge called the Ahnai Tangi, the greatest natural obstacle on the way to Wana, 4 miles to the south. This gorge rises as an almost insignificant feature on the landscape, only 80 yards in length and 30 yards wide, yet it became the scene of some of the fiercest fighting of the entire campaign. A strong *lashkar* of up to three thousand Mahsuds was entrenched at this position, which had to be taken in order for the artillery and baggage, along with supply convoys, to get through and proceed to Wana.

'The fighting commenced at dawn as our leading troops moved up the valley,' writes Major Walter James Cummings, an officer of the South Waziristan Scouts who took part in the battle.

> The enemy had chosen well their ground for this, their strongest opposition to our invasion of their country. The battle raged in all directions and casualties mounted alarmingly, but our troops managed to hold back the attackers from gaining any position that would enable the enemy to fire into the *nullah* itself, where the vulnerable brigade train of animals which followed close on the advance were then herded for safety. Camels, mules, wounded and followers were packed like sardines that night into the small place, which providentially was available for us to use. The precipitous side of our emergency camp gave protection and picquets were closed in all around.

The Mahsuds brought their marksman skills into play with deadly accuracy, defying every attempt to dislodge them from the hillsides as they shot up the troops who were sheltering behind rocks and those who were trying to erect defensive picquets. 'The enemy now turned their attention to picking off individual stragglers of our withdrawing troops, who had been driven from their positions on the right,' says Cummings.

> Some of these unfortunate lads, trying to escape the hail of bullets, were attempting to find a way back to the main body along a narrow path on the face of the north cliff. As they felt their way along the goat track the Mahsuds picked them off. It was terrible to see their bodies toppling down to the floor of the Taki Zam. We were powerless to help them. We could only lie where we were and watch with horror. Once the Mahsud snipers had accomplished that gruesome work there was nothing to prevent them from looking elsewhere for targets and their bullets now came in our direction.

Cummings spent the better part of the afternoon rescuing two wounded airmen who had crash-landed their plane in a field. The RAF officers were hit as they were dragged to safety, as were the two sepoys sent to bring them in.

> By this time darkness was approaching, and with dusk came respite from further attacks and bullets. The enemy were licking their

> wounds and we were licking ours. The *lashkars*, which had suffered at least five hundred casualties in their persistent attacks, were in no mood or condition to continue the battle that night, and for all the troops it was just as well. The battle had lasted for twelve hours and more, and everyone was cold and weary, as well as hungry.[3]

The striking column took heavy losses on that day, with some four hundred dead and wounded, including fourteen British officers, most of them killed. Mahsud losses were estimated at a thousand. The next morning, well aware of the proclivity of the Mahsud for stripping and mutilating the dead and even digging up their graves to loot their clothes and blankets, the British dug a deep trench under the cliff and then detonated a heavy charge of explosives to bring down a slice of the rockface to cover their dead. A party of tribesmen did come out, but this was to offer a peace overture which was flatly rejected. After seeing how the Mahsuds had summarily torn up the peace terms signed at Jandola on 29 December, the commanding officers were by now all too familiar with this delaying tactic. The fighting went on well into April, nearly a year after the start of the Afghan War. The Mahsuds finally tired of the struggle and agreed to hand over a number of rifles and pay their fine, although both fell short of the terms agreed at a *jirga* held five months previously. On that basis, it could have been considered yet another pyrrhic victory for the Government. The Derajat Column had fought its way into the tribe's territorial heartland, where the force established a permanent garrison and began work on a road network, which caused the Mahsuds great remorse and shame. But the Army had taken a severe blow in the fighting. 'In the early stages of the campaign, the troops had sustained defeats of a kind never before seen in Frontier warfare and which would have lasting effects on the organisation and training of the Indian Army,' says Robson. 'Above all, the Mahsuds had not been brought to heel.'[4]

This most recalcitrant of the Pathan tribes was back on the rampage in a matter of months, and in due course the Government was forced to take renewed punitive action. So it went for the next few years, until early 1925 when squadrons of RAF bombers and fighters concentrated a series of attacks on a small body of Mahsud rebels, who emerged very badly mauled from the bombardment and strafing that followed. From that time onward, it was gloves off with the tribesmen. Scorched earth tactics were a common tactic on these RAF raids, involving the petrol bombing of crops and strafing of livestock. The Mahsuds took notice, and for more than a decade tribal outrages were limited to sporadic raids by diehard fanatics.

The most colourful episode to relieve the relative ennui of Frontier life in the 1920s was the abduction of a pretty 17-year-old English girl by Pathan tribesmen in 1923. This was the Molly Ellis affair, a cause célèbre which the British press pursued with predictable vigour, for this was an outrage against English maidenhood. Molly was the daughter of a staff officer in Kohat, who happened to be away on tour the night that a gang of Afridis broke into the family bungalow. The raiders' plan was to kidnap mother and daughter, but Molly's mother put up a fight and was murdered, while the girl was whisked away to the hills of Tirah, still in her nightdress. There was a frantic effort to negotiate Molly's release with the kidnappers, who were contacted through intermediaries a few days later. The Afridis, who, as it turned out, were hunted criminals, were holding Molly as hostage on a demand that the Government grant them a pardon for past crimes. There was no question of a military expedition into Tirah, where no European had set foot since General Lockhart's 1897 invasion. In any case, this would have been a futile exercise, for the abductors would be sure to murder the girl if the Government sent in troops.

The situation grew increasingly desperate as the weeks dragged on with no word from the abductors. The outlaws were being hunted by British agents, as well as a party of their own tribesmen and some Afghans, to whose territory they had fled. As Sir John Jaffey, Chief Commissioner in Peshawar, vividly recounts: 'A sudden tragedy befell which found the vast civil and military departments of Government as helpless as men with hands tied behind them. An English girl in the hands of ruffians somewhere across the border! All the King's horses and all the King's men could only make matters worse, and British prestige shone dim.'[5]

This was destined to become a Frontier epic with all the romantic trimmings, for just as the situation looked bleakest, in stepped the plucky English heroine. It was pointless to send men in to negotiate with the kidnappers: Government emissaries had twice tried and failed to get through. It was then that Mrs Lillian Starr, a nursing sister at the Peshawar Mission Hospital and the widow of a doctor who had also been murdered by an Afridi housebreaker, was summoned to Jaffey's official residence. Her mission, should she choose to accept it, was to undertake a journey to Tirah, track down Molly's abductors, and negotiate the girl's release. She took on the task without flinching. Wearing traditional Pathan dress, Lillian Starr rode off one morning with two native guards towards Tirah, and before sunset she became the first white woman to enter the forbidden land of the Afridis. On the road she passed the Dargai Heights, and stopped to pay her respects at the graves of the Gordon Highlanders who had fallen in that action. Two days later she entered the village of Khanki Bazaar, where she was brought before an influential mullah who at first denied all knowledge of the kidnapping. Mrs Starr had intelligence to the contrary, and continued to demand information from the white-bearded preacher, who was astonished to find himself under interrogation by a European Christian woman, a species he probably had not set eyes upon before. Quite to her astonishment, he eventually gave in and produced two of the murderers. The negotiations for Molly's release dragged on through the day and, with the mullah's intercession, Mrs Starr was able to whittle down the raiders' demands to what she considered an acceptable compromise. 'Under the blighting influence of the Mullah's hostility they agreed,' she later wrote, 'after some half-hearted argument, to surrender their captive in exchange for the release by Government of two men of the Bosti Khel section who were held in the Kohat gaol.'[6] She had been authorised by Jaffey to accept these terms, for the prisoners in question were merely thieves, not murderers, and men of no special account. While waiting for news that the exchange prisoners were on their way, Mrs Starr went about treating these ferocious Pathan warriors as so many rustics in a rural English hamlet, wandering off to take some photographs and distributing pills for the villagers' ailments. When word arrived that the two thieves had been freed and were on their way, Mrs Starr was taken to see Molly, to whom she refers throughout her account as 'Miss Ellis'. The girl was lying on a bed in a dark room in the mullah's house, smiling and unharmed after her ordeal.

The party returned to Peshawar, while the bandits made good their escape into Afghanistan. In their desperation, they even made an attempt to kidnap another Englishwoman and her husband one night in Parachinar, close to the Afghan border. This left the pair of them with their hands drenched deeper in blood, for when the unarmed husband rushed to his wife's defence, the two men hacked the couple to death with their Khyber daggers. One of the bandits was eventually caught and hanged by the British. The other was seized by the Afghans and merely deported to Turkestan. The Molly Ellis affair was one of those rare occasions in which Englishwomen were catapulted centre stage in India. Unlike the horrors endured by the mothers and daughters who were caught up in the upheaval of 1857, this affair had a happy ending.

Jaffey could hardly contain his delight at the success of Lillian Starr's heroic exploit. This was understandable, for had things gone the other way it could have fared badly for the man who sent her on the mission. He summed up the affair in a fitting gush of hyperbole: 'With the charm of her fair face and a woman's courage she carried our standard for us behind those iron hills where no Englishman may pass. She had the great joy of bringing back to us the English girl unscathed and uninjured, and she made a British mark on the heart of Tirah better than all the drums and tramplings of an army corps.'[7]

The calm was broken a few years later by a wave of political disturbances that swept across the North-West Frontier. These events spawned two figures who became a thorn embedded in the Government's side, from the early 1930s to the very day the Raj rolled up the carpet. The men in question and the unrest they brought to the Frontier cannot be taken in isolation, for this was a time of agitation throughout India. Mahatma Gandhi and his followers were on the march, and the Government was forced to face up to the reality that the days of the Raj were numbered. Britain was by fits and starts beginning to loosen its grip on the reins of power, leading inevitably to full independence, though not necessarily the dismembering of the subcontinent that took place in August 1947.

The British tradition has always been to govern by rule of law, the country's former colonies being no exception. There was never an attempt to advance or restrict the march towards Indian sovereignty using royal or viceregal decree. A series of legislative reforms was enacted in this period, starting with the Indian Councils Act, known as the Morley-Minto Reforms of 1908, which represented a significant landmark in the history of constitutional development towards Indian self-government. These reforms became part of the India Act 1909 that provided for the appointment of sixty Indian representatives to the viceroy's councils and up to fifty to the provincial legislative councils. The next major piece of legislation, the Government of India Act 1919, attempted to devise a system of gradual devolution of power, while setting out the maximum concessions that the Government was prepared to make at that time. It was a case of two steps forward and one back. This Act, and the Montagu-Chelmsford Report that was embodied in the law, touched off street protests that were vigorously repressed, the Amritsar massacre being the most brutal example. Gandhi launched a nationwide protest against the Rowlatt Acts, which introduced stringent anti-terrorist laws to deal with growing civil disorder in British India. After a series of round table discussions held in London between 1930 and 1932, the Government of India Act 1935 was passed, upholding the move towards Indian sovereignty first outlined in the 1919 law. The drive towards Indian self-rule only served to stir up resentment and further alienate the Pathans from the momentous changes taking place in the rest of the country. The North-West Frontier Province was not taken into account under any of these reforms, and the Pathan homeland remained firmly in the iron fist of the Frontier Crimes Regulation.

Mirza Ali Khan and Abdul Gaffar Khan were Pathan nationalist leaders with different agendas. They were almost complete opposites in appearance as well. Mirza Ali was a small, wiry man who suffered from severe asthma, a hunted outlaw and something of a genius in guerrilla warfare. Abdul Gaffar was a beefy giant, 6ft 4in, the son of a family of aristocratic landowners, whose avowed pacifism earned him the nickname of 'the Frontier Gandhi'. His vision went beyond the opportunistic ambushing of British patrols. Abdul Gaffar's cause was 'Pakhtunistan', the creation of a separate and independent Pathan homeland, to be achieved through non-violent means, and as such he represented a far more dangerous threat to British India. Mirza Ali was also to embrace the cause of Pakhtunistan, but not until circumstances made it expedient for him to do so, much later in his career. What both men shared was a determination to drive the British from the North-West Frontier.

Civil disobedience was the order of the day in 1930, with Gandhi's Congress Party calling for a boycott of British textiles imported into India, as well the picketing of shops selling alcohol and violation of the laws that imposed restrictions on the felling of trees. 'The police just managed to keep the upper hand, save in Peshawar,' says the historian Lawrence James. 'Here political life was dominated by Abdul Gaffar Khan, the leader of the Khudai Khidmatgar or "Servants of God".' James describes Gaffar Khan as 'a tolerant Muslim' who had been educated at a Christian mission and believed 'almost uniquely for a Pathan, in women's rights and education'.[8]

Like other nationalist leaders of his day, Gaffar Khan was possessed by a utopian vision of a society founded on the exaltation of race and hard work. He had no truck with the fascist movement of the 1930s nor, on the other hand, was he prepared to sit cross-legged in front of a loom. He was, above all, a man of action, peaceful of spirit, though not averse to sending a mob against the police.

Abdul Gaffar Khan was a genuine idealist with a sincere belief in his own principles. From the standpoint of the established authority, he represented the most dangerous breed of populist leader. As a young man Gaffar Khan fell under the influence of various religious and nationalist movements. He was a frequent visitor to the fundamentalist Deoband seminary, 75 miles north of Delhi, the embryo of the madrasa network that established itself as the training ground for Muslim extremism in South Asia and the alma mater of future Taliban militants. Deobandi Islam was to become the religious inspiration of the

Taliban leadership, including the fugitive Mullah Mohammed Omar who in April 2000 made an appearance in Peshawar as the keynote speaker at an international Deobandi Conference.

Gaffar Khan also took part in the Khilafat Movement, which between 1919 and 1924 organised mass protests whose specific target was British post-war policy in Turkey, although the agitation was eventually directed against British rule in India. Gaffar Khan participated in the movement's 1920 *hijrat*, which is a Muslim exodus from infidel land. In that year, tens of thousands of Muslims from Sind and the North-West Frontier trekked into Afghanistan, wherever they could foil the Border Police, with the open connivance of the Amir Amanullah, who embraced this mass migration from British India as an attractive opportunity to embarrass the Raj. When their numbers swelled to some sixty thousand Amanullah realised that his impoverished country could not support this vast influx of refugees. On his return, Gaffar Khan was arrested and sent back to prison. As part of his apprenticeship in the theory and practice of sedition, the Frontier Gandhi also travelled to Kabul to take counsel from the luckless Amanullah, who was only too happy to encourage the young idealist in his struggle against the British. Within a short time, Gaffar Khan had put his infrastructure in place and mustered the popular support he needed to launch his crusade.

The year 1930 brought unrest to the North-West Frontier on a scale rivalling that of the Third Afghan War and even the 1897 Pathan Revolt. The root cause of these disturbances was Gaffar Khan's political-religious movement, the Khudai Khidmatgar, also known as the 'Red Shirts' after the uniform worn by his followers. The authorities found this latter detail decidedly irksome, for it raised fears amongst the Russophobes in Government that Gaffar Khan might have allied himself with the Bolsheviks. In fact, the Frontier Gandhi had as little sympathy for the Russians as he did for the Raj – his was exclusively a Pathan nationalist movement whose ideology was founded on Islam and Pathan statehood. Gaffar Khan's principles did not, however, prevent his making common cause with unlikely confederates. He had already met Gandhi in 1919, during the period of agitation over enactment of the Rowlatt Acts. Gaffar Khan developed a deep admiration for the Mahatma, despite his being a Hindu, and he later became a member of Gandhi's inner circle.

The Red Shirt movement got moving in earnest when Gaffar Khan returned from an All-India National Congress conference in Lahore in December 1929. The meeting was hosted by Jawaharlal Nehru, who was to become independent India's first prime minister. The Hindu leader told the gathering that he would settle for nothing short of full independence for India and he laid the groundwork for widespread public protests to achieve his objective.

> Badshah Khan [he was given this title, meaning 'king of kings', by his followers], as vice president of the Frontier Congress Committee, attended, along with other activists from the Frontier. He endorsed the Congress programme completely and in early 1930 the Peshawar Congress Committee named Abdul Gaffar Khan with his newly founded Khudai Khidmatgar movement as their ally in a forthcoming civil disobedience campaign.[9]

The Amritsar massacre in April 1930 had raised the political temperature to maximum level across India. The North-West Frontier and especially Peshawar did not escape a wave of protests orchestrated by Red Shirt activists. On the day that news of the massacre reached the Frontier, the Red Shirts sent their followers into the streets of the capital. These were mainly members of the Khudai Khidmatgar Frontier Youth League, a paramilitary body that was organised into companies, put through regular drilling, and given military training. The police went straight for Gaffar Khan, who, along with eleven of his supporters, was arrested on charges of sedition and unlawful assembly under the Frontier Crimes Regulation. Gaffar Khan took this in his stride, for he had been convicted for seditious activities as early as 1920 and was no stranger to prison life. Word of his arrest sparked an outbreak of rioting in the city. The disturbances spread like wildfire across the Vale of Peshawar, bringing thousands of Afridis down from the hills, most of them drawn by the scent of loot. The rioters spread chaos in the district by cutting telegraph wires, firing on trains and generally causing havoc wherever they could. After about three hours of pandemonium the crowds were dispersed with the help of mounted patrols and armoured cars, but sadly not before several soldiers had opened fire and killed an indeterminate number of people. Indian National Congress sources put the fatalities at two hundred, though the actual total was almost certainly lower. By now it was open to debate whether the real power in Peshawar district was Gaffar Khan's underground government or the British administration.

The riot was over but it took the Army four days to restore order to the city. The shockwaves of the Peshawar disturbances were felt as far away as Waziristan, where several sections of the Wazir tribe attacked a garrison of the Tochi Scouts at Datta Khel, who had to defend themselves with machine-gun fire. The situation grew so critical that twelve RAF bombers were called in to disperse the tribesmen, but they failed to break off the siege of Datta Khel. Finally, two bomber squadrons consisting of forty-eight aircraft, an almost unheard of number for one Frontier sortie, arrived to bomb and strafe the Wazirs and their villages. No sooner had the Wazir maliks agreed the Government's peace terms, than the Red Shirts operating in South Waziristan began galvanising the Mahsuds into action, while elsewhere on the Frontier Gaffar Khan's agents were busy stirring up rebellion in Tirah. Some seven thousand Afridis set off on a march to Peshawar, drawn by the prospect of fighting and booty. It took a flying column of Guides, Lancers and Hussars, supported by the RAF, to disperse the *lashkar* across the plain, where they were strafed and bombed back into Tirah. Within days the tribesmen, mostly young hotheads, had begun another march to Peshawar, where they were met by armoured cars and RAF bombers. The Government found it necessary to declare martial law, and that more or less eliminated the threat to the city, apart from a few minor sporadic incidents over the next few days.

In March 1931, Gandhi prevailed on the Viceroy, Lord Irwin, to release Gaffar Khan from gaol. The Mahatma's argument, which was indeed hard to fault, was that the incarceration of his Frontier alter ego provided a rallying point for extremist agitators and that this could only result in further violence. Gaffar Khan was freed and the ban on his Frontier Youth League was lifted. The Pathan leader enjoyed a few months of freedom but was rearrested at the end of 1931 for his savage anti-British speeches, and for dispensing justice through his own 'courts' to the point that, in the public eye, the British administration was beginning to resemble a lame duck.

Gaffar Khan's life as a free man became something of an interlude between prison terms: in December 1934 he was detained again, only three months after his previous release. This time he was expelled from his homeland with an order not to enter the North-West Frontier Province. He then went to Bombay to preach civil disobedience before an assembly of Christian nationalists.

Gaffar Khan's influence was by now on the wane, while Congress took the view that the young militants of the Khudai Khidmatgar had become a political liability. Nehru ordered the Frontier Youth League disbanded and the following year, 1932, the Red Shirts were dissolved, although the organisation continued to operate as an underground movement.

'It should be conceded, however, that its efforts had not been without some results,' writes Arthur Swinson. 'That year the North-West Frontier Province was raised from a Chief Commissionerate to a Governor's Province, and from now on its political rights and institutions were equal to those in the rest of India. In 1935 the Province shared the further advance towards self-government marked by the Government of India Act.'[10] The Indus had ceased to act as a barrier to political and social intercourse between the North-West Frontier and the rest of India.

The Frontier now enjoyed a new status and with this came a modest degree of self-government. To be sure, the real power rested with the Governor of the Province, but in a gesture of goodwill towards the Pathans Sir Abd-ul-Qaiyum, a retired civil servant, was appointed First Minister with responsibility for non-strategic matters, such as health and education. His long years of service in the British administration made him a soft target for the Red Shirts, who launched a vigorous propaganda campaign accusing him of accepting the role of British flunkey.

It was an extraordinary irony that, in 1937, when Congress was invited by the Governor of the province to form a ministry, the man selected for the post of Chief Minister should have been Dr Khan Sahib, Gaffar Khan's elder brother and likewise a devoted follower of Gandhi. Sir Abd-ul-Qaiyum, who was dismissed after a vote of no confidence, cast his lot with Muhammed Ali Jinnah's Muslim League, which in 1947 was to lead the first government of independent Pakistan.

The Khan brothers had little in common beyond their blood relationship and a shared belief in the Pathan cause. Khan Sahib, though having served time in gaol after the Rowlatt Act agitation, was cut from a totally different cloth than his visionary brother: he had served as medical officer to the Corps of Guides and taken a degree at Edinburgh University. Moreover, he had a strong British connection through marriage, as his wife was from Yorkshire. Once Gaffar Khan had returned from his internment outside the North-West Frontier, he worked alongside his brother to push through a programme of social reforms, placing special emphasis on curbing the powers of the *nawabs*, a clique of autocrats who ruled the villages under an almost feudal system of hereditary power, and also on extending inheritance rights to women.

The Congress government of the North-West Frontier Province, along with the tribes, applied the brakes to anti-British activities following the outbreak of war in Europe in 1939. Khan Sahib's government resigned in protest, as did all Congress ministries in India, in token opposition to Britain's war effort. In 1942, the Frontier was hit by a number of disturbances that were incited by Gandhi and Red Shirt militants, but for the most part it was business as usual. The following year Jinnah's Muslim League formed interim ministries wherever it could put its people into government, including the North-West Frontier. The Congress majority in the Legislative Assembly boycotted the sessions until the end of the Second World War, when Khan Sahib and Congress were returned to power.

'The fact that the militantly Muslim Pathan Frontier was a stronghold of Congress power in the decade before independence remains one of the great paradoxes of Indian political history,' writes James Spain, who was a personal acquaintance of Gaffar Khan.[11] The explanation of this unholy alliance lay in Gaffar Khan's pragmatism.

He believed in Gandhi's social and economic ideals, but his chief concern was to find a strong backer for the Khudai Khidmatgars, in order to give his movement legitimacy and a national profile. The answer was Congress, and since Congress had mounted the most effective challenge to British rule, Gandhi was chosen as the Red Shirts' natural ally.

Uncharacteristic of most politicians, Abdul Gaffar Khan never wavered from his principles, and continued to espouse the cause of Pakhtunistan to his dying day in 1988, at the ripe old age of 98. In spite of the violent clashes between Hindus and Muslims that took place in the countdown to Partition, he kept his weakened movement in alliance with Congress until the end of British rule. When the North-West Frontier Province was given the choice in a referendum of joining India or Pakistan, the majority of Khudai Khidmatgars refused to vote in favour of Pakistan, in compliance with Gaffar Khan's attack on the British for failing to include the choice of an independent Pathan state. This more or less marked the Red Shirts' last gasp in the political arena, for the movement quickly disintegrated after Partition. Not to be deterred, Gaffar Khan pressed on with his political career and in 1948 he was elected president of the newly-created Awami National Party, the successor to the Khudai Khidmatgar movement. A month later he was arrested for 'sedition against the state' under the Frontier Crimes Regulation and spent the next three years in prison. Amongst other charges, the Pakistanis suspected Gaffar Khan of conspiring with a shadowy Muslim agitator from Waziristan, a mullah who had spent many years on the run, first from the British and later from the Pakistani authorities.

Mirza Ali came into prominence in March 1936, on the heels of a crisis triggered by the so-called Islam Bibi affair. Earlier that year several of the Pathan tribes were on the verge of insurrection over a court verdict that had been handed down in the case of the forced conversion and marriage of a 15-year-old Hindu girl. Ram Kori, known as Islam Bibi through her conversion, had married a Pathan student from Bannu, Syed Amir Noor Ali Shah, who carried his bride off to a village in Waziristan. Islam Bibi's relations brought a charge of abduction against Shah and this in turn resulted in the intervention of British troops to recover the girl.

The Islam Bibi scandal also triggered a radical change in Mirza Ali's life. Until that time he had lived a quiet existence as an obscure imam at a mosque in Ipi, a village in the Daur territory of the lower Tochi Valley of North Waziristan. He was regarded as a man of principle and saintliness, one who, moreover, had never shown any unfriendliness towards the British. When the protests began to heat up, the Political Officer in Waziristan, accompanied by two companies of Tochi Scouts, with a squadron of RAF bombers circling overhead, persuaded the tribesmen to allow Islam Bibi to plead her case before a tribal *jirga*. But before this could take place, the troops intervened and whisked the girl and her family off to the Punjab. The husband was arrested and charged with abduction of a minor. He was found guilty and sentenced to two years' imprisonment. That was when the gentle holy man from Waziristan, known till then as Mirza Ali, donned the mantle of the notorious Faqir of Ipi.

The Daurs were in a state of high agitation, to the point that a *lashkar* was raised and several thousand tribesmen were threatening to stage a protest march on Bannu, an act that was certain to degenerate into a looting spree. The Faqir of Ipi, who was about 44, though his exact age was never known, saw this assemblage of warriors as a signal from God to take up the sword of Islam against the infidel. The Daurs were made of lesser stuff than their Mahsud and Wazir neighbours, so when the Government sent a flying column of Tochi Scouts to disperse the marchers, the tribesmen quietly dispersed without a shot being fired. 'The Faqir from Ipi fled in disgust, after laying his curse on the Daurs for their defection and on the Wazirs for not supporting him sufficiently,' writes Frank Leeson, a British officer who in 1936 was serving in the region with the North Waziristan Khassadars. 'Ipi found refuge at a place called Biche Kashkai in the lower Khaisora Valley, where he built himself a house and a mosque, and . . . set himself actively to foment trouble.'[12] There the Faqir cleverly forged an alliance with a Mahsud priest, Mullah Fazal Din, the son of the infamous Mullah Powindah who for years had been the chief instigator of numerous Mahsud attacks against British interests.

The Government was resolved to take stern measures to abort the emergence of a Red Shirt-type movement in Waziristan. The Wazirs and Mahsuds represented the most serious threat to stability because of their unyielding hostility to the British, influenced to no small degree by their close ties with Afghanistan. The Faqir already had five hundred armed Afghans under his command. These men had slipped across the border from Birmal, the only part of Waziristan on the Afghan side of the Durand Line. General Sir John Coleridge, the popular, avuncular commander nicknamed 'Daddy Coleridge', led two columns of British troops and Indian sepoys into the Khaisora Valley, where the Faqir was holed up, as a show of strength and in order to clear the way for road building in the area. The river valley is strategically located south of the Tochi road, from where it was an easy matter to threaten communications with Razmak and the administered areas around Bannu. If the Army's purported peaceful advance were to encounter resistance, Coleridge planned to employ all the force at his disposal to take the Faqir into custody, thus nipping in the bud the mullah's fledgling career as an anti-Government troublemaker.

What had been envisaged as almost a large-scale *gasht*, or patrol, quickly turned into some of the bitterest fighting ever seen in Waziristan. The Government troops marched straight into a trap that had been laid by a *lashkar* of several thousand heavily armed Pathans from both sides of the border. The route lay through a scrub-covered valley pock-marked with hillside caves. Two Wazir snipers lay concealed in these caves, waiting until the lead troops were at short range, when they opened fire with deadly accuracy. Eleven men fell in the first fusillade. It was not until darkness was nearly upon the road that an Army machine-gunner, spotting the rifle flashes, was able to silence the snipers. On 26 November, the first day of hostilities, two British majors and a soldier were among fifteen Indian other ranks killed and sixty-six wounded. The Faqir of Ipi's prestige soared after this engagement and the tribesmen lost no time in pursuing the retiring columns into the Tochi Valley.

In late December Coleridge was ordered back to Khaisora to retaliate for a humiliation which the Government, in its weakened state, could not allow to go unpunished. The Faqir had set up his command post in the region's cave network and on New Year's Eve the RAF carried out its first attacks on this inaccessible area, using high explosives, incendiary and anti-personnel bombs. Yet the bombs failed to hit their target and the Faqir of Ipi escaped unharmed.

On 4 March of the following year the Faqir raised the stakes by calling on all Muslims in Government service to abandon their posts and join a general jihad against the British. Those who failed to do so, he emphasised menacingly, would be denied Muslim funeral ceremonies. This was highly persuasive rhetoric and it set alarm bells ringing in the ears of many ignorant tribesmen. The fear of eternal damnation had, in past conflicts, not failed to trigger desertions in the ranks. 'Support for him continued to increase and reinforcements came in again from southern Waziristan,' says Frank Leeson. 'Owing to the threat to the roads the Army began running its traffic only on certain pre-selected days . . . in convoys with armoured car and infantry escorts.'[13] This became an established tactical routine in Waziristan in the 1930s and it continued as standard operational procedure for ten years, through the Second World War. It was called Road Opening Days. Under this system, eight times a month a military lorry convoy left Bannu to take supplies and personnel up a 70-mile road to Razmak, the main centre of Indian Army presence in Waziristan. 'The dates were kept secret to discourage anyone with evil intention to plan their activities,' recalls Rodney Bennett, a former intelligence officer with the 2nd Punjab Regiment in Waziristan.

> The high ground on either side of the road had to be occupied by the Army, the Frontier militia or Khassadar units. Tribal emissaries were sent to Bannu to gauge the Army's strength, and then plan their tactics accordingly. By the sixth week one had to be careful, for the tribesmen had infinite patience and would watch and wait to see if we lowered our guard. The tribesmen's tactics were similar to a football pitch. The danger came from someone on the wing who passes the ball to a player by the goal post. A Pathan gang would fire at a certain position whilst a knifing party would go in from the other side.[14]

Bennett acknowledged that the Army's weakness lay in the fact that the initiative was with the tribesmen, who could choose the time and place to engage the convoys. This soldier's frustration found its expression in verse:

When we plan for modern war,
Common sense is to the fore,
But up here that is a thing that can't be said.
The Pathan can do his worst,
Because we let him shoot us first,
And we cannot answer back before we're dead.

This was the predicament in which the Army found itself on 29 March, when the Faqir raised one thousand Wazirs to attack an infantry brigade out on Road Opening Day duties. The action turned into a melée of machine gun fire and dagger thrusts that lasted for the better part of the day, with heavy casualties on both sides. The Mahsuds stepped into the fray a few days later when they ambushed a large motorised convoy on the road, resulting in another sharp engagement and a total disregard for the dangers of machine guns and armoured cars on the part of the Pathans. In one battle a section of armoured vehicles raced to help some machine-gunners whose position had been overwhelmed by knife-wielding tribesmen. They found the enemy casually stripping the rounds from the machine gun belts and leading away the transport mules.

After a short lull in the fighting, a third campaign was mounted in the Khaisora district. Part of the motive for this operation was to exact revenge for the murder of two British officers. Captain John Anthony Keogh of the 12th Frontier Force Regiment and Lieutenant Ronald Nicholson Beatty of the Tochi Scouts were gunned down in road ambushes within twenty-four hours of one another. There is a twist to the Beatty killing which reveals something of the tribesmen's ability to keep the upper hand. The Government had collected 50,000 rupees in fines from the maliks under the terms of submission handed down after the second Khaisora campaign. Beatty was driving to the Daur district with 32,000 rupees in cash to pay allowances to a unit of khassadars stationed there. The ambush party killed Beatty at close range and then made off with the money, effectively recovering nearly two-thirds of the fine, with which to purchase arms and ammunition.

General Coleridge's plan was to deal the Faqir's men a definitive blow by inflicting the heaviest losses possible. By wiping out large numbers of enemy fighters, with aerial bombardments on open positions and heavy use of mountain batteries and machine guns, Coleridge hoped to convince the Pathans that they were playing a losing game. This was a strategy endorsed by many military commanders who were becoming increasingly frustrated by having to confront hit-and-run guerrilla tactics.

One veteran Frontiersman sums up the unabashed hardliner school: 'In operating against tribesmen we have two objectives in view. Emphatically to kill as many as possible, that being by far the most convincing form of argument. To destroy his villages and stores of food, and capture his cattle and sheep.'[15] A brigade of Coleridge's division set up camp at Biche Kashai, one of the Faqir's strongholds, where the men settled down for the night in preparation for launching their offensive the following morning. The Pathans had other plans: a thousand tribesmen waited for nightfall before moving in for the attack, using grenades and home-made bombs. The troops were kept up all night in a pitched battle to prevent the Wazirs breaking through the camp perimeter. The men were so exhausted after this all-night engagement that the advance had to be postponed, with a consequent demoralising effect on the Army. The strike force eventually moved into action on 29 April with heavy artillery fire and carpet bombing raids by an RAF squadron. The tribesmen were driven into the hills and on 3 May Coleridge marched his troops back to Razmak, the operation having been pronounced a success.

The peace that descended on Waziristan was, as usual, a short-lived interlude between campaigns. Within weeks the Faqir was back raiding in British administered territory, looting and kidnapping at will. Coleridge led his columns to the Faqir's base of operations, destroyed a number of villages, and then turned his guns on the Mahsuds to the south. Towards the end of 1937 the fighting died down with the onset of winter. The Government had suffered nearly a thousand casualties out of a force of forty thousand men, and the Faqir was well out of reach, holed up in Afghanistan. The pursuit continued, but the Faqir always managed to stay one step ahead of the authorities, enjoying the sanctuary of his Afghan hosts when needed and, it goes without saying, the protection of his Waziristan co-religionists.

It might be useful from a historical perspective to consider some of the parallels between the hunt for the Faqir of Ipi and the operations that are taking place, seventy years later, against Osama bin Laden and his followers. There is no doubt that both these preachers of jihad were funded by foreign paymasters. Bin Laden's global terrorist network has backers throughout the Muslim world, and Al Qaeda is known to operate an efficient worldwide drug and money laundering operation. The coffers of Al Qaeda were filled from sources as diverse as the West and Saudi Arabia during the fight against the Soviets in Afghanistan. Protection racket money from the Saudis and other Gulf states finds its way into Al Qaeda cells, along with hefty subsidies from tame Islamic charities and income from the booming Afghan poppy crop, boosted of course by America's 'war on terror' in Afghanistan which has restored the power of local warlords. Ipi's funding came from various sources, all of which shared a common interest in fomenting destabilisation in British India, and later in Pakistan. The Faqir collected Soviet subsidies in the 1920s and early 1930s. Congress was also a contributor to his anti-British cause, and during the Second World War the Faqir was pocketing money from Axis donors. The Germans, who had stationed 150 agents in Afghanistan, as well as the Italian legation in Kabul, were disbursing regular sums to the Faqir. In 1940, this enabled him to carry out on average two outrages a week in British India.

Ipi and Bin Laden are very much their own men, with agendas that do not necessarily conform to their sponsors' objectives. Bin Laden pays lip service to the cause of international jihad and the destruction of Israel: his personal targets are Saudi Arabian oil and Pakistani nuclear weapons. The Faqir of Ipi became an impassioned devotee of Pakhtunistan and never took seriously the calls by Congress and Nazi Germany for the overthrow of British rule in India.

At the height of the Waziristan campaign the Government had the equivalent of nearly three divisions in the field, whose mission was to track down and capture the elusive demagogue of Ipi. The Faqir, like Bin Laden, who has almost certainly found a refuge in Waziristan, initially fled to a network of remote caves, out of reach of the Army's mountain batteries and the RAF's bombers. It will be remembered that Osama bin Laden's first hideout after the terrorist attacks of 11 September 2001 was the Tora Bora cave complex close to the Pakistani border. Both fugitives could count on sanctuary and active support in tribal territory, above all in Waziristan, which today, as in the past, remains the main stronghold of anti-government hostility within tribal territory. The debacle the Pakistani Army suffered in its South Waziristan offensive of 2005 was in many ways a replica of the pounding that General Coleridge's troops took in 1936 in the very same theatre of operations. No moral is implied here – this is simply to highlight the extraordinary coincidences that exist between the two men's careers. However, it may be useful to draw attention to the fact that, despite a vast outlay of funds and deployment of ground troops and air power, neither the British nor the Pakistanis ever managed to lay their hands on the Faqir of Ipi, who continued to preach jihad and stir up tribal revolt until his death in 1960.

The Partition of India is a vast and painful subject that falls outside the remit of this book, except in one respect. When Prime Minister Clement Attlee announced the Government's plan for Indian independence to the House of Commons in early June 1947, the North-West Frontier Province was left dangling as a conundrum that could only be peacefully resolved through a referendum. It was essential to have the tribes under the flag of Pakistan or India, the former being the logical choice. If the Muslim part of the Punjab opted for Partition, which it did, the Frontier province would find itself in isolation and easy prey to Afghan intrigues. Jinnah was delighted with this arrangement, which he confidently expected to precipitate the ouster of Congress from Frontier politics. It was an accurate forecast: on 20 July 1947, for the first time in history, the Pathans expressed their opinion through the ballot box. As has already been recorded, the Red Shirts boycotted the ballot. However, slightly more than 292,000 tribesmen went to the polls to cast an overwhelming vote in favour of union with Pakistan. The exact result was 286,370 for and 2,874 against, with a turnout of 50.99 per cent of the eligible electorate, an impressive show of political enthusiasm when compared with the average voter turnout in a US election.

In 1933 Choudary Rahmat Ali, an Indian law student at Cambridge University, proposed the creation of a separate Muslim state in India. He gave it the name of 'Pakistan', using letters from five territories of British India: 'P' for Punjab, 'A' for 'Afghan' North-West Frontier Province, 'KI' for Kashmir, 'S' for Sind and 'TAN' from Baluchis*tan*. On 14 August 1947 this acronym, dreamt up in a Cambridge college, became the Islamic Republic of Pakistan. For the British, Partition was in many ways the end of a love affair, for it would be hard to find other words to express this emotional commitment to an unlikely bedfellow. The lament of one British officer reflects the sadness felt on departure by the many thousands of soldiers, civil servants and *box-wallahs* who served the Raj. 'That is the end: an order is given by the British officer commanding the company, and in one second abandonment has given place to discipline. The fire is stamped out, and in orderly ranks the battalion melts away in the darkness as the final note of the "Last Post" vibrates in the night.'[16]

SEVEN

'Did we not fight well?'

Nature abhors a vacuum but to a government it is absolute anathema, more so when it involves an unguarded border. The British departure from India left a gaping power vacuum on the North-West Frontier. The Raj usually kept between thirty thousand and forty thousand troops stationed on the Frontier in the years before Partition. Naturally, these units could count on naval and air support from the rest of British India. 'With the British withdrawal, all this disappeared, except that minority portion of the British Indian military establishment which fell to Pakistan,' says James Spain. 'This totalled something less than 200,000 men in all.'[1] This may seem a sizeable force, except that almost immediately most of these troops were diverted to Kashmir to deal with their country's border dispute with India.

Within a month of Partition the wheel had turned full circle: the fledgling Government of Pakistan began withdrawing regular army units from tribal territory, following recommendations issued by a commission that had begun its review of post-independence military policy for the Frontier as early as 1944. Pakistan needed all the troops it could muster to cope with the rapidly deteriorating political conflict in Kashmir. The strategy was to garrison the army outposts on the Frontier with a beefed-up corps of native levies, and this plan was given the code name 'Operation Curzon'. It was an endorsement of the policy laid down by the man who, fifty years earlier, had deployed Pathan militia units along the border with Afghanistan. The transfer of troops was completed in the first half of December. The last outpost to be handed over to the militias was Razmak near Bannu, in North

Waziristan, which also happened to be the largest and costliest fort on the North-West Frontier.

The march from Razmak began on 18 December, though the exact date of withdrawal was kept a closely-guarded secret to the last minute in order to minimise the risk of the columns walking into an ambush on the road. The *Daily Telegraph* correspondent who accompanied the 4,700-strong column described it as

> a general withdrawal through hostile territory – the first major military operation the Pakistan Army had undertaken and the largest of its kind in the long and tragic history of the Frontier. Almost every yard of the 70-mile road winding through mountain passes north of Waziristan will bring its chance of ambush by tribesmen who are still under the influence of the Faqir of Ipi.[2]

There was in fact almost daily loss of life from sniping on the seventeen motor convoys that wended their way along the icy road to Bannu.

Sir George Cunningham, Governor of the North-West Frontier Province, volunteered to join the march as a show of goodwill to the departing troops, but the military authorities refused to accept responsibility for his safety. His loss would have thrown the province into convulsion, for Cunningham was revered as 'one of us' by the tribesmen. On 14 August, only hours after the handover ceremony to Pakistan, the Governor drove through the streets of Peshawar to find his car mobbed by nearly a thousand people, all shouting 'Pakistan Zindabad!' and 'Jinnah Zindabad!' To Cunningham's astonishment the crowd then began to cheer, 'Cunningham Governor Zindabad!' 'Indeed, it was rather like the Rectorial installation in St Andrew's all over again,' he recalls. 'At one point a band, rather surprisingly, struck up *God Save the King!*'[3]

Shortly after Operation Curzon came into force, the Pathan tribes were out on the warpath, only this time the enemy was not the British master. In October 1947 thousands of tribesmen were gathered in Peshawar and loaded into lorries. The motorised columns drove due east to Kashmir to claim this predominantly Muslim territory for

Pakistan. Much has been made of this 'spontaneous' rush by the Pathans to defend their religion and homeland. Cunningham, for one, was convinced that the whole operation had been orchestrated by the Pakistanis. In his diary entry for 25 October, he states that the Pathans were speeding almost unopposed towards Srinagar, whose large European population faced the imminent threat of widespread looting and disorder if the tribesmen were to take the city. 'I sent for Abdul Qayum, my Chief Minister . . . and told him that I knew, or suspected, pretty well all that had been going on in the [North-West Frontier] Province, and who had been instigating our tribesmen to go to Kashmir. He grinned.'[4] Apart from the political forces behind this 'jihad', it was an open secret that the ruler of Swat was bankrolling the Kashmir campaign.

'On 22 October, thousands of tribesmen invaded Kashmir, bent upon Hindu women, loot and murder,' says Michael Edwardes. 'Though the Pakistan government denied any responsibility for the tribal invasion, it undoubtedly supplied the tribes with transport, machine guns, mortars and light artillery, while Pakistani army officers, ostensibly on leave, led the contingents.'[5]

Jinnah himself turned a blind eye to the Pathan offensive on the grounds that it could only be a good thing if it managed to thwart the intention of Hari Singh, Maharajah of Kashmir, to seek accession of his realm to India. In the end, Pakistan failed to prevent this happening, with the result that Kashmir has since been a battleground threatening global as well as regional stability. But in October 1947, Kashmir's fate was hanging by a thread. Military intelligence in Peshawar fully expected the Pathan *lashkars* to be in Srinagar by nightfall on 26 October. It was only the swift airborne deployment of Indian troops to the area that brought the Pathan advance to a halt 25 miles from the city. Had the paratroopers delayed a day or two longer, what is now divided Kashmir would have fallen entirely to Pakistan. Fortunately for India, the Pathans got bogged down in bitter feuding over the spoils of war when they stood almost at the gates of Srinagar. The *lashkars* had by then lost their momentum and thus failed to capture the city's vital airstrip, which was taken by a company of Sikh Rifles.

In a very short while thousands of Pakistani troops found themselves tied down in Kashmir, a dispute that was to ignite two fully fledged wars with India. Now it was Afghanistan that stepped to centre stage, blatantly trumpeting support for the 'Pakhtunistan' cause, the historic battle cry of the Faqir of Ipi and Abdul Gaffar Khan, who were still out there spreading the gospel of Pathan nationhood. It goes without saying that Pakhtunistan, as envisaged by Afghanistan, meant rolling the Durand Line eastward, back to the Indus. To this end, Kabul spared no effort pouring money and arms into pro-Pakhtunistan movements, while training young Pakistani Pathans in the art of guerrilla warfare.

In the late 1950s the Frontier was rocked by a series of terrorist attacks, the handiwork of these Pathan youths who had been indoctrinated and trained in Afghanistan. In 1961 Pakistan broke off diplomatic relations with Kabul, an understandable reaction under the circumstances, but one that was to raise the temperature between the two countries and which allowed Kabul an even freer hand in stirring up political turmoil on the Frontier.

Hardly had the ink dried on the handover of power than the new state of Pakistan found itself bogged down on two fronts: to the east a war of guns in Kashmir and to the west a war of words with Afghanistan, a showdown that was on the brink of escalating into open hostilities. The Soviet Union was unhappy over an initiative taken by the USA to develop close ties with the government of Pakistan. India had found a willing ally in Moscow, a relationship that over the longer term carried its cost in political and economic integration with the developed world. The Americans were naturally keen to check Soviet expansionism in the subcontinent. This objective was to be achieved by taking Pakistan under the US wing. Now it was down to the Soviets to shift the next piece on the board, and the way forward was through open as well as covert support for Afghanistan, a country that even Washington had acknowledged in all but name as a client state of Moscow. Part and parcel of this alliance was Russia's encouragement of Afghan agitation for Pakhtunistan.

The first salvo in the political row over Pakhtunistan was fired in September 1947, a few days before the start of the shooting war on the Kashmir front. Afghanistan was the only UN country to vote against Pakistan's bid for membership. By this action, the North-West Frontier was catapulted into the arena of global politics, for Kabul argued that it could not recognise the new state of Pakistan until the Pathans had been allowed to decide their own destiny. Afghanistan demanded a plebiscite on Pathan independence though, oddly enough, there was no call for the Frontier's integration with the several millions of Pathans living west of the Durand Line, in Afghanistan itself.

Gandhi's Congress Party had in fact petitioned the Viceroy, Lord Mountbatten, to include a third option in the Frontier referendum, which was independence from Pakistan and India. Mountbatten's reply was a flat refusal: Nehru, he explained, had already rejected this idea, therefore it was pointless to reintroduce it only weeks before Partition was to take effect. None of the three leading figures involved – Nehru, Gandhi or Mountbatten – was prepared to allow the Frontier issue to derail the Indian Independence Act.

There was little tangible evidence of broad-based popular support amongst the Pathans for the idea of a separate Frontier state, which suggests that the tribal lands were being exploited as a pawn to keep Pakistan on the defensive. Cunningham, in his role of Governor of the North-West Frontier Province, held a *jirga* of tribal elders in November 1947, three months after Partition, to ascertain their views on Pakhtunistan. The elders and maliks were the men who shaped opinion at home and had the power to put the *lashkars* on the march. 'I interviewed the *jirgas* of all the tribes from end to end of the Frontier,' he reported, 'and without exception they stated and confirmed in written statements that they were part of Pakistan, and wished to preserve the same relations with Pakistan as they had with the British.'[6]

Afghanistan's crusade for an independent Pathan state thrust Kabul deeper into the welcoming arms of Soviet Russia. In the early 1950s, Afghanistan recognised and supported the Faqir of Ipi as 'president' of a Pakhtunistan that existed solely in the imagination of the firebrand mullah and his followers. The Faqir ran his 'government' from a network of caves in Waziristan adjacent to the Afghan border. There was almost nothing that resembled a formal structure in this fanciful country that was run by ministers, departments and even a 'national assembly'. The entire apparatus lost its drive and finally ceased to exist after the Faqir's death in 1960. His nephew Niaz Ali Khan assumed the mantle of jihad and was occasionally a nuisance to the Government, but Ali lacked his uncle's personality and leadership qualities. On the other hand, he was only too happy to accept bribes from the Political Agent as payment for good behaviour, and he spent most of his time hiding out in caves on the border and never causing much trouble in North Waziristan.

By and large, the most noticeable change in policy after the British departure was an almost total absence of punitive expeditions against the unruly Frontier tribesmen. From the day of independence to the Pakistani army's 2005 incursion into South Waziristan, only one serious incident of military action took place in tribal territory. It could be argued in the Government's defence that in this particular instance, Afghanistan was widely believed to be the instigator of a tribal revolt in remote Bajaur. This occurred in May of 1961. Pakistan's President Mohammed Ayub Khan announced that an Afghan military force of five to seven brigades was massed on the border opposite Bajaur Agency, where a few light skirmishes had taken place in September of the previous year. The Pakistani Air Force staged a bombing raid on a village where Afghan agents were suspected of having set up an ammunition dump. In retaliation, Afghan troops opened fire with mortars and machine guns on a border post near Bajaur, sparking fresh aerial bombardments to dislodge what Karachi claimed was a force of one thousand Afghan troops that had infiltrated Pakistani territory.

The principal Afghan agent accused of stirring up trouble among the tribes was a shadowy figure named Badshah Gul. According to Pakistani sources, Gul had been distributing ammunition to the Bajaur tribesmen with such munificence as to bring about a dramatic drop in the price of bullets. Within the space of a few months, the cost of ten rounds for a .303 rifle fell from thirty-three to as little as five rupees. Gul was also supplying the tribesmen with money and transistor radios in the hope of yielding a crop of disaffection and rebellion against the Government. Pakistani intelligence sources concede that Gul's efforts to buy support from local tribal leaders met with some success. They point the finger at the Khan of Jandal and Nawab of Dir, though both failed to rally their kinsmen to stage a full-scale uprising. Pakistan's reaction, apart from the air strike, was to sever diplomatic ties with Afghanistan and shut the international border. Kabul came out the loser in this episode, for with the border closure Afghanistan was driven deeper into the Soviet camp. As the US diplomat on the spot, James Spain, noted, 'The result was Afghanistan's virtually complete dependence on the Soviet Union for transportation and communication facilities and a necessary cutting back of U.S. assistance programmes, supplies and equipment, which normally flowed through Pakistan.'[7]

The Bajaur conflict marked another episode in a conflict that had been rising to a violent head since 1955, when Pakistan merged its four provinces to create the One Unit of West Pakistan. The two units, East and West Pakistan, coexisted on either side of the Indian border until the system was dissolved in 1970, one year before Pakistan and India went to war over East Pakistan, which broke away to become Bangladesh. The temporary disappearance of the North-West Frontier Province was not to Afghanistan's liking. The Afghan monarch, King Zahir Shah, and the country's prime minister, Mohammed Daud Khan, went so far as to hoist the Pakhtunistan flag at a rally in Kabul. The amalgamation of the provinces into the One Unit structure deprived Afghanistan of its most effective tool for thrashing Pakistan and for taking the spotlight off political and social failings at home. The rabble-rousing exercise achieved its objective. Afghan mobs took to the streets, with the compliance of the police, who stood idly by as the rioters ransacked Pakistan's Embassy in Kabul and legations in Jalalabad and Kandahar. In retaliation, Pathan tribesmen in Peshawar demolished the Afghan consulate and a *lashkar* of Wazirs assembled to march on Kabul. Fortunately, calmer heads prevailed in Karachi and the Government persuaded the tribesmen to call off what would have amounted to an invasion of foreign territory. The situation took a menacing turn when Afghanistan mobilised its armed forces and recalled its ambassador to Pakistan, dragging the two countries closer to war than at any time since Pakistan's independence. The crisis was defused only by last-minute Saudi mediation, but it brought home the message that Pakhtunistan represented far more than a domestic issue. Indeed, Afghanistan's ultimate ambition envisaged the carving-up of the existing state of Pakistan, a move that would have led to open warfare and the almost inevitable involvement of India and the Soviet Union.

As evidence of Kabul's territorial designs, as early as June 1947 the Afghan prime minister Mohammed Hashim Khan unabashedly stated in an interview in Bombay that if there was not to be an independent Pakhtunistan, sovereignty over Pakistan's North-West Frontier Province should be transferred to Afghanistan so that this land-locked country might gain an outlet to the sea, presumably with the eventual annexation of Baluchistan.[8] 'The denunciation of the Durand Line implicit in the claim of Hashim Khan, was an essential preliminary in the prosecution of Afghan irredentism advancing its territorial claim to the Arabian Sea,' says Pakistani author Musa Khan Jalalzai.[9] It was of course very much in Moscow's interest to encourage Afghanistan to pursue this demand. Since the days of the Great Game the Russians had aspired to a warm water outlet and Afghanistan, a weak state dependent on Russian aid, was just the vehicle for achieving this objective.

It would be a mistake to ignore the legitimate political aspirations of 37.6 million people, which is the number of Pathans living on either side of the Frontier, making this the world's largest tribe. But this is quite different from manipulating the doctrine of self-determination, a tactic that Afghanistan has employed with varying degrees of success over the years. The problem is complicated by the Pathan tribes being divided by an ill-conceived political border, although for the Pathans living in Pakistan this does not preclude the granting of some form of autonomy within a federal framework. There are historical and contemporary precedents for such an arrangement. One might consider, for instance, the case of the Spanish and French Basques. The latter live in Europe's most centralised state, politically indistinguishable from their fellow citizens of Normandy or Haute Savoie. The Basques living south of the Pyrenees, while of the same ethnic stock, enjoy a large measure of self-rule within the federalist Spanish state.

Even the British, in occasional moments of calm and with the end of the Raj in sight, acknowledged the case for tribal self-government. A policy paper issued only three years before Partition tacitly admitted the failure, after nearly a century, to bring the tribesmen into the fold of 'civilised' society. The Government recognised that the Frontier lived under varying shades of anarchy, from a 'passive state of political depression' in the northern tribal areas to an active state of internal disorder coupled with open guerrilla hostility in Waziristan. 'In short our diagnosis is that the patient is suffering from a lack of good government, just as a human being might suffer from a lack of Vitamin B,' the report states. 'If this diagnosis is correct, then the obvious treatment is to supply the good government that is lacking.' The question was whether this was to be imposed from without by force of arms – a line of approach that in the past had not met with resounding success – or through internal self-government. The second view would imply the abandonment of the policy of non-interference in tribal domestic affairs and its substitution by one of constructive interference. 'It is possible', the Government statement continues, 'to visualise a series of self-governing tribal units covering the whole length of the border, each possessing a clearly defined constitution, federated possibly under a central tribal body, and maintaining ordered relations with the central and provincial governments.'[10]

It says a great deal about the British Government's concern for India's welfare that colonial civil servants devoted their time to drawing up post-war policy documents, with Britain engaged in desperate fighting in Europe and with few giving long odds on the outcome. The Government had even set up a 'Commission for Post-War Planning, North-West Frontier Province', whose remit was to devise a scheme for the economic development of FATA. The official thinking was that any such plan needed to be built and implemented in a workable political framework of government for the tribal areas. This is where the Commission's efforts came unstuck, for the Indian Independence Act had not yet been promulgated and no one could forecast how Government relations with the tribes would fare in the short term. The head of the Commission addressed these concerns in a letter to the Governor, Sir Olaf Caroe:

> Since political conditions in the tribal areas are at present uncertain and insecure, it seems to me inevitable that any approach to the tribesmen on the subject of the economic development of their country would be met by questions, if not also suspicion, as to the ultimate intentions of Government in regard to the political future of the tribes.[11]

The question put to Caroe was whether the North-West Frontier authorities were in a position to hasten a decision on tribal self-government, since in the present state of uncertainty it was almost impossible to progress on the economic development front. The Governor was a true friend of the Pathans and felt a genuine concern for their welfare. Whatever his views on the subject, however, all efforts to improve the lot of the tribesmen were shortly swept into the background by the rush to Indian independence.

The Commission's findings embodied some noble thoughts, but it was not to be. Instead, it was left to Pakistan to try and make good on Britain's belated, half-hearted attempts to mend its fences with the Pathans. The fatal flaw in British policy was that from the outset the Raj treated the tribes as a military instead of an economic problem. This was tacitly acknowledged in the Commission's letter to Caroe, which went on to add a caveat to the drive for economic development, one which brings home the state of undeclared war that existed for nearly one hundred years between the Pathan tribes and the Government of India. The underlying fear was that, whatever material improvements were brought to the tribal areas, these would be channelled into warlike instead of economic pursuits. It was therefore imperative first to resolve the question of the Frontier tribes' political status. 'Any wealth which the tribesmen would acquire through the economic development of their country . . . would almost certainly be devoted to the collection of arms and to the organisation of their people on a military basis for resistance against a foreign invader or even for the purpose of aggressive action against British India,' the Commission concludes.[12]

Pakistan, on the other hand, has by and large taken a more enlightened view of its Pathan citizens. Of course, the government that took over after Partition had the benefit of sharing a religion with the Frontier tribes, a fact whose importance cannot be overemphasised. It is doubtful, not to say unthinkable, that British negotiators could have sat down with the chief maliks of the Pathan tribes and obtained their sworn allegiance to an alien government. With the termination of British rule, all agreements and treaties that bound the tribal areas with the Government of India were abrogated under the Indian Independence Act. Parenthetically, this was also one of the arguments used by Afghanistan to declare the Durand Line null and void. A lively legal wrangle still continues over whether a successor state can enforce a treaty signed between a foreign power and a government that has ceased to exist. Constitutionally, after Partition the Pathan territories lying outside the administered districts became independent. It was therefore up to Pakistan to enter into fresh agreements and treaties with the tribal leaders.

'For this purpose, the new state of Pakistan secured through its political agents in the tribal agencies an agreement with the maliks in 1947', according to a research paper by a leading Pakistani think tank.

> Under this agreement the maliks declared the tribal areas as part of Pakistan and pledged to provide any help to the new country whenever the need arose. They also made a commitment to be peaceful and law-abiding and to maintain friendly relations with the people of the settled districts. In return and on the foregoing conditions, the Government of Pakistan pledged to continue the existing benefits.[13]

The 'benefits' in question were the tribal allowances, some 50 million rupees a year, a sum greater than Afghanistan's total annual budget, which the British doled out to the tribal maliks in exchange for undertakings to keep the roads open and restrain the tribesmen from raiding towns and police posts in administered territory. Pakistan has also exempted the tribes from income tax, though it could be argued that it was hardly worth the risk to send revenue agents into remote areas to collect a pittance in taxes from heavily armed, hostile tribesmen.

That was the carrot: the stick was the Frontier Crimes Regulation. After independence, the Muslim League administration in power in the North-West Frontier Province found the FCR a useful tool for clamping down on political opponents like the Red Shirts. Abdul Gaffar Khan was tried and convicted several times under this statute, which excludes legal counsel, trial by jury and habeas corpus, and which vests in the Political Agent authoritarian powers that reduce the defendant to the status of a medieval serf.

Since independence, there have been repeated calls for the reform and even the repeal of the 1901 law governing the tribal areas. It is argued that the ultimate objective has to be the inclusion of the tribal areas within the national framework. 'The present order, though it has survived for more than a hundred years is, nevertheless, patently an anachronism in the modern day world,' says the noted Pakistani diplomat Humayun Khan. 'It would be difficult to identify many nations which concede that large areas of their land and millions of their inhabitants are immune to their laws and not subject to their control. The plan becomes all the less tenable when these areas and these people occupy the marches along a sensitive border.'[14]

The Frontier Crimes Regulation exists as a self-perpetuating evil in at least two respects. The writ of Pakistan does not run in FATA. The responsibility of administering the tribal areas rests with the Federal Government through the Governor of the North-West Frontier Province. What this means in practice is that the Pakistan Constitution does not apply to FATA, and only the President of the country has the authority to extend any federal laws to the area. Political parties are not allowed to function in tribal territory and the maliks who contest regional elections do so as independents. The Soviet invasion of Afghanistan in 1979 and Al Qaeda's attacks on the

USA in 2001 propelled the Pathan homeland into the front line of global conflict, where it is firmly rooted today thanks to the infiltration of Taliban remnants and foreign terrorists, and also the flourishing drug trade. The ebb and flow of Afghan hostility towards Pakistan has also kept political tension along the Durand Line on high alert over the years. From a tactical point of view, it is far more pragmatic for Islamabad to make use of the FCR, however despotic, than to have to work through due process of law in order to exercise control of the border region and its inhabitants. Secondly, as long as the people of FATA remain the poorest in Pakistan, the Pathans will continue to treat any Government presence in their territory with suspicion and truculence, making a hard-line policy the most expedient option for dealing with the tribes.

The life of the Frontier Pathan can hardly be described as enviable. A British journalist on a tour of FATA in the 1950s expressed his joy at the absence of police stations, road signs and all the paraphernalia we associate with organised Western society. He called the tribal belt 'the last free place on Earth'. Of course, the reporter filed his report from a well-heated, comfortable London newsroom. The story is different in the barren, parched hills of Waziristan, for instance. Of the seven tribal agencies, only Kurram is blessed with enough arable land to call agriculture a basic economic activity. On the other hand, 85 per cent of the tribal belt is considered unfit for cultivation, and only a small portion of the land can be used for animal husbandry. This has compelled the tribesmen to seek other pursuits, most notably transport, much of which involves smuggling of every conceivable type of merchandise, from drugs and arms to top-of-the-range Japanese cars and tobacco. A Pathan is to be found at the wheel of almost every one of the psychedelically painted juggernauts one sees rumbling up the Khyber Pass, belching out huge clouds of black diesel fumes. His consignment might well be a container load of television sets or refrigerators that has 'fallen off the back' of a tanker docked at Karachi port. He will drive the lorry into Afghanistan, in compliance with his bill of lading, and making appropriate payments at informal checkpoints along the route, and once across the border the lorry will be turned round and driven back to the smugglers' bazaars of

Peshawar. Contraband costs the Pakistani exchequer a huge amount in lost revenue, but the upside is that this flourishing trade has eliminated the tribesmen's need to go raiding in the settled districts.

Pakistan held provincial elections in October 2001, three years after General Pervez Musharraf seized power in a bloodless coup. The outcome of the vote in the North-West Frontier Province confirmed the trend towards Islamist radicalisation that has taken root in the region since the Soviet invasion of Afghanistan, when thousands of mujahidin fighters fled across the border. During the Soviet occupation of Afghanistan, Pakistan's Inter-Services Intelligence (ISI) sent cadres of mujahidin recruits to fight the Russians. These Pakistani youths came into contact with anti-Soviet guerrillas who had arrived in Afghanistan from the Middle East and other countries with a large Muslim population. After the Soviet withdrawal in 1989, the ISI sent many of these young Pathan fighters along with foreign elements to infiltrate and carry out terrorist activities in Kashmir. With the opening of a dialogue between Pakistan and India on the future of Kashmir, the insurgents started returning to FATA, where many of the Arabs, Chechens and others settled in tribal agencies, mainly in Waziristan, and married into Pathan families. These people continue to be loyal to the Taliban and they have helped a lot of Pakistani and Afghan extremists to slip across the border into FATA. Together, they have fomented an unwholesome political radicalisation of the region, which bore fruit in an overwhelming victory in the October 2001 elections for a coalition of six Muslim fundamentalist parties.

The Muttahida Majlis-i-Amal (United Action Council), known as the MMA, won an absolute majority in the regional legislature and took sixty of the 342 seats in the country's National Assembly. The MMA is bitterly opposed to General Musharraf and his American allies, and they make no secret of their pro-Taliban sympathies. In fact, much of the Taliban leadership was trained in the madrasas of Jamiat Ulma-e-Islam, the faction that dominates the MMA coalition. The mullahs who have taken over the Frontier government are working to install a strict sharia, or fundamentalist, regime in the

North-West Frontier Province. So far, the 'reforms' they have brought in have been largely trivial and of a cosmetic nature. The MMA ordered the closure of the bar at the Pearl Continental Hotel in Peshawar, Pakistan's only hotel bar that served as a watering hole for the foreign press. Pictures of women were removed from advertising hoardings, and passengers travelling to the Province by coach were obliged to suffer the inconvenience of having their headphones collected after crossing the bridge at Attok, in compliance with a ban on music on public transport.

To the Government's consternation, the MMA has also begun some more serious muscle-flexing exercises. After prayers on 30 March 2003, groups of white-bearded clerics led two hundred thousand people through the streets of Peshawar calling for the death of George W. Bush. It was one of the biggest political demonstrations ever staged in Pakistan, and a dramatic reminder of the North-West Frontier's potential for radical activism.

A few weeks after that march, an incident took place that suggested that the Government had been badly shaken by the demonstration and was determined to take action against the MMA. Maulana Azam Tariq, the head of a proscribed radical political party, the SSP, which had been declared a terrorist organisation by Pakistan and was placed on a terrorist watch-list by the United States, was freed from custody. This unsavoury bigot faced about sixty criminal charges, including murder and incitement to sectarian violence, yet he emerged as the leader of the Millat-e-Islamia, or Party of the Islamic Nation, a sanitised reincarnation of the SSP. In their study of Islamist terrorist networks, the French academics Mariam Abou Zahab and Olivier Roy state their conviction that Azam Tariq was granted his freedom in exchange for an undertaking to counteract the MMA's radicalisation of the North-West Frontier.

'Although Azam Tariq denied it, there is every reason to believe that his release and his election to the National Assembly [he stood as an independent candidate in 2002] were the result of a deal with the Government which apparently wanted to use him to undermine the Muttahida Majlis-e-Amal.'[15] The authors of these comments are not alone in their belief that Azam Tariq was acting for the Government in an attempt to sabotage the religious rulers in Peshawar – he was gunned down in the street in Islamabad in October 2003.

One can easily sympathise with the Government's fear of creeping 'Talibanisation' in the North-West Frontier Province, but a clamp-down on the MMA, which Musharraf could impose by decree using his presidential prerogative, would only serve to place a halo of martyrdom on the mullahs' heads. The National Assembly has the power to overturn laws passed by the provincial assembly. But it is of vital importance to avoid over-reacting to this perceived threat to stability. The Frontier has survived intact under far more trying circumstances than the present situation. The Soviet invasion of Afghanistan in 1979 touched off an almost unprecedented refugee movement, but one that caused little disruption to civil order in the tribal and settled areas of the Frontier. More than three million people, about a third of Afghanistan's population, had to be given shelter and fed in Pakistan's neglected and poorest province. In spite of the pressure this wave of immigrants put on the local economy and job market, there was no noticeable increase in prices, no food shortage and no depression of wage rates due to the influx of thousands of job seekers.[16]

There is just cause to assert that the threat to stability posed by the MMA is more perceived than real. The clerics have declared it contrary to sharia law for male coaches to train women athletes and for male journalists to cover women's sports events, but, imbecilic as these rulings are, it is not lost that they have not extended the bans to female athletes or sporting events. Indeed, women face far more serious problems in the settled districts and their plight in the tribal areas can be described as desperate. The literacy rate in FATA is an appalling 17.4 per cent overall, while in the case of tribal women the level drops to 3 per cent. The number of secondary schools is less than two hundred in the seven tribal agencies, but girls have access to only eighteen of them. Village women are treated more or less on a par with livestock, and a wife caught committing adultery can consider herself lucky to escape with her life – amputation of the nose is the standard less drastic punishment.

All this speaks volumes for decades of Government neglect that goes back to the inception of Pakistan. There was never a concerted effort to bring the tribes into mainstream Pakistan, for the simple reason that the country had to contend with a hostile Afghanistan on its border. Successive governments found it more expedient to continue providing the tribesmen with allowances and using FATA as a buffer. After Partition, the Political Agents in FATA were encouraged to think in terms of development schemes for their particular jurisdictions, but very little was done to implement this proposal. There was some progress in developing Kurram, a bit of road building in the Mohmand Agency, and some schools and hospitals in the Khyber Agency. The new corps of Pakistani administrators quickly learnt, like their predecessors of the Raj, that the tribal areas were not the easiest place to innovate, especially as all negotiations had to be conducted with the conservative maliks and *jirgas*. Nevertheless, the Government and the tribes at some point will have to forge a compromise agreement to gradually bring the Frontier Pathans into the mainstream of health, education and the job market, while allowing them to retain their time-honoured traditions. The North-West Frontier will for the foreseeable future be on the front line of global conflict, but it does not follow that it has to remain on the periphery of national life.

Rudyard Kipling was once on a walk up the Khyber Pass when a bandit took a shot at him, but, as he assures us, 'without malice'. The North-West Frontier Province, with its neatly laid-out cantonments, its rows of rose bushes behind the walls of the colonial bungalows, the manicured garden of its Peshawar Club, its English language of everyday life in commerce and government, even its British churches and cemeteries, stands as an undeniable legacy of the Raj. For a hundred years, British soldiers and Indian sepoys fought pitched battles against Pathan tribesmen in every corner of the Frontier. Rarely did a month pass without a column riding out from some garrison to punish an Afridi or Mahsud raiding party. There was wholesale butchery and brutality on both sides, yet one cannot help sensing that the shooting, as Kipling remarked, was in some way 'without malice'. Whatever the wording used in official reports, to the troops in the field the Pathan fighters were always spoken of as the 'hostiles', never the 'enemy'. This gives some indication of an underlying mutual respect and, one is inclined to argue, a genuine admiration between battlefield opponents.

This relationship is epitomised by an episode that took place after the 1908 campaign against the Zakka Khel, when the tribal leaders came to tender their submission to the British officer in charge, who happened to be George Roos-Keppel. As the maliks crowded round their adversary, one of them stepped forward to ask, 'Did we not fight well, sahib?' Roos-Keppel looked him straight in the eye, for a Pathan will trust no man who fails to do so, and replied, 'I wouldn't have shaken hands with you unless you had.'

EPILOGUE

Osama, Where Art Thou?

Until a very few years ago, Waziristan was a meaningless name in the West to all but a handful of South Asian scholars and defence analysts. Since the terrorist attacks of 11 September 2001, hundreds of millions of television viewers and newspaper readers have come to associate Waziristan with Osama bin Laden. Indeed, the founder of Al Qaeda was himself a relatively unknown personality before he launched his terrorist campaigns in the late 1990s. The name Bin Laden and the gaunt, 6ft 4in, bearded figure who appears in propaganda videos today prompt instant recognition from the vast majority of the world's population.

If Bin Laden is still alive, and there is every reason to believe he is, the odds are that he has found sanctuary in South Waziristan, FATA's heartland of anti-West fanaticism, where he would have been warmly received as a hero. One could hardly conceive of a more suitable hideout. Waziristan is geographically and socially on the extreme periphery of Pakistani society, therefore the lack of information about the region and its people is not surprising. The tribal agency is located in the Suleiman range of rugged mountains, ridges and ravines, and is considered one of the border region's least accessible areas. Of all the Pathan tribes of the Frontier, the Wazirs and Mahsuds of Waziristan are deemed to be the most independent. This autonomous status extends even to their own tribal maliks and elders, whom they are under no obligation to obey. The Wazirs make up a more cohesive unit than the other tribes: their interpretation of *badal*, in the code of Pakhtunwali, for instance, is that revenge is only to be taken against the perpetrator of a murder or other offence. Internal feuds are therefore dramatically reduced, for there is no call for reprisals against the culprit's family.

The Pakistani authorities seem to subscribe to the view that Waziristan is indeed Bin Laden's safe haven. Acting under US pressure, early in 2005 Pakistan took the unprecedented step of sending an invasion force into the tribal belt, its own national territory, with the objective of rooting out 'top level foreign terrorists'. The Pakistanis had drawn up a list of Al Qaeda militants suspected of sheltering in South Waziristan. There is little doubt that the Government's target was Bin Laden, the world's most wanted terrorist, and who carries a $25 million price tag on his head.

The 'Wana Operation', as it was dubbed, began in January 2005 and by the time the Pakistani forces had withdrawn, some six months later, the invasion had cost the Army nearly seven hundred casualties. Losses on the tribal side were three hundred killed and six hundred arrested on suspicion of carrying out terrorist activities or harbouring foreign guerrillas. The Army came up against a level of resistance it had not expected to encounter. The troops found themselves under fire from tribesmen armed with a panoply of powerful weaponry, much of it a legacy of the Soviet invasion of Afghanistan, some of it materiel that had been smuggled into FATA. No high-ranking Al Qaeda operatives were to be found among the dead or captured. Since then Pakistan has set up some six hundred checkpoints and stationed eighty thousand troops along the border with FATA. From the tribesmen's perspective, this can hardly be taken as a goodwill gesture. Whatever the political or military outcome, it would be impossible to estimate the years it will take to repair the damage done in terms of bad blood this offensive has created between the Government and the Pathans of Waziristan.

The US intelligence services also seem convinced that Bin Laden is holed up somewhere in Pakistan's tribal territory, an assumption based more on logical deduction than documentary evidence. Bin Laden disappeared from Kabul shortly before the USA launched its full-scale invasion of Afghanistan to exact revenge for the attacks on the World Trade Centre and Pentagon. Based on reports from informers and captured militants, two days before the fall of Kabul, on 12 November, the Al Qaeda leader and his followers fled Kabul with the intention of shifting their command post to Tora Bora, a network of caves and underground bunkers in the mountains bordering FATA, which was constructed in the 1980s with Saudi money and under the direction of Pakistan's ISI intelligence service. Bin Laden drove first to Jalalabad, on the main road from Kabul to Peshawar, in a convoy of four-wheel drive lorries and armoured vehicles. By now the US aerial bombing campaign had become intense and Bin Laden found himself in a dangerously exposed position. Afghan intelligence sources estimated that the Tora Bora complex held up to 1,600 of Bin Laden's élite battle-hardened Arab and Chechen fighters. The Al Qaeda chief knew the place well, for it was from here that he had fought the Soviet invaders in the 1980s. Somewhere towards the end of November 2001 Bin Laden, along with a handful of his loyalists, escaped the US military net, heading on foot in the direction of Parachinar. They crossed the border into one of FATA's more remote and inaccessible regions and from there, with the help of Pakistani sympathisers, it would have been an easy journey to Waziristan.

That is where US Special Forces and surveillance teams lost the scent of their elusive prey. Satellites that can read a car's number plate from miles above the Earth and state-of-the-art computer decryption methods are of little value in tracking a handful of men stealing their way under cloud cover along goat paths through remote mountain wilderness.

Peter L. Bergen, in his analysis of Islamist terrorism, highlights the failure of US intelligence to successfully infiltrate any spies within Bin Laden's group. Bergen cites a CIA officer as saying: 'The CIA probably does not have a single truly qualified Arabic-speaking officer of Middle Eastern background who can play a believable Muslim fundamentalist and who could volunteer to spend years of his life with s****y food and no women in the mountains of Afghanistan. Most case officers live in the suburbs of Virginia. We don't do that kind of thing.' 'It is of little avail that the US National Security Agency spends billions of dollars every year intercepting phone calls,' says Bergen. 'Theoretically, the NSA can track the communications of Bin Laden and his followers via satellite intercepts and quickly detect the man himself through his voiceprint. But Bin Laden has been aware of that at least since 1997, when he stopped using satellite phones to communicate his orders, preferring to deliver them via radio or in person.'[1]

Where does one begin to search in an inhospitable area of 10,500 square miles, a land inhabited by people whose tribal code of Pakhtunwali requires them to offer asylum to a Bin Laden or anyone else who comes asking for sanctuary? That question was addressed in the autumn of 2001 by a small team of US specialist agents who were to be found in the archive room of a renowned London map collection, poring over old charts of the Pathan borderland, pinpointing those very goat tracks and cross-referencing the maps with contemporary travelogues. It was a well thought-out mission, but at the time of writing this their efforts have yet to bear fruit.

Thousands of fugitives are today on the run in every corner of the world: murderers, drug barons, terrorists, evildoers of all descriptions. Osama bin Laden is merely the most high-profile criminal of the lot. His eventual capture or assassination is not so much a function of the resources thrown at the manhunt as the potential for betrayal within the ranks. This is where the world's most wanted terrorist has the upper hand. Twenty-five million dollars has no meaning to a fanatical Wazir, a tribesman who probably lives outside the cash economy and who is, moreover, bound by honour to protect his house guest. As for his Al Qaeda bodyguards, or other militants who may be aware of Bin Laden's whereabouts, the horrific reprisals that would await an informer can be taken as a guarantee of silence.

Even without a network of henchmen willing to provide cover, or the benefit of remote and inaccessible surroundings, it is usually not difficult for a determined fugitive to stay one step ahead of the law. Consider the case of Eric Rudolph, the Atlanta bomber of the 1996 Olympics, who managed to remain on the run for five years. This was not in South Waziristan, but in a country with multiple law enforcement and espionage agencies on the federal, state and local levels, and where CCTV cameras festoon virtually every lamp-post and shopping mall in the land.

Washington's deployment of vast resources of manpower and money to track down a single fugitive distorts the greater geopolitical picture. The hunt for Bin Laden also embodies a political risk which, though this may not rank high on Washington's agenda, will surely have a long-term impact on Pakistan's relations with the Frontier tribes. Each bombing by the US military of a village in Waziristan, Bajaur or elsewhere, in which Bin Laden or his top lieutenants are suspected of holing up, is manna for the likes of the MMA and other Muslim extremist organisations. These attacks, which have so far failed to net any 'high value targets', cause immeasurable damage to the Pakistani Government's efforts to build bridges to the people of FATA. The USA forces will one day depart this conflict zone, with or without Bin Laden's head, and it will be left to Islamabad to pick up the pieces. This is precisely what happened when the Soviets withdrew from Afghanistan in 1989 and the USA, having achieved its objective, turned its back on the mujahidin fighters that the American security services had spent years arming and funding. This, of course, is what triggered the anti-American crusade of the former CIA ally, Osama bin Laden.

The manhunt for Bin Laden serves to perpetuate a misleading image of this Saudi gunman as a towering figure of darkness resembling Darth Vader in the film *Star Wars*, instead of what he really is: an ailing fanatic on the run who periodically issues unheeded calls for worldwide jihad. The question is, leaving aside its value as a psychological victory in the war on terrorism, whether there is any justification for the huge effort under way to capture or kill Bin Laden.

For comparison's sake, the capture of Saddam Hussein in Iraq was undeniably a spectacular propaganda coup for the Bush administration. However, looking at the breakdown in law and order that has swept the country in the wake of Saddam's arrest, it could be argued that the operation amounted to little more than a publicity stunt, and one that leaves his captors with an awkward problem on their hands. Saddam's eventual execution is likely further to fan the flames of insurrection against the US occupation of Iraq.

The North-West Frontier's potential as a linchpin in global politics should not be underestimated. After all, in the days of the Raj the region we now know as FATA was the epicentre of a protracted stand-off between the world's two greatest imperial powers. Charles Allen is one of several specialists on the subject who has grasped the need to comprehend the grievances of the people believed to be sheltering Bin Laden and his followers. 'On the Afghan-Pakistan border, Osama bin Laden's Fanatic Camp survives,' writes Allen, 'in part because he and his remaining "Arabs" and Taliban allies have been offered sanctuary, but also because of the active connivance of the jihadised Pathans of the North-West Frontier Province – supported to a significant degree by the greater Pakistani populace.'[2] Allen argues that by allowing such grievances to continue, the West has done Islamist fundamentalism a huge and continuing favour. It is a matter of simple common sense. From the Frontier Pathans' point of view, anybody who drops bombs on their villages or invades their territory is, quite understandably, perceived to be a mortal enemy.

Humayun Khan, who served as Political Agent in North Waziristan, Malakand and Swat, is one of Pakistan's foremost authorities on tribal matters. He is also one of the most articulate critics of treating FATA as a military problem, a tactic that for one hundred years proved disastrous for the British. 'The Americans should be made to see that a political approach to this problem is required,' he says. 'This would involve a considerable investment of funds, but not more than what is being spent on military operations. These funds could be injected into the tribal areas, with a flow of benefits that would be more or less immediately visible to the tribes. If this were to happen, I think the future of FATA could be promising.'[3]

The capture of Osama bin Laden has become a political bugbear, as misguided as the missiles being fired at civilian targets in tribal territory. Al Qaeda, in Arabic, translates as 'the base'. To fell a tree, one does not chop away at the canopy. It is the base that needs to be attacked. However, if this is done without taking into account the sensitivities of the tribesmen who are shielding Taliban and Al Qaeda militants in their homeland, the spread of Islamist radicalisation on the North-West Frontier will become a self-fulfilling prophecy.

Notes

CHAPTER 1. PEOPLE OF A LOST ORIGIN

1. Arnold Toynbee, *Between Oxus and Jumna*, Oxford University Press, 1961, pp. 4–5.
2. Aurel Stein, 'Notes on Tirah', *Journal of the Royal Asiatic Society*, July 1925, pp. 402–3.
3. Mountstuart Elphinstone, *An Account of the Kingdom of Caubal*, Indus Publications, vol. 1, pp. 207–8.
4. *Ibid.*, p. 207.
5. Thomas Pennell, *Among the Wild Tribes of the Afghan Frontier*, Seeley & Co., 1909, p. 32.
6. James W. Spain, *The Pathan Borderland*, Indus Publications, 1963, p. 40.
7. Olaf Caroe, *The Pathans*, Macmillan & Co., 1958, p. 3.
8. General Sir Andrew Skeen, *Passing it On*, Gale & Polden Ltd, 1932, p. 1.
9. Caroe, *The Pathans*, p. xiii.
10. Skeen, *Passing it On*, p. 3.
11. *Ibid.*, p. 4.
12. William Barton, *India's North-West Frontier*, John Murray, 1939, p. 9.
13. *Report of the Indian Statutory Commission*, HMSO, 1930, vol. 1, p. 102.
14. Toynbee, *Between Oxus and Jumna*, p. 156.
15. *A Dictionary of the Pathan Tribes of the North-West Frontier of India*, Superintendent Government Printing, Calcutta, 1910, p. 146.
16. OIOC, *Report Showing the Relationship of the British Government with the Tribes Independent and Dependent on the North-West Frontier of the Punjab*, MF1/20 (microfiche), 1856, p. 55
17. Walter James Cummings, *Frontier Fighters*, unpublished memoirs, author's collection, p. 14.
18. John Masters, *Bugles and a Tiger*, Michael Joseph, 1956, p. 199.
19. Evelyn Howell, *A Monograph on Government's Relations with the Mahsud Tribe*, Government of India Press, 1931, pp. 90–1.
20. Stein, 'Notes on Tirah', p. 403.
21. Spain, *The Pathan Borderland*, p. 47.

22. Robert Warburton, *Eighteen Years in the Khyber*, John Murray, 1900, p. 210.
23. Lal Baha, *N.W.F.P. Administration under British Rule*, National Commission on Historical and Cultural Research, 1978, p. 56.
24. C. Collin Davies, *The Problem of the North-West Frontier*, Curzon Press, 1932, p. 67.
25. Spain, *The Pathan Borderland*, pp. 55–6.
26. OIOC, Selections from the Records of the Government of the Punjab (New Series no. XIV), V/23/343, 1871–82, pp. 11–16.
27. Caroe, *The Pathans*, p. 421.
28. Edward Oliver, *Across the Border*, Chapman & Hall, 1890, p. 145.
29. Caroe, *The Pathans*, p. 437.
30. Arthur Swinson, *The Siege of Saragoda*, Corgi, 1968, Preface.

CHAPTER 2. A FRONTIER IS BORN

1. Stephen Tanner, *Afghanistan: A Military History from Alexander the Great to the Fall of the Taliban*, Oxford University Press, 2002, p. 136.
2. Philip Mason, *A Matter of Honour*, Jonathan Cape, 1988, p. 225.
3. Swinson, *The Siege of Saragoda*, pp. 78–9.
4. H.L. Nevill, *Campaigns on the North-West Frontier*, Sang-e-Meel Publications, 2003, p. 14.
5. *Ibid.*, p. 18.
6. *Ibid.*, p. 20.
7. Charles Allen, *Soldier Sahibs*, Abacus, 2001, p. 288.
8. Nevill, *Campaigns*, p. 25.
9. Charles Allen, *God's Terrorists*, Little Brown, 2006, p. 19.
10. W.H. Paget and A.H. Mason, *Record of Expeditions against the North-West Frontier Tribes*, Whiting & Co., 1884, p. 247.
11. *Ibid.*, pp. 445–6.
12. Frederick Roberts, *Forty-One Years in India*, Macmillan & Co., 1914, p. 34.
13. *Ibid.*, p. 35.
14. Beaumont, *Sword of the Raj*, Bobbs-Merrill Co., Inc., 1977, p. 106
15. *Ibid.*, p. 107
16. Roberts, *Forty-One Years in India*, p. 35.
17. Allen, *God's Terrorists*, p. 125.
18. Davies, *The Problem of the North-West Frontier*, p. 5.
19. Paget and Mason, *Record of Expeditions*, p. 95.

20. George Younghusband, *The Story of the Guides*, Macmillan & Co., 1918, p. 2.
21. Khaled Hosseini, *The Kite Runner*, Bloomsbury, 2003, p. 140.
22. Roberts, *Forty-One Years in India*, p. 441.
23. Paget and Mason, *Record of Expeditions*, p. 52.
24. Michael Barthorp, *The North-West Frontier*, Blandford Press, 1982, p. 59.
25. Nevill, *Campaigns*, p. 61.
26. *Ibid.*, p. 63.
27. OIOC, *Tribes Independent and Dependent on the North-West Frontier*, microfiche MF1/20, 1856, p. 55.
28. Philip Woodruff, *The Men who Ruled India*, Jonathan Cape, 1953, vol. 2, p. 291.

CHAPTER 3. POACHERS TURNED GAMEKEEPERS

1. Tanner, *Afghanistan: A Military History*, p. 205.
2. Letter from Lord Salisbury to Queen Victoria, 26 April 1899, Royal Archives, RA/VIC/A 75/61.
3. Roberts, *Forty-One Years in India*, pp. 511–12.
4. *Ibid.*
5. *Ibid.*, p. 493.
6. Charles Chevenix Trench, *The Frontier Scouts*, Jonathan Cape, 1985, p. 9.
7. Woodruff, *The Men who Ruled India*, pp. 294–5.
8. James G. Elliott, *The Frontier 1839–1947*, Cassell, 1968, p. 110.
9. OIOC, *North-West Frontier Policy*, L/MIL/17/13/11, 1920.
10. Frank Leeson, *Frontier Legion*, The Leeson Archive (privately printed), 2003, p. 119.
11. Algernon Durand, *The Making of a Frontier*, Oxford University Press, 2004, p. 119.
12. *Ibid.*, pp. 2–3.
13. Abdur Rahman, *The Life of Abdur Rahman*, John Murray, 1900, vol. 2, p. 158.
14. Kerr Fraser-Tytler, *Afghanistan*, Oxford University Press, 1950, pp. 188–9.
15. *Ibid.*, p. 169.
16. Ahmed Rashid, *Taliban*, I.B. Tauris, 2002, p. 187.
17. Ijaz Hussain, 'Is the Durand Agreement Dead?', in *Tribal Areas of Pakistan: Challenges and Responses*, Islamabad Policy Research Institute, 2005, pp. 161–2.
18. Davies, *The Problem of the North-West Frontier*, p. 7.

CHAPTER 4. THE HUNDRED YEARS WAR

1. Swinson, *The Siege of Saragoda*, p. 207.
2. Durand, *The Making of a Frontier*, pp. 199–200.
3. Nevill, *Campaigns*, p. 177.
4. Spain, *The Pathan Borderland*, p. 174.
5. Davies, *The Problem of the North-West Frontier*, p. 96.
6. OIOC, L/PS/18/A54/3 Secret Correspondence between the Amir and the Viceroy, 31 January 1885.
7. OIOC, *Parliamentary Papers, 1898* (C. 8714), Appendix G, p. 39.
8. Winston Churchill, *The Story of the Malakand Field Force*, Leo Cooper, 2002, p. 33.
9. *Ibid.*, p. 25.
10. Allen, *Soldier Sahibs*, pp. 222–3.
11. Spain, *The Pathan Borderland*, p. 179.
12. Churchill, *Malakand Field Force*, p. 230.
13. *Ibid.*, p. 71.
14. *Ibid.*, pp. 127–8
15. OIOC, L/MIL/17/13/19, p. 388.
16. Thomas Holdich, *The Indian Borderland*, Methuen & Co., 1901, p. 347.
17. *Ibid.*, p. 347.
18. Warburton, *Eighteen Years in the Khyber*, p. 299.
19. OIOC, *Official History of Operations on the North-West Frontier*, 1882.
20. Nevill, *Campaigns*, p. 276.
21. Warburton, *Eighteen Years in the Khyber*, p. 301.

CHAPTER 5. A MOST SUPERIOR PERSON

1. Mason, *A Matter of Honour*, p. 393.
2. Peter King, *The Viceroy's Fall*, Sidgwick & Jackson, 1986, p. 38.
3. Caroe, *The Pathans*, p. 370.
4. OIOC, Supplementary Despatches of Duke of Wellington, vol. 4, pp. 592–601.
5. Warburton, *Eighteen Years in the Khyber*, p. 37.
6. Barton, *India's North-West Frontier*, p. 61.
7. Churchill, *Malakand Field Force*, p. 215.
8. *Ibid.*
9. OIOC, Debate in the House of Lords, 7 March 1898.
10. *Ibid.*

11. Swinson, *The Siege of Saragoda*, p. 255.
12. OIOC, George Nathaniel Curzon, *Frontiers*, 8008/cc/41, 1907, pp. 5–6.
13. OIOC, William Lockhart, Letter to Secretary of State of the Government of India, 1898.
14. Baha, *N.W.F.P. Administration*, p. 111.
15. *Ibid.*, p. 13.
16. Howell, *Government's Relations with the Mahsud Tribe*, pp. 90–1.
17. OIOC, L/PS/10/42 Political and Secret Department, pp. 47–55.
18. Thomas D. Farrell, 'The Founding of the North-West Frontier Militias', *Journal of the Royal Central Asian Society*, June 1972, pp. 170–1.
19. Winston Churchill, *My Early Life*, Eland Publishing, 2000, p. 130.
20. Khalid Aziz, *Frontier Crimes Regulation and Administration of the Tribal Areas*, Government of India Regulation No. III (1901), sections 21–39.
21. Mumtaz A. Bangash, 'FATA: Towards a New Beginning', in *Tribal Areas of Pakistan*, Islamabad Policy Research Institute, 2005, pp. 64–5.
22. Aziz, *Frontier Crimes Regulation*, p. 119.
23. Pennell, *Among the Wild Tribes*, p. 29.
24. Spain, *The Pathan Borderland*, p. 67.
25. OIOC, *Official History of Operations on the North-West Frontier*, 1882.
26. Davies, *The Problem of the North-West Frontier*, p. 149.
27. OIOC, L/PS/10/45, Secret Papers, Letter from the Viceroy to the Amir Habibullah Khan, 10 May 1907, p. 86.
28. OIOC, George Roos-Keppel, correspondence with the Viceroy in *North-West Frontier Policy*, 1920.
29. David Omissi, 'The RAF in Iraq and India in the 1920s', *Journal of the T.E. Lawrence Society*, vol. 13, no. 2, p. 73.
30. Edgar O'Ballance, *Afghan Wars*, Oxford University Press, 2003, pp. 59–60.
31. *Ibid.*, p. 67.
32. Brian Robson, *Crisis on the Frontier*, Spellmount, 2004, p. xiv.

CHAPTER 6. THE RED SHIRTS ARE COMING

1. Robson, *Crisis on the Frontier*, p. 149.
2. Quoted in *ibid.*, p. 170.
3. Cummings, *Frontier Fighters*.
4. Robson, *Crisis on the Frontier*, p. 236.
5. Lillian Starr, *Tales of Tirah and Lesser Tibet*, Hodder & Stoughton, 1924, p. 161.

6. *Ibid.*, p. 231.
7. *Ibid.*, p. 162.
8. Lawrence James, *Raj: The Making of British India*, Little Brown & Co., 1997, p. 527.
9. Mukulika Banerjee, *The Pathan Unarmed*, Oxford University Press, 2000, p. 57.
10. Swinson, *The Siege of Saragoda*, p. 319.
11. Spain, *The Pathan Borderland*, p. 172.
12. Leeson, *Frontier Legion*, p. 82.
13. *Ibid.*, p. 85.
14. Rodney Bennett in conversation with the author.
15. J.P. Villiers-Stuart, *Letters of a Once Punjab Frontier Force Officer*, Sifton, 1925, p. 25.
16. Quoted in *The Times*, 21 April 1926.

CHAPTER 7. 'DID WE NOT FIGHT WELL?'

1. Spain, *The Pathan Borderland*, p. 260.
2. *Daily Telegraph*, 19 December 1947.
3. OIOC, George Cunningham, *Private Correspondence*, 1947.
4. OIOC, European Manuscripts, MSS Eur D670/6.
5. Michael Edwardes, *The Last Years of British India*, Nel Mentor, 1967, p. 215.
6. S.M. Burke, *Foreign Policy of Pakistan*, Oxford University Press, 1973, p. 70.
7. Spain, *The Pathan Borderland*, p. 243.
8. As quoted in Khalid B. Sayeed, *The Political System of Pakistan*, Houghton Mifflin, 1967, p. 376.
9. Musa Khan Jalalzai, *The Foreign Policy of Afghanistan*, Sang-e-Meel Publications, 2003, p. 210.
10. OIOC, European Manuscripts, MSS Eur D714/70.
11. *Ibid.*
12. *Ibid.*
13. Mansoor Akbar Kundi, *Federally Administered Tribal Areas of Pakistan*, Asia Printers, Islamabad Policy Research Institute, 2005, pp. 16–17.
14. Humayun Khan, *The Role of the Federal Government and the Political Agent*, Islamabad Policy Research Institute, 2005, p. 114.
15. Mariam Abou Zahab and Olivier Roy, *Islamist Networks*, Hurst & Co., 2004, p. 25.

16. Asif Ashraf, *Economic Impact of Afghan Refugees in NWFP*, Pakistan Academy for Rural Development, 1988, pp. 33–5.

EPILOGUE. OSAMA, WHERE ART THOU?

1. Peter L. Bergen, *Holy War, Inc.*, Weidenfeld & Nicolson, 2001, p. 249.
2. Allen, *Soldier Sahibs*, p. 297.
3. Humayun Khan in conversation with the author.

Bibliography

PRIMARY SOURCES

British Library, Oriental and India Office Collection (OIOC)

OIOC *Report of the Indian Statutory Commission*, vol. 1 (London, HMSO, 1930), p. 102

OIOC *Report Showing the Relationship of the British Government with the Tribes Independent and Dependent on the North-West Frontier of the Punjab*, MF1/20 (microfiche), 1856, p. 55

OIOC, Selections from the Records of the Government of the Punjab (New Series, no. XIV), V/23/343, 1871–82, pp. 11–16

OIOC L/MIL/17/13/11 *North-West Frontier Policy*, 1920

OIOC L/PS/18/A54/3 *Secret Correspondence between the Amir and the Viceroy*, 31 January 1885

OIOC *Parliamentary Papers*, 1898 (C. 8714), Appendix G, p. 39

OIOC *Official History of Operations on the North-West Frontier*, 1882

OIOC *Supplementary Despatches of Duke of Wellington*, vol. 4, pp. 592–601

OIOC L/MIL/17/13/19, 1920, p. 388

OIOC *Debate in the House of Lords*, 7 March 1898

OIOC L/PS/10/45, Secret Papers, Letter from the Viceroy to the Amir Habibullah Khan, 10 May 1907, p. 86

OIOC, George Roos-Keppel, correspondence with the Viceroy in *North-West Frontier Policy*, 1920

OIOC, George Nathaniel Curzon, *Frontiers*, 8008/cc/41, 1907, pp. 5–6

OIOC, William Lockhart, *Letter to Secretary of State of the Government of India*, 1898

OIOC L/PS/10/42 *Political and Secret Department*, pp. 47–55

OIOC, George Cunningham, *Private Correspondence*, 1947

OIOC European Manuscripts, Mss Eur D670/6

OIOC European Manuscripts, Mss Eur D714/70

Royal Archives, Windsor Castle

RA/VIC/A 45/61, Letter from Lord Salisbury to Queen Victoria, 26 April 1899

Newspaper Accounts

The Times, 21 April 1926

Daily Telegraph, 19 December 1947

Reports and Journals

Ashraf, Asif, *Economic Impact of Afghan Refugees in NWFP* (Peshawar, Pakistan Academy for Rural Development, 1988)

Aziz, Khalid, *Frontier Crimes Regulation and Administration of the Tribal Areas*, Government of India Regulation No. III (1901)

Bangash, Mumtaz A., 'FATA: Towards a New Beginning', in *Tribal Areas of Pakistan* (Islamabad, Islamabad Policy Research Institute, 2005)

Farrell, Thomas D., 'The Founding of the North-West Frontier Militias', *Journal of the Royal Central Asian Society*, June 1972

General Staff Army Headquarters, *A Dictionary of the Pathan Tribes of the North-West Frontier of India* (Calcutta, Superintendent Government Printing, 1910)

Howell, Evelyn, *A Monograph on Government's Relations with the Mahsud Tribe* (Simla, Government of India Press, 1931)

Hussain, Ijaz, 'Is the Durand Agreement Dead?', in *Tribal Areas of Pakistan: Challenges and Responses* (Islamabad, Islamabad Policy Research Institute, 2005)

Khan, Humayun, *The Role of the Federal Government and the Political Agent* (Islamabad Policy Research Institute, 2005)

Kundi, Mansoor Akbar, *Federally Administered Tribal Areas of Pakistan*, (Islamabad, Asia Printers, Islamabad Policy Research Institute, 2005)

Omissi, David, 'The RAF in Iraq and India in the 1920s', *Journal of the T.E. Lawrence Society*, vol. 13, no. 2

Stein, Aurel, 'Notes on Tirah', *Journal of the Royal Asiatic Society*, July 1925

SECONDARY SOURCES

Allen, Charles, *Soldier Sahibs* (London, Abacus, 2001)

Allen, Charles, *God's Terrorists* (London, Little Brown, 2006)

Baha, Lal, *N.W.F.P. Administration under British Rule* (Islamabad, National Commission on Historical and Cultural Research, 1978)

Banerjee, Mukulika, *The Pathan Unarmed* (Karachi, Oxford University Press, 2000)

Barthorp, Michael, *Afghan Wars* (London, Cassell & Co., 1982)

Barthorp, Michael, *The North-West Frontier* (Dorset, Blandford Press, 1982)

Barthorp, Michael, *The Frontier Ablaze* (London, Windrow & Greene, 1996)

Barton, William, *India's North-West Frontier* (London, John Murray, 1939)

Beaumont, Roger, *Sword of the Raj* (Indianapolis, Bobbs-Merrill Co., Inc., 1977)

Bergen, Peter L., *Holy War, Inc.* (London, Weidenfeld & Nicolson, 2001)

Burke, S.M., *Foreign Policy of Pakistan* (Karachi, Oxford University Press, 1973)

Caroe, Olaf, *The Pathans* (London, Macmillan & Co., 1958)

Chevenix Trench, Charles, *The Frontier Scouts* (London, Jonathan Cape, 1985)

Churchill, Winston, *The Story of the Malakand Field Force* (Longmans, 1898; London, Leo Cooper, 2002)

Churchill, Winston, *My Early Life* (1930; London, Eland Publishing, 2000)

Cummings, Walter James, *Frontier Fighters* (Unpublished memoirs, author's collection)

Davies, C. Collin, *The Problem of the North-West Frontier* (London, Curzon Press, 1932)

Durand, Algernon, *The Making of a Frontier* (Thomas Nelson & Sons; Karachi, Oxford University Press, 2004)

Edwardes, Michael, *The Necessary Hell* (London, Cassell & Co., 1958)

Edwardes, Michael, *The Last Years of British India* (London, Nel Mentor, 1967)

Elliott, James G., *The Frontier 1839–1947* (London, Cassell, 1968)

Elphinstone, Mountstuart, *An Account of the Kingdom of Caubal* (1808; Karachi, Indus Publications)

Fraser-Tytler, Kerr, *Afghanistan* (London, Oxford University Press, 1950)

Hensman, Howard, *The Afghan War of 1879–80* (Lahore, Sang-e-Meel Publications, 1999)

Hodson, R.V.E., *The Story and Gallantry of the North-West Frontier* (Southampton, Clio Publishing, 2002)

Holdich, Thomas, *The Indian Borderland* (London, Methuen & Co., 1901)

Hosseini, Khaled, *The Kite Runner* (London, Bloomsbury, 2003)

Jalalzai, Musa Khan, *The Foreign Policy of Afghanistan* (Lahore, Sang-e-Meel Publications, 2003)

James, Lawrence, *Raj: The Making of British India* (London, Little Brown & Co., 1997)

Keppel, Arnold, *Gun Running and the Indian North-West Frontier* (Lahore, Sang-e-Meel Publications, 2004)

King, Peter, *The Viceroy's Fall* (London, Sidgwick & Jackson, 1986)

Leeson, Frank, *Frontier Legion* (The Leeson Archive [privately printed], 2003)

Macmunn, George, *Afghanistan from Darius to Amanullah* (Lahore, Sang-e-Meel Publications, 2002)

Mason, Philip, *A Matter of Honour* (London, Jonathan Cape, 1988)

Masters, John, *Bugles and a Tiger* (London, Michael Joseph, 1956)

Miller, Charles, *Khyber* (London, Macdonald & Jane's, 1977)

Nevill, H.L., *Campaigns on the North-West Frontier* (1910; Lahore, Sang-e-Meel Publications, 2003)

O'Ballance, Edgar, *Afghan Wars* (Oxford, Oxford University Press, 2003)

Oliver, Edward, *Across the Border* (London, Chapman and Hall, 1890)

Paget, W.H. and Mason, A.H., *Record of Expeditions against the North-West Frontier Tribes* (London, Whiting & Co., 1884)

Pennell, Thomas, *Among the Wild Tribes of the Afghan Frontier* (London, Seeley & Co., 1909)

Rahman, Abdur, *The Life of Abdur Rahman* (London, John Murray, 1900)

Rashid, Ahmed, *Taliban* (London, I.B. Tauris, 2002)

Roberts, Frederick, *Forty-One Years in India* (London, Macmillan & Co., 1914)

Robson, Brian, *Crisis on the Frontier* (Kent, Spellmount, 2004)

Salim, Ahmad, *Loya Jirga* (Lahore, Sang-e-Meel Publications, 2006)

Sayeed, Khalid B., *The Political System of Pakistan* (New York, Houghton Mifflin, 1967)

Schofield, Victoria, *Old Road, New Highways* (Karachi, Oxford University Press, 1997)

Shah, Sayed Wiqar Ali, *Ethnicity, Islam and Nationalism* (Karachi, Oxford University Press, 1999)

Skeen, General Sir Andrew, *Passing it On* (London, Gale & Polden Ltd., 1932)

Spain, James W., *The Pathan Borderland* (Karachi, Indus Publications, 1963)

Starr, Lillian, *Tales of Tirah and Lesser Tibet* (London, Hodder & Stoughton, 1924)

Swinson, Arthur, *The Siege of Saragoda* (London, Corgi, 1968)

Tanner, Stephen, *Afghanistan, a Military History from Alexander the Great to the Fall of the Taliban* (Karachi, Oxford University Press, 2002)

Thapar, Romila, *Early India* (Harmondsworth, Penguin, 2002)

Thorburn, S.S., *Bannu, or Our Afghan Frontier* (Lahore, Sang-e-Meel Publications, 1999)

Toynbee, Arnold, *Between Oxus and Jumna* (London, Oxford University Press, 1961)

Villiers-Stuart, J.P., *Letters of a Once Punjab Frontier Force Officer* (London, Sifton, 1925)

Warburton, Robert, *Eighteen Years in the Khyber* (London, John Murray, 1900)

Woodruff, Philip, *The Men who Ruled India* (London, Jonathan Cape, 1953)

Younghusband, George, *The Story of the Guides* (London, Macmillan & Co., 1918)

Zahab, Mariam Abou and Roy, Olivier, *Islamist Networks* (London, Hurst & Co., 2004)

Index